THE MIRAGE OF AMERICA IN CONTEMPORARY ITALIAN LITERATURE AND FILM

BARBARA ALFANO

The Mirage of America in Contemporary Italian Literature and Film

UNIVERSITY OF TORONTO PRESS
Toronto Buffalo London

ISBN 978-1-4426-4405-2

Printed on acid-free, 100% post-consumer, recycled paper with vegetable-based inks.

Toronto Italian Studies

___

Publication cataloguing information is available from Library and Archives Canada.

___

This book has been published with the assistance of a grant from Bennington College.

University of Toronto Press acknowledges the financial assistance to its publishing program of the Canada Council for the Arts and the Ontario Arts Council.

Canada Council **Conseil des Arts**
for the Arts **du Canada**

University of Toronto Press acknowledges the financial support of the government of Canada through the Canada Book Fund for its publishing activities.

Contents

Acknowledgments

In July 1999, I crossed the sky between Europe and America. The history of this book begins then. I took my first ten-hour flight to the United States. It was a rocky flight. I knew nothing of the world I was about to enter, except for what I had seen in films and read in books; and I had just discovered that I knew very little of the world I was leaving behind. However, I was not afraid of the unknown. I was afraid of flying. The book I took with me on this trip was Alessandro Baricco's *City*, which I did not read on the plane. Instead, I spent that time pondering the many aspects of fear. I could not imagine that *City* would become material for a chapter of *The Mirage of America in Contemporary Italian Literature and Film*. I had no idea the book would ever exist, let alone fathom its content. I carried *City* with me because it was my best friends' gift for my departure. The playful dedication reads, "We will miss you … but maybe not too much?" My first thankful thoughts go to those in Italy who let me go.

I have stated the following many times, in different ways. I'll say it again. Juana Djelal, my friend, inviting me to cross the pond was a great idea. Thank you. Here is the end result.

I did eventually read *City* a couple of years later, when I began connecting the dots between the two shores. I, the writer of this book, am fully part of its content. My life is the unwritten chapter between its lines. I cannot possibly acknowledge here everyone who helped me arrive at the typing of this last page. However, if you were on my path, I see you from here.

I am immensely grateful to Bennington College for supporting entirely the publication of the book. They lifted a weight that made my life and the writing process much easier. I felt honoured by this early acknowledgment of my work.

At the University of Toronto Press, I found in Ron Schoeffel and Judith Williams professional wisdom, sagacity, and exemplary skills. Thank you for rescuing *The Mirage of America in Contemporary Literature and Film* from what I did not see, understand, realize, or imagine. To the unknown colleagues who have read the manuscript for UTP goes my immense gratitude for the careful responses and intellectual stimulus they provided.

This book has gone through many changes, but it owes its core and original form to the guidance, wisdom, advice, and patience of Djelal Kadir, a wonderful mentor and a true friend.

My heartfelt thanks to my friends and colleagues Roberta Tabanelli, Steven Thomas, and Quentin Youngberg for reading parts of the manuscript, and for giving me advice that has shaped it up. I am also indebted to the jolly members of a too short lived support reading group, born at Bennington in a small apartment administered by a big grey cat: Karen Gover, Valerie Imbruce, and Carol Pal, thank you so much for your caring, reading, suggesting, and correcting! Thanks are in order also for Jason Laine, Ron Montesi, and my dear friend Judy Matz, who, at different stages, took on the difficult task of taming my wayward English. You gave me a chance to admire your patience and kindness.

Many of the stories I like have fairy godmothers disguised as great women and wonderful friends. I have two, in my life – Juana Djelal and Sherry Roush. *The Mirage of America* would not exist without their loving friendship, unyielding support, smart advice, and magic wisdom. This book and I owe you a lot.

Friendship has nourished me in the Berkshires and at Bennington, while I was going through the last stages of my writing. Asma Abbas, Carol Pal, and Valerie Imbruce: with you I found a home away from home.

To my parents and sister goes my gratitude for letting me camp in their sitting room for many summers, two months at a time, and for giving up their music and television hours to respect the religious silence I imposed on them during those times. Yet, my gratitude will never be an appropriate measure for the extent of their love. To them I dedicate this work.

THE MIRAGE OF AMERICA IN CONTEMPORARY ITALIAN LITERATURE AND FILM

Introduction

"Ma tu, cosa ci sei venuto a fare?"
["What did you come here for, then?"][1]

Gina Lagorio, *L'arcadia americana*

A mirage is an optical illusion; by analogy, it is "something that appears real or possible but is not in fact so."[2] The works of the contemporary Italian intellectuals considered in this study (writers, filmmakers) reflect a specific image of America – never simply the United States of America, but that cultural construct that Italy has called America since the New World entered its collective imaginary. In the novels and films under examination here, while America may sometimes correspond to the United States, overlapping with the geopolitical space, more often it may be only a metaphor, an idea, a dream, or a myth. The reader will know the difference, since I refer to the nation as the United States and to the cultural construct as America.

"Mirage" comes from the French *se mirer*, "to be reflected"; it is a deceptive image that contains also a reflection of the self, of one's own desires and beliefs. The authors discussed in this work are observed subjecting themselves to a process of reflection while subjecting America to a searching examination. *The Mirage of America in Contemporary Italian Literature and Film* consists, then, in tracing the record of this spectral process which stands at the intersection of Italian culture, its representations of the American myth, ethics of the individual, and issues of transculturation.

This study offers a new reading of America as imagery in Italian narrative and film created between the 1980s and the first decade of the

2000s, which chart an ethics of the subject who, although culturally bounded, projects the range of her or his agency beyond national and cultural boundaries. In these works, America represents the topos of a real or metaphorical destination. The individual who sets out on a voyage for America, as geographical place or as ideal concept, also begins a search for the self. America, as a metaphor for a new land, as an icon, or in its reality as a geopolitical space, becomes the inevitable phenomenon with which this individual must come to terms. In *Morals and Stories*, Tobin Siebers writes, "A claim can be theoretically grounded only when it is thematically grounded" (6). Here America is the theme.

Analysing texts narrated from both first-person and non-first-person perspectives, and filmic productions, I consider the ways in which images associated with the United States inflect and shape the ethicality of the individual. The aim is to define what function and significance narrative images of the United States hold in the evolution of the engaged subjects who explore the possibilities of their cultural and historical agency. My chief interest lies in the contemporary Italian intellectual whose ethics encompass the rejection of a certain image of America – America as the land of unlimited possibilities for human social and ethical accomplishment. I choose America because of the ample space it has occupied in the cultural history of Italy as the ultimate utopia of self-realization.

The Mirage of America highlights the importance of Italian literature and film as a locus for the formation of an individual's ethics that encompasses the ability to function on a cross-cultural scale. Historically, due to the vicissitudes of the formation of Italy and a long history of particularism, Italian intellectuals have a weak sense of national identity or boundaries, and, conversely, a strong sense of individual responsibility towards universal, moral values. They are historically in constant displacement – political or metaphorical – and this position of displacement allows them to negotiate issues of identity and alterity that are relevant to the encounter and cohabitation with different cultures. In other words, the Italian intellectual focuses on an ethical self, and I explain here how and why this self needs to confront America, and ultimately does, in the search for a viable transcultural ethics that relies on the individual. In this regard, *The Mirage of America* extends Julia Kristeva's concern with the contemporary "decline of individualities":

The values crisis and the fragmentation of individuals have reached the point where we no longer know what we are and we take shelter, to preserve a token of personality, under the most massive, regressive common denominators: national origins and the faith of our forebears. (*Nations without Nationalism* 2)

Investigating the possibility of transcultural ethics becomes crucial in a historical moment when Italy has become the America of many migrants who come to her from south and east in search of not simply a better life, but first of all a liveable life. On a larger scale, in a globalized context of cohabitation with very different cultures, it becomes paramount to explore the importance that the individual holds not so much as a representative of a specific cultural identity, but as the singular bearer of ethical values across cultures and nations.

This book examines five novels and five films released during a twenty-five-year period, between 1981 and 2006: Alessandro Baricco's *City*, 1999; Francesca Duranti's *Sogni mancini*, 1996 (*Left-Handed Dreams*, 2000); Gina Lagorio's *L'arcadia americana*, 1999 (The American Arcadia); Andrea De Carlo's *Treno di panna*, 1981 (*The Cream Train*, 1987); Melania Mazzucco's *Vita*, 2003 (translation with the same title, 2005); and the films *Non ci resta che piangere*, 1984 (Nothing Left but to Cry, directed by Roberto Benigni and Massimo Troisi); *Lamerica*, 1994 (Gianni Amelio); *Caro diario*, 1994 (*Dear Diary*, Nanni Moretti); *The Last Customer*, 2002 (Nanni Moretti); and *Nuovomondo*, 2006 (*Golden Door*, Emanuele Crialese).

These narratives ultimately declare that though setting out for America, either as a geographical space or as a concept, can be tantamount to setting out to discover the self, discovering the self does not, or should not necessarily, lead to America. In 1943, in his essay on Elio Vittorini's *Americana*, Giaime Pintor wrote:

> In our words dedicated to America much may be ingenuous and inexact, much may refer to arguments extraneous to the historical phenomenon of the United States as it stands today. But this does not matter because if the continent did not exist our words would not lose their significance. This America has no need of Columbus, it is discovered within ourselves; it is the land to which we turn with the same hope and faith of the first immigrants, of whoever has decided to defend at the price of pains and error the dignity of the human condition. (244–5)

Contrary to what America meant for the writers and intellectuals working in the first half of the twentieth century, such as Pintor, Cesare Pavese, and Vittorini, my analysis of contemporary works indicates that the concept of America does not empower the individuals concerned. This is a concept on which I elaborate fully in my third and fourth chapters, where I pursue an extensive comparison of some of my primary sources with Jean Baudrillard's *Amérique* and Ben Morreale's play "Ava Gardner's Brother-in-Law."

The works under consideration in chapter 5, all produced after 2000, mark a turn in how artists and intellectuals look at America, which now loses much of its ideological component and returns to be the historical dream that moved the poor masses of Southern Italy to cross the ocean during the great migration, between the last decades of the nineteenth century and the restrictive U.S. immigration laws of 1921 (the Quota Act) and 1924 (the National Origins Act).[3]

The Vantage of the *I*: Prospecting in Perspective

For those countries whose histories have been marked by the presence and the political and military action of the United States, or whose cultures have been strongly influenced by its political and economic power, or simply by its existence as the destination of their migrations, all of which apply to Italy, America has played a role in the formation of their cultural identities beyond its geography.

I examine this role through the lens of subjectivity as a locus for ethics formation within an Italian cultural and historical context. My ultimate goal is to define what function America, as construct and as imagery, may hold in the formation of subjective ethics. In the texts that I analyse in chapters 1, 3, and 4, the self comes in the form of a first-person narrator, which creates an ideal setting for the exploration of issues of subjectivity related to issues of space in the formation of identity. Looking at creative writing and film through the form of first-person narratives offers the chance to deal with the subject in its problematic singularity, an aspect that much of the academic discourse on identity, culture, and globalization (in several disciplines besides literature, such as geography, history, and sociology) has chosen to leave aside, preferring to deal exclusively with theories of identity that bypass singularity, often in order to smoothly accommodate issues of collective political and sociocultural struggles. In chapter 2, America is the object (indeed, the subject) of observation itself.

First-person narratives explore those zones of the self that save the subject from its historic and materialistic reification as perpetrated by certain academic discourses exclusively on behalf of an identity that overrides the individual as a *locus* of struggle for, and performativity of, ethical agency and choices. But my subject is not only an "I"-narrator.[4] It is also the individual(s) of *City*, a third-person narrative, and the intellectual at the centre of this essay. This polymorphic subject has an ethical aspect. The subject of *The Mirage of America* is, then, grounded in an understanding of subjectivity as forms of relation of the self to itself, forms that represent operative ethical choices. I base this usage in the Foucauldian definition of the self, that is,

> not a substance, it is a form, and this form is not primarily or always identical to itself. You do not have the same type of relationship to yourself when you constitute yourself as a political subject who goes to vote or speaks at a meeting and when you are seeking to fulfill your desires in a sexual relationship. Undoubtedly there are relationships and interferences between these different forms of the subject; but we are not dealing with the same type of subject. In each case, one plays, one establishes a different type of relationship to oneself. (Foucault 291)

What I am interested in, and what leads me to the analysis of mainly first-person narratives, is the dimension of the self that Foucault surprisingly brings into his materialistic discourse by simply reconstituting an old, haunting ghost: "Oneself." Michael Hardt and Antonio Negri, referring to Foucault's final works on the history of sexuality, explain the presence of this dimension as "humanism after the death of Man":

> The ethical care of the self reemerges as a constituent power of self-creation. How is it possible that the man who worked so hard to convince us of the death of Man [...] would in the end champion these central tenets of the humanist tradition? [...]. Foucault asks in his final work a paradoxical and urgent question: What is humanism after the death of Man? Or rather, what is an antihumanist (or posthuman) humanism? [...]. If we are to conceive Man as separate from nature, then Man does not exist. This recognition is precisely the death of Man [...]. The humanism of Foucault's final works, then, should not be seen as contradictory [...]. Once we recognize our posthuman bodies and minds, once we see ourselves for the simians and cyborgs we are, we then need to explore the *vis viva*, the creative powers that animate us as they do all of nature and actualize our potentialities. This is humanism after the death of Man: what Foucault calls "le travail du soi sur soi," the continuous constituent project to create and recreate ourselves and our world. (*Empire* 91–2)

This dimension of self-creation cannot be set apart from a level of subjectivity as individuality, a dimension well represented in first-person fictional works. Hardt and Negri do not directly refer to individuality, but it is undeniable that Foucault, by simply saying "oneself" and stating "le travail du soi sur soi," recognized this individual dimension as necessary to the understanding and analysis of subjectivity.

Foucault did not exclude the dimension of the individual from the theoretical approach to the understanding and analysis of social forms. In *Labor of Dionysus* Hardt and Negri write:

> Subjectivity must be grasped in terms of the social processes that animate the production of subjectivity. The subject, as Foucault clearly understood, is at the same time a product and productive, constituted in and constitutive of the vast networks of the social labor. Labor is both subjection and subjectivation – "Le travail du soi sur soi" – in such a way that all notions of free will or the determinism of the subject must be discarded. Subjectivity is defined simultaneously and equally by its productivity and its producibility, its aptitudes to produce and be produced. (11)

This is a notion that clearly does not leave room for a theoretical consideration of individuality. But "le travail du soi sur soi" implies a site of individuality where this production happens that cannot be discarded and that is represented not only by the relation of the self to the community, but also by – again – a relationship of the self to itself – even if it exclusively, and obviously, happens through the interaction of social forces.

Why is this important? Because globalization issues of displacement and otherness, as can be understood in Kristeva's *Étrangers à nous-mêmes*, carry with them a dimension of individuality as a site of struggle for the formation of social ethics. Taking into consideration this aspect of the self does not mean falling back into transcendence, but simply focusing on a particular aspect of the labour of subjectivity: the self. It is an aspect that looks at the labour of the individual on her/his own self and that does not transcend at all a "Subjectivity [...] defined simultaneously and equally by its productivity and its producibility," because this labour of the self does not escape the laws of materialism. Unless we want to fall into what Hardt and Negri call the Marxian paradox "of confiding the liberation of the revolutionary subjectivity to a 'process without subject'" (*Labor of Dionysus* 11), we have not only to recognize Foucault's humanism, but also to give credit to it by trying to understand how "le travail du soi sur soi" works. Foucault proposed a question, not merely an affirmative theoretical principle: What work should one do on oneself? Displacement and otherness draw attention to the ethical responsibility of the individual. If fiction still makes sense as representation of social relations in the age of post-nationalisms, that sense is also, and especially, to be found in its capacity to express and represent this "travail du soi sur soi" urged by displacement and otherness.

In *The Mirage of America* the quest resides in this multifold relationship of the self to itself as performed through space and in the encounter with its alterities, since the "I" going towards (to or against) America is the representation of "a relationship of the self to itself." As if sitting in a hairdresser's chair, in order to talk about "America" Italian intellectuals hold a mirror of irony to their back, so that reflecting upon America becomes a way to reflect upon themselves and their function in society. In his *America in Modern Italian Literature*, Donald Heiney writes that for Italian intellectuals to discuss America has always meant to discuss themselves.

On the level of representation, as we shall see further in considering *Caro diario*, *L'arcadia americana*, and *Sogni mancini*, images of U.S. culture are significantly woven into narratives of self-description and are used to shape a specific relationship of the narrating "I" to itself. This relationship plays itself out through spatial iconography. The protagonists of my texts all move, in the beginning, from spaces whose barriers have disintegrated, losing in the process their original significance, to zones of uncertainty that reveal themselves to be zones of the self. I will pass from one text to the other to evaluate these movements of the subject and to see where and which America lies in these transitions and passages.

As far as the politics of the subject in its relationship to space is concerned, this study explores ideas of space and place as framed by the cultural references of the beholder. The analysis relies on Djelal Kadir's definition of place and space:

> The mathemata and metaphorics of space, whether global, local, virtual, real, or hyperreal, are ultimately ideologically bounded and defined within the circumscriptive parameters of cultural habitus. In this sense space and place function as concomitants, and landscape, whether geometrically naturalized or aesthetically skewed, frames the cultural habitat of the inhabitants, who see themselves as its human agencies and who frame the space of that landscape in turn. (24–5)

The ethical subject of my inquiry, in its relationship with space, is just such a human agency.

The Ethics of the Subject

Let us begin with a dictionary. The *Oxford English Dictionary* defines ethics as "The moral principles by which a person is guided. The rules of conduct recognized in certain associations or departments of human life." Gina Lagorio, when questioned about ethics, provided the link between the moral principles by which that person is guided and the association of human life around her/him. She said, "Credo che nessun essere umano sufficientemente dotato di ragione possa vivere senza seguire una linea di condotta di solito ereditata dall'ambiente in cui è nato (è quel che chiamiamo etica) [...]" (Oberti 5; "I believe that no human being sufficiently endowed with reason can live without following a line of conduct usually inherited from the environment where he or she was born. This is what we call ethics [...]").

I quote Gina Lagorio to give a working definition of ethics in this book because, having established the theoretical frame that defines the subject as singular – the individual – I am now framing this individual within her historical and cultural aspects: in this book, s/he is the Italian leftist intellectual. Gina Lagorio, herself, is exemplary of such subjectivity.

Historically, as we shall see in the next two sections, the Italian intellectual feels the moral duty to participate in the development of civil society and regards her/his role as fundamental in that development. It is in this light that one has to understand Lagorio's definition of ethics as a local, cultural construct. For Italian intellectuals, to be ethically engaged in their social milieu has always entailed the consideration of human relationships on a larger scale than just the local (I shall be dealing with this further in the next section of this chapter). When Gina Lagorio refers to "a line of conduct usually inherited from the environment where he or she was born," she does not confine the works of ethics geographically, she talks about inheritance. Lagorio shares with her reader the understanding that the inheritance of that line of conduct which relies on the individual bears universal values. Italian intellectuals are those individuals who constantly focus on themselves and on the work they do on themselves for the sake of civil society. Each of them is the subject as defined previously with the help of Foucault. In his preface to the American edition of *Travels in Hyperreality*, Umberto Eco writes,

An American interviewer once asked me how I manage to reconcile my work as a scholar and university professor, author of books published by university presses, with my other work as what would be called in the United States a "columnist" [...]. My answer was that this habit is common to all European intellectuals, in Germany, France, Spain, and naturally, Italy: all countries where a scholar or scientist often feels required to speak out in papers, to comment, if only from the point of view of his own interests and special field, on events that concern all citizens [...]. But many Italian scholars and literary critics also write columns where they take a stand on political questions, and they do this not only as a natural part of their work, but also as a duty. (ix–x)

The same attitude pertains to writers and filmmakers. I explain in the next pages how and why this position of the Italian intellectual came into being historically.

What Italian intellectuals do, then, once they have established their position as an influential factor in civil society, is to criticize that society for the sake of its betterment and moral change. With this we move to the level of representation, because the intellectuals do so through their work.

Tobin Siebers explains the place of ethics in literature, and I would extend his definition to representation as far as my work is concerned:

My theme and theory privilege place, as craftsmen privilege the hammer, as a way of talking about literature and ethics. We have an attraction to where we are not only because it is the site of work and living but because we make our tools and ideas work there [...]. More specifically, I will focus on the idea of character as that "place" – for the Greek *ēthos*, in addition to suggesting "character" and "ethics," originally meant "to be found somewhere" – in which ethical ideas and literary ones gather together to help us work out the best way to live with other people in the places where people live. There literature and ethics join forces in the search for the good life for a human being. (5)

A literal and literary example of such characters as sites are *City*'s subjects, who, rather than travelling somewhere like the protagonists of the other works discussed here, are themselves "places," as one of the protagonists of the novel defines individuals (see chapter 2).

We will ultimately discover that for the contemporary Italian intellectual to reject the myth of America as the land of salvation, whether real or metaphorical, means to be striving for an ethical accomplishment directed at "the search for the good life for a human being." With this, I hope to have clarified the meaning of an individual as a site for ethics formation.

The Self and Italian Narrative

I refer more than once in this text to Donald Heiney's assertion that, for Italian intellectuals, to discuss America means to discuss themselves. Heiney was not simply expressing an idea; he was basing his claim on a centuries-old cultural tradition that sees the self as protagonist of narratives portraying historical and social scenarios whose components are projected beyond national boundaries. With regard to nineteenth-century Italian narratives, Gian-Paolo Biasin writes, "In little more than a century, the course of the Italian historical novel has been, first, to accompany the emergence of the national state, and then to transcend both regional and national boundaries to become cosmopolitan and marketable worldwide" (154). He refers to historical novels as stemming from narratives of the self and narratives of an individual's vicissitudes.

From Ugo Foscolo to Antonio Tabucchi and Gianni Celati, Biasin traces the changing but nonetheless central relationship between the self and narrative in Italian literary tradition, focusing on Luigi Pirandello, Italo Svevo, Elsa Morante, Italo Calvino, and other important authors. However, the connection between narrative and the self is older than the formation of the nation state. Without going back to Dante, we can stop at Christopher Columbus and Amerigo Vespucci, who, according to Gérman Arciniegas, were in a sense the founders of American literature.

In his essay "Italy and the Invention of America," Theodore Cachey shows us how, in the High Renaissance, national identity for Italians was constructed through narrative "abroad," and not at home (in an Italy politically weak and practically stateless, or rather having too many states): "Like Petrarch, who overcomes his stateless status through travel and writing across a wide variety of patronage contexts, Columbus makes a place for himself in this world through a scriptural network of notarial documents, an extensive epistolary, and the journals and letters of the four voyages" (23). Cachey quotes Antonio Gramsci to support the notion of a cosmopolite Italian who, paradoxically, finds his national identity abroad. In his *Prison Notebooks*, Gramsci writes: "for many centuries Italy had an international-European function.

Italian intellectuals and specialists were cosmopolites and not Italians, not national" (Cachey 19). Biasin concludes, "Contemporary Italian literature is not only Italian but also international as far as its geographical referents are concerned, as befits an increasingly homogenized but still multicultural world, and a growing instability of the very notion of the Self" (170). Among the several authors he mentions as international are Andrea De Carlo and Francesca Duranti, both of whom are treated in this study.

Italian literature and film provide a rich and significant context to explore matters of self and of an ethics that entails the relationship to the Other on a global scene. My work finds a self that is geographically unstable, indeed, but morally strong, advocating increased moral responsibility for the individual, universally. This self moves on the threshold between two worlds, assuming a liminal position. Nanni Moretti in *Caro diario* is constantly moving from one place to the next, seeming to wander pointlessly. The protagonist of *Sogni mancini* lives between two worlds, Italy and America; the narrator of *L'arcadia americana* is on a trip to the United States, as is the protagonist of *The Cream Train*; Benigni and Troisi (*Non ci resta che piangere*) and the Albanians of *Lamerica* are all travelling. All travel towards themselves. The protagonists of *City*, for their part, are already beyond movement. They do not even need to travel any longer; they are in a web of exploded places where boundaries have collapsed. These subjects in movement, or beyond movement, confront a dream of final, happy dislocation called "America." In doing so, they are still an integral part of the Italian literary tradition from which they emerge. As we have seen, if for the self the national character can ensue traditionally from wandering/wondering "abroad," physically or metaphorically, then it becomes almost inevitable for that self to confront the utopian space "America," either in its iconic or geopolitical manifestations. The construction of the self and how the self relates to itself involves a confrontation. It is a matter of self-representation.

Matters of Space: "L'America sta qua."
The Place of the New World in Italian Literature

"L'America sta qua," "America is here," sings an Italian song of the 1980s entitled "Una domenica italiana," "An Italian Sunday."[5] The song repeats what the Italians say about their country whenever they refer to it as a place where living a comfortable life can be easier than in other countries, a place one does not really need to leave if she or he wants to be happy. In other words, says the Italian, we are in America[6] without realizing it, so "America is here" is an everlasting epiphany, a moment of realization of one's own stupidity. Even if we are in America already, we do not know it, since our mind is displaced, and we are constantly looking for America somewhere else: America as an ideal place where one's own identity can be definitively found and played out.

This ideal space becomes textual, of course, as Cachey very convincingly explains in "Italy and the Invention of America." After all, why did Columbus and Vespucci leave Italy? They sought to find their fortunes and their identities somewhere else, an identity ultimately accomplished through the narrative of their voyages.

The importance of subjectivity in Italian literary tradition cannot be underestimated, and in the case of works such as Moretti's *Caro diario* it is tightly linked to the concept of America as a new space, since the film is a first-person narrative that reinforces (in order to undermine) the idea of constantly being or going somewhere else so as to be, feel, and live better.

Along the same lines, by saying "L'America sta qua" the Bel Paese evokes in three words the history of Italian emigration to the Americas, implying that those who remained, or those who seek refuge, today, and migrate to Italy, knew and know better. But little does the average Italian know about the economic misfortunes of Amerigo, who had never been a sailor before Don Fernando sent him after his friend, Columbus, to see what the real deal was, in the Indies, and whether, in fact, those even were the Indies. Amerigo liked maps and ships with all the love of a curious businessman who tries to make his living from them, "pero meterse Amerigo en una nave para ir al Atlántico jamás lo había hecho [...]" ("but he had never gone aboard a ship to go to the Atlantic [...]"), writes Germán Arciniegas in *Amerigo y el Nuevo Mundo*. "El astrolabio," Arciniegas continues, "le era familiar desde los tiempos en que el tío Giorgio Antonio lo hizo pintar en el retrato de San Augustín: pero lo conocía así: pintado. Explicado en los libros. Acariciado en tierra" (183; "he had been familiar with the astrolabe since his uncle Giorgio Antonio had it painted in the portrait of Saint Augustine, but he knew it like this: painted. Explained in books. Cherished on land"), like a dream one cherishes; and it is the dreamy space of Italian America that I wish to explore, trying to map out those fields of intellectual battle where America is for Italy the text and pre-text for narrating its own history and culture.

In his writing on Vittorini's *Americana*, Pintor drafted the ethical space of metaphorical America, "to defend at the price of pains and error the dignity of the human condition" (245). However, much less metaphorically, like many future Italian emigrants, what Amerigo needed to defend when he left Italy, when he set sail for the Indies, was indeed his own human condition and economic integrity, since his trade business in Italy, as in Spain, had been a failure. His own harsh economic reality forced him to decide to cross the ocean, and by his writing he ended up doing more than just reinvigorating his bank account, or helping to discover new lands. As Arciniegas points out, Columbus and Vespucci initiated American literature:

La literatura americana es la única de la cual conocemos el momento, el día exacto en que comienza, y quiso la suerte que los dos escritores italianos que la iniciaron – Colón y Vespucci – fueran capaces de imprimir a sus páginas la frescura y el golpe de milagro que corresponde a un hallazgo semejante. (190)

[American literature is the only one of which we know the moment of birth, the exact day on which it begins, and it was fate that made the two Italian writers who started it capable of giving its pages the freshness and magic touch that correspond to such a discovery.]

Since then, America has been for Italy a text to be written and rewritten. Dissenting intellectuals in Fascist Italy looked at the United States as the space, either real or imaginary, of freedom.

The situation is reversed in contemporary intellectual Italy. The films *Caro diario*, *Lamerica*, and *Non ci resta che piangere*, Alessandro Baricco's novel *City*, Francesca Duranti's *Sogni mancini*, as well as Gina Lagorio's *L'arcadia americana* are examples of how America tends to be negated and negativized on the level of both discourse and representation.[7] If Baricco tries to meld the United States' culture into the larger space of Western, globalized civilization, thereby depriving America of its own peculiarities, Moretti places America in a negative space of unviable ethics. The Italian actors and directors Roberto Benigni and Massimo Troisi find a drastic, paradoxical solution to the problem. In *Non ci resta che piangere*, a Florentine Communist schoolmaster, Saverio, and his even more Communist Neapolitan janitor, Mario, magically travel back in time five centuries and find themselves in 1492 Florence. When they realize the importance of the event, besides trying to warn Savonarola about the imminent end of his involvement in Florentine politics, they travel to Palos to prevent Columbus from setting out on his voyage. As luck would have it, they fail, for although they reach Palos on what they believe is the right day, it turns out that history had given them a wrong piece of information: they arrive too late.

The America that once took thousands of emigrants into its bosom comes back as the spectre of an unfulfilled dream of social justice in Gianni Amelio's *Lamerica*, where, for the Albanian immigrants, Italy itself turns into the new "America."

Scholarship and the History of the American Myth

I have gathered the historical observations that follow (and those that preceded) from several seminal works on the history of America in Italian literature and culture, and in European culture in general: Donald Heiney's *America in Modern Italian Literature* (1964), Antonello Gerbi's *The Dispute of the New World* (1973), Gérman Arciniegas' *Amerigo y el Nuevo Mundo* (Amerigo and the New World, 1990), Stefania Buccini's *The Americas in Italian Literature and Culture: 1700–1825* (1990), and Martino Marazzi's *Little America: Gli Stati Uniti e gli scrittori italiani del novecento* (Little America: The United States and the Italian Writers of the Twentieth Century, 1997). The books that concern Italy specifically, although focusing on different periods of time (they overlap at least in the case of Marazzi and Heiney), all aim at tracing a historical survey of the representation of America in Italian literature and culture, and, to a certain necessary extent, they also sketch the influence of American literature and film on Italian culture.

Concerning modern and contemporary Italy, Donald Heiney's work focuses on some major Italian modern writers and scholars, up to 1969, such as Cesare Pavese, Elio Vittorini, Italo Calvino, and Fernanda Pivano; thirty-three years later, Martino Marazzi can stretch that window to include famous and less famous contemporary authors. Heiney's and Marazzi's analyses of the subject differ in at least two ways. Heiney is an American scholar who looks at how illustrious Italian authors portray America in their works; but, at the same time, his interest lies just as much in displaying the Italian ethos that underlies those portrayals. He is concerned with the encounter between the two cultures and the subsequent clashes. Marazzi's work is more centred on the fortune and significance of America in twentieth-century Italian literature. My study differs from both because it is not a historical overview; rather, it focuses on specific works over a twenty-year time span. My objective is not to portray the fortunes of America in Italian literature and film, but to outline, through the analysis of literature and film, the role America plays in the ethicality of a subject: Italian intellectuals, who project their agency on a scale of values that they consider universal. I shall draw the features of this intellectual subject shortly.

What influenced modern Italy, as far as its myth of America goes, came from different sources: the letters from the emigrants during the Great Migration (1870–1921), and before that, Jean-Jacques Rousseau, René de Chateaubriand, Bernardin de Saint-Pierre, James Fenimore Cooper: the texts that formed the European myth of America in its more positive and more negative manifestations, as developed from Thomas More to Georges Louis Leclerc de Buffon. Italy fully participated in the "dispute of the New World," as Antonello Gerbi calls it, which saw, on one side, the detractors of America such as Buffon and DePaw, and, on the other, those who praised the "natural" ethics of the noble savage and America as the land of the Golden Age, of freedom, and of the possibility for a renewed and better Christian society. I can recall here Lodovico Antonio Muratori and his 1743 *The Happy State of Christianity in the Missions of the Fathers of the Society of Jesus in Paraguay*, translated into English and French a few years after its first publication. Muratori fully espouses the position of Bartolomeo de Las Casas about the atrocities committed by the Spaniards in South and Central America, and still sees those lands, two centuries after Las Casas' experience, as capable of being restored to a Golden Age by inducing their peoples "to profess a primitive and innocent Christianity" (Buccini 7). In his *Scienza Nuova*, Giambattista Vico placed the Indians in the age of the gods and talked of them as one race scattered over two continents, in which he distinguished only the Patagonians because he was influenced by the myth of the gigantic people.

More than Vico's, it is Antonio Genovesi's position that is relevant to my discourse, as an example of how Italian intellectuals talked about themselves while talking of America. Genovesi was a Neapolitan intellectual and, like many others in Italy, tended to agree with Voltaire's negative view about America and its *sauvages*, rather than with Rousseau's idyllic vision of them. Enlightened Italian intellectuals defended their concepts of civilization. Genovesi compares African and American savages to European savages like those who, in his perspective, formed the lower classes in the Kingdom of Naples. According to him, those classes were an expression of irreversible barbarity. Other authors, such as Carlo Goldoni in some of his plays, sustain the myth of the noble savage as represented in French literature. In the eighteenth century, the cultural link between North America and Italy became stronger around the time of the American Revolution, during which a singular figure stands out. Filippo Mazzei, an Italian physician, who became a prominent personality as a diplomat for the Union, helped the diffusion of revolutionary ideas both in Italy and in North America, where he sojourned for many years. He became a theoretician of Independence and was a friend of Franklin and Adams, whom he met in England. The two Americans convinced him to move to their country as a farmer, which he did (there he worked at a cooperative). When he arrived, he was welcomed by George Washington, and in 1779 he was appointed agent for Virginia and sent to Europe to obtain loans for the continuation of the war.

As for other Italians who contributed to the relationship between the Americas and Italy at that time, one can recall Lorenzo Da Ponte, Mozart's librettist, who moved to Pennsylvania to escape creditors. Carlo Botta wrote a history of the American War of Independence to give an example of how a revolution should be conducted.[8] Giacomo Leopardi tried to separate facts from fantasy in the maze of narratives about the Americas. He had never been there, but he knew well all the arguments of the dispute over the New World, and he shared with Rousseau the idea that society corrupts an innate human goodness. In his *Zibaldone*, Leopardi talks about the Native Americans to distinguish among different stages of civilization. He differentiates between savages (not touched by civilization at all); barbarians, the first nuclei of civilizations; and the civilized. Examples from the three categories are to be found among American Native populations, where Mayans and Aztecs are considered the civilized peoples.

To conclude this brief historical overview, I must also mention Giuseppe Garibaldi, known as the hero of the two worlds, for his support of and active participation in the South American struggle for independence, and his political appreciation in the United States.

Italian Modernism and America

Until 1930, Italian imagery of America consisted of letters from emigrants – the first big wave of emigration had already occurred at the end of the nineteenth century – and of works by Edgar Allan Poe, who was read in Baudelaire's French translation, Fenimore Cooper, and

Chateaubriand; and by Giacomo Puccini's *La Fanciulla del West*, based on David Belasco's *The Girl of the Golden West*, which was staged at the very beginning of the twentieth century.

In the 1930s, a revolution of the myth occurred. American jazz, American film (the Western), and the new American literature exploded in Europe as symbols of freedom and of the possibility of a new life reinvigorated by new democratic ideals that were to oppose European decadence. The attempt of Fascism, in Italy as elsewhere, to silence the invasion of American culture only had the effect of producing even greater interest in it. In fact, Elio Vittorini, Giaime Pintor, Cesare Pavese, and other Italian intellectuals were called "americanisti" even before Fascism came to an end. Vittorini's *Americana*, an anthology of American literature, represented a milestone for the "americanisti." Vittorini, like Pavese, was reading American literature clandestinely during Fascism. They read Caldwell, Steinbeck, Saroyan, Sinclair, Melville, and Hawthorne. When Vittorini and Pavese were reading American literature half-secretly, almost in an atmosphere of conspiracy, translations in French were not always available; hence, they learned English. Vittorini became one of the greatest Italian Americanists and translators by reading American books with the dictionary at his side. He taught himself English by translating *Robinson Crusoe* word for word. Pavese wrote a thesis on Whitman at the University of Turin in 1930, and translated Melville, Dos Passos, Faulkner, and others.

Unlike Pavese, Vittorini was not university trained. He studied when he did not work. He was the son of a railroad man, and he started off in literature as a proofreader for an Italian magazine. Both Pavese and Vittorini had problems with censorship, of course, but they were backed by editors like Giulio Einaudi and Valentino Bompiani. When asked by Bompiani, Vittorini edited an anthology of American literature. As soon as the book was ready to be released in 1941 it was censored and republished without Vittorini's prefaces to the American authors. Some uncensored copies were rescued, one of which ended up in Giaime Pintor's hands, another in Pavese's. Notwithstanding the censorship, the prefaces had a strong influence on Italian Americanists at a time when American literature was influencing the style and content of these authors' creative output.

Pintor worked as a translator for the Franco-Italian armistice commission, starting in 1940. Due to his public position, he was not credible as an anti-Fascist, though he was a very subtle one. Later, through the British secret services, he decided to join the partisans in the armed struggle to help the liberation of Italy, but died while trying to cross the enemy's line on the southern front in order to organize the resistance around Rome. In December 1943, at age twenty-four, he was torn apart by a German mine. Vittorini's *Americana*, which he read in 1943 (two years after Vittorini had given him a copy), made Pintor a more open opponent of the Fascist regime, although the essay in support of *Americana* was not published until after the liberation of Italy (in *Aretusa*), when Pintor had already died. In his text, Pintor uses the position of the American myth in Italian culture to accuse Fascist intellectuals, criticize German literature, and declare dead the old Italian convention of literary criticism based on aesthetics alone. In other words, he takes the opportunity to talk about Italy while writing of America. At the end of his article on Vittorini's *Americana*, Pintor honestly admits that what he has written may have little to do with the historical reality of the United States.

Pavese too interprets the interest of the Italian intellectuals in American literature from a political point of view ("Yesterday and Today"). He tells us, now that there is no ideal of liberty and democracy to fight for, that the literature coming from the United States no longer seems as interesting. Little did he know, in 1947, what the Beat Generation would mean for Italian intellectuals a decade later.

The Left "I": A Close-up on the Italian Leftist Intellectual[9]

Before focusing on the novels and films that I have chosen for this book, it is necessary to clarify the position of the contemporary Italian intellectual towards civil society, to explain why this prominent figure happens to be, at least in this work, a Leftist, and why, despite being a Leftist, and being influential, s/he is rarely registered with any leftist political party. My goal is to paint the background that will help the reader understand why, for example, authors such as Nanni Moretti and Gina Lagorio, who support leftist ideals, are critical of the leftist political establishment; or why the protagonist of *Left-Handed Dreams* declares "io *sono* di Sinistra," "I *am* on the Left," but leaves Italy, unwilling to join the struggle of the Italian Communist Party, and with no desire to know the new leftist parties born from the ashes of the previous one.

David Ward, who has written extensively on modern Italian culture, writes:

On the face of it, contemporary Italian intellectuals have a more prestigious existence than their Anglo-Saxon counterparts. Whether as writers,
academics, journalists or film directors, Italian intellectuals are courted by
political parties of all persuasions to add luster to their slates at election
time, and wooed by the media as influential opinion makers. The contact
Italian intellectuals have with the institutions of civil society comes from a
long tradition going back to the Middle Ages. Indeed, Italian society has
consistently relied on its intellectuals, rather than its political class, to sup-
ply the nation's agent for social change. (81)

Courted and wooed, indeed. Gina Lagorio was a deputy of the Independent Left for five years. She was asked to run for re-election after
her term expired, but she refused for reasons that are still unknown but
imaginable; she declared more than once that she was disgusted with
official politics. Lagorio wrote a diary of her experience as a deputy
that, she said, could only be published *post mortem*.

Dante was the first intellectual who "set a trend that was to be repeated as Italy made its way towards unification in the second half
of the nineteenth century" (Ward 82) by trying to constitute an Italian
ethos in a divided country with his search for a literary idiom, among
the many Italian dialects, that could be a unifying element. As Cachey
reminds us, and Ward reiterates, the history of Italian intellectuals is the
history of the gap between being Italian and living in a state that does
not satisfy their need for an ethical, national identity.

Until their position shifted towards the people, after and because of
Fascism, Italian intellectuals were unable and unwilling to bridge high
culture and the masses. The consequences of Fascism brought about the
necessary change theorized by the founder of the Italian Communist
Party, Antonio Gramsci. Seeing the failure of Benedetto Croce's Liberal
philosophy, whose bourgeois intellectual clinging to high culture could
not really lead the masses towards change, Gramsci understood that it
was the task of the "organic intellectual" (organic to the class of origin)
to promote change within civil society.[10] "In Gramsci's thought, it is
intellectuals who lay the cultural foundations on which moral and intellectual leadership are established in society" (Ward 87). We shall
have many chances to see how Moretti, Lagorio, Duranti, Amelio,
Baricco, and Benigni are keenly aware of their leading function as intellectuals, and strongly feel this responsibility as *individuals*, not belonging necessarily to any political lobby.

The Communist Party became a strong pole of attraction for intellectuals after Fascism, but "the question of the leadership between culture and politics [...] remained open" (Ward 89). At this point in his essay, as an example of the fracture between intellectuals and political power, Ward recalls the public argument on the autonomy of the intellectual between Elio Vittorini and Palmiro Togliatti, leader of the Communist Party, in the 1950s. Togliatti thought that Vittorini's *Politecnico*, a review founded to support social change from the Left, would "be a useful tool in the construction of the PCI's [Communist Party] cultural hegemony – Gramsci's precondition for assuming the leadership of the society" (Ward 90). Vittorini, however, was directing a literary magazine devoted, among other things, to the spreading of Italian Realism and Neorealism, whose experimental poetics "drew on European and American influences" (Ward 90), and not to the formation of a Communist nation. Togliatti was extremely displeased with Vittorini's literary interests that were not all directed towards the domestic goals of the Party. I refer to their disagreement not only because Vittorini was one of the leftist intellectuals who were deeply engaged with the idea of "America," but also because, half a century later, Gina Lagorio makes reference to that argument in her introduction to *Raccontiamoci com'è andata* (Let's Tell Each Other How It Went, 2003) to remind the reader of her intellectual independence from the leftist establishment, even while writing a book that supports and celebrates the accomplishments of the Left during the Resistance against Fascism.

It is important to stress the independence of Italian intellectuals who see themselves as *individually* bearing and promoting fundamental values, and whose national identity is historically weak. This is what makes them the subject of my work, which aims at leaping over literary national boundaries.

What are, then, the social background and history of this individual who does not necessarily belong to any leftist party, but is still a Leftist, and of whose cultural landscape America is a substantial part? To answer this question, in the attempt to define the iconic myth of America in Italy, Umberto Eco imagines a character whom he names Roberto. About Roberto, Eco writes,

Roberto abitava piuttosto il territorio extrapartitico delle attività culturali, delle case editrici, delle cineteche, dei giornali, dei concerti, è proprio in questo senso è stato culturalmente molto influente [...]. Roberto potrebbe essere nato tra il 1926 e il 1931. (Eco, Ceserani, and Placido 14)

[Roberto inhabited a territory outside of any political party, made of cultural activities, publishing houses, film libraries, newspapers, and concerts, and in this sense he has been culturally very influential [...]. Roberto could have been born between 1926 and 1931.]

As Roberto was then educated under Fascism, his only possible means of rebellion was to be absorbed by American culture, as we have already seen. I want to report, in its entirety, Eco's vivid and acute description of Roberto because no paraphrase could possibly be as incisive and crucial to the understanding of the intellectual examined in this book.

Once an adult, Roberto,

Dopo la guerra fu o membro o compagno di strada di un partito di sinistra. Rispettò Stalin, fu contro l'invasione americana in Corea, protestò per la morte dei Rosenberg. Abbandonò il partito con gli eventi ungheresi. Fu fermamente convinto che Truman fosse un fascista [...] adorò Hammett e si sentì tradito quando la *hard-boiled novel* passò sotto l'amministrazione del maccartista Spillane. Pensò che il passaggio a nord-ovest per un socialismo dal volto umano fosse sulla "road to Zanzibar" con Bing Crosby, Bob Hope, and Dorothy Lamour. Riscoprì e divulgò l'epica del New Deal, amò Sacco, Vanzetti, e Ben Shan, conobbe prima degli anni Sessanta (quando ridivennero celebri in America) i *folk songs* e le ballate di protesta della tradizione anarchica Americana e ascoltò con gli amici, alla sera, Pete Seeger, Woody Guthrie, Alan Lomax, Tom Jodd e il Kingston Trio. Era stato iniziato al mito di Americana, ma ora il suo *livre de chevet* era *On Native Grounds* di Alfred Kazin. Ecco perché quando la terza generazione, quella del '68, lanciò la sfida, magari anche contro gli uomini come Roberto, l'America era già un modo di vivere, anche se nessuno di quei ragazzi aveva letto *Americana*. (Eco, Ceserani, and Placido 17)

[After the war was a member, or just the pal of a Leftist political party. He respected Stalin, was against the American invasion of Korea, protested the death of the Rosenbergs. He abandoned the party with the events of Hungary. He was firmly convinced that Truman was a Fascist [...] he adored Hammet and felt betrayed when the hard-boiled novel came under the aegis of the McCarthyist Spillane. He thought that the Northwest Passage for a humane Socialism was on the "road to Zanzibar" with Bing Crosby, Bob Hope, and Dorothy Lamour. Rediscovered and divulged the epic of the New Deal, loved Sacco, Vanzetti, and Ben Shan, he knew before the seventies (when they became famous in America) the folk songs and ballads of protest of the American anarchic tradition and listened with his friends, at night, to Pete Seeger, Woody Guthrie, Alan Lomax, Tom Jodd, and the Kingston Trio. He had been initiated to the myth of *Americana*, but now his *livre de chevet* was Alfred Kazin's *On Native Grounds*.

That's why, when the third generation of '68 launched the challenge, probably even against the likes of Roberto, America was already a way of life, even if no one of those young people had read *Americana*.]

Roberto was the intellectual father, so to speak, of the authors treated here. Gina Lagorio represents here RobertA, with the capital "A" as a reminder, since Eco forgets to mention the importance of women intellectuals for the Resistance in Fascist Italy, and for the rebuilding of the country after the war. They too listened to jazz and walked the same cultural paths, as Lagorio reminds us (see chapter 4). They chanted in the streets with men during 1968, they were feminists in the 1970s and 1980s. And while I do not gender the reading of the texts I have chosen, I nonetheless have to point out that Roberto was not singing the *folk songs* alone. RobertA, alias Gina Lagorio, Dacia Maraini, Elsa Morante, Natalia Ginzburg, Oriana Fallaci, Francesca Duranti, to mention a few, was present and active.

The polymorphism of the attitudes and feelings towards America, which Eco describes in the Italian intellectual of the 1940s and 1950s, carries over into the 1960s and 1970s. The cherished or hated aspects of America vary, of course. By the time Moretti, De Carlo, Amelio, and Benigni operate, Roberto, and RobertA with him, have changed:

Il nuovo Roberto è stato forse un membro di un gruppo marxista-leninista del 1968, ha lanciato qualche bomba Molotov contro un consolato Americano nel 1970, alcuni cubetti di porfido contro la polizia nel 1972, e contro la vetrina di una libreria comunista nel 1977. Nel 1978, evitata la tentazione di unirsi a un gruppo terrorista, ha raccolto qualche soldo ed è volato in California, diventando magari rivoluzionario ecologo o ecologo rivoluzionario. L'america è diventata per lui non l'immagine di un rinnovamento futuro ma il luogo ove leccarsi le ferite e consolarsi di un sogno distrutto (o dato per morto troppo in anticipo). (Eco, Ceserani, and Placido 18)

[The new Roberto was perhaps a member of a Marxist-Leninist group in 1968, launched a few Molotov cocktails against an American consulate in 1970, some cubes of porphyry against the police in 1972 and against the window of a Communist bookshop in 1977. In 1978, avoiding the temptation to join a terrorist group, he gathered some money and flew to California, becoming perhaps a revolutionary ecologist, or an ecological revolutionary. For him, America became not the image of a future renovation, but the place where he could lick his wounds and console himself for a dream destroyed (or declared dead too early).]

Indeed, Roberto here, in his old and new versions, is a summa of what characterizes, in a more complex way – but not in the same way for each of them – the intellectuals examined in this book, either portrayed or portraying. Eco wrote the above text in 1983; *Treno di panna* had already been published, so its protagonist, Giovanni, had already flown to California. What happens in the Italian sociopolitical landscape in the mid-1980s and the 1990s is explained in chapters 1 and 3, and recalled when needed in the other chapters.

Very different was and is the case of the Italian intellectuals on the Right, conservative, and centre-to-the-right side of the political spectrum. The roots of what is usually indicated as "antiamericanismo di destra" (Rightist anti-Americanism, in opposition to the "antiamericanismo di sinistra," Leftist anti-Americanism), are already to be found in the strong anti-U.S. sentiment of the Fascist regime, at the end of the 1920s. With regard to that period, Massimo Teodori explains,

Dalle colonne di "Critica fascista" Giuseppe Bronzini indicava nel materialismo e nell'edonismo i mali tipici della moderna civiltà che trovava nell'America la sua massima espressione. [...] In America è il "dio denaro" che regna su una società individualistica senza valori spirituali, segno evidente della decadenza della razza. [...] Il pericolo Americano, per l'Europa e l'Italia, sta nel dinamismo economico senza remore e senza controlli e nel suo carattere espansivo che guida le scelte politiche orientandole aggressivamente in senso imperialistico e militare. (*Maledetti americani* 55–6)

[From the columns of "Critica fascista," Giuseppe Bronzini pointed at materialism and hedonism as the typical evils of modern civilization that found in America its main expression [...] In America, money reigns over an individualistic society without spiritual values, which is a clear sign of the decadence of race. [...] The American danger, for Europe and Italy, is to be found in the economic dynamism void of either hesitations, or controls, and in its expansive mark that leads the political choices, orienting them aggressively towards imperialism and militarism.]

Italian foreign policy becomes overtly and completely hostile to the United States after the mid-1930s. However, by the end of the great migration, Fascist Italy did not appreciate the severe reduction of the migration fluxes that the United States imposed, as the huge migratory wave to the United States had helped Italy, since its unification, to alleviate the tragic social problem of the poor, starving masses of Southern Italy.[11]

Although the political and economic relationship between Italy and the United States has obviously greatly changed since the end of the Second World War, the attitude of the conservative intellectuals towards America has not changed:

> Allora, negli anni Ottanta come oggi, non sono le scelte di politica estera o le risposte al terrorismo ad essere messe sotto accusa: il bersaglio è molto più generale, è la civiltà Americana con i suoi disvalori, collocati ai livelli più bassi di una scala che ha al vertice le tradizioni italiana ed europea. (Teodori, *Maledetti americani* 54)[12]

> [Then, during the eighties, as well as nowadays, what is under accusation are not the choices in foreign politics, or the response to terrorism: the target is much more general, it is American civilization with its negative values, collocated at the lower levels of a scale that has Italian and European traditions at the top.]

The rejection of what is perceived as American life-style is at the centre of Marcello Veneziani's discourse in "Non voglio fare l'americano," an article published in *Il Giornale*, after 9/11. Marcello Veneziani is a conservative journalist and writer, an intellectual of what is called in Italy "la nuova destra," "the new Right":

> Non mi piace dell'America l'indifferenza, se non il disprezzo, verso il resto del mondo […] il primato assoluto del denaro e del profitto […] il disprezzo per la storia, la civiltà altrui e la cultura […] le rigidità furiose dell'anima quacchera, puritana e protestante, la subordinazione della politica agli interessi economici […] l'assenza di quel tessuto comunitario e urbano che costutuisce la nostra anima e la nostra richezza: ma chi non ha un passato, non può darselo, non è colpa loro …

> [About America, I do not like the indifference, if not the scorn towards the rest of the world […] the absolute supremacy of money and profit […] the

disdain for history, the civilizations and cultures of others [...] the furious
rigidity of the Quaker, puritan, and protestant soul; the subordination of
politics to economic interests [...] the absence of that communitary and
urban texture which constitutes our soul and our richness: but those who
do not have a past, cannot invent it; it is not their fault ...]

We find in Veneziani's words the same criticism that the conservative
establishment directed to the United States throughout the twentieth
century.

His words are echoed in those of another prominent conservative
intellectual, the historian Franco Cardini, who, in an interview to *Il
Foglio* in 2002, explained his anti-Americanism as follows: "Il mio 'stare
a destra' ha sempre condannato l'espansione dell'Occidente sul mondo
e la distruzione delle culture 'altre' accompagnata dall'imposizione di
un primato economico, finanziario, produttivo, tecnologico, militare"
(Guardì; "my 'being on the Right' has always condemned the expan-
sion of the Western world and the destruction of other cultures, accompanied by the imposition of an economic, financial, productive,
technological, and military primacy").

Over the decades of the twentieth century, these values recognized as
negative have been the target of Italian Catholicism as well.[13]

After September 11, at a moment when the cultural anti-Americanism
of the Left and of the Right converged against the U.S. war in
Afghanistan, the Catholic writer (essayist and columnist) Vittorio
Messori said to the daily *Il Corriere della Sera*:

Q. "Messori, perché dice di non stare né con bin Laden né con Bush?"

A. "Perché non stia con i terroristi, mi pare ovvio. Ma non posso stare
neanche con Bush. Come si fa ad approvare quella che è il primo caso nella
storia di guerra contro ignoti?"

Q. "Veramente un 'noto' c'è: Osama bin Laden."

A. "Appunto. Nella loro mentalità hollywoodiana, gli americani hanno
sempre bisogno del capo della banda Bassotti, di qualcuno che faccia la
parte del cattivo. Ma è chiaro a tutti che il problema del terrorismo non si
può ricondurre al solo bin Laden." (Messori)

[Q. "Messori, why do you say you are neither on bin Laden's side, nor
on Bush's?"

A. "The reason why I am not on a terrorist's side is obvious. But I cannot
take Bush's side either – how can anyone approve the first launching of a
war, in history, against unknown persons?"

Q. "Actually, there is a well-known person: Osama bin Laden."

A. "Excactly. In their Hollywoodian mind-set, Americans always need to find the boss of the Beagle Boys, someone who plays the villain's part. However it is plain for everyone to see that terrorism cannot be traced back exclusively to bin Laden."]

What I want to point out is not Messori's opinion against the invasion of Afghanistan, not different from many other opinions, either pro or contra the war. In his criticism, Messori conflates "Americans" with Hollywood, thus repeating old stereotypes about U.S. culture that have rarely, if ever, been overcome or seriously questioned by intellectuals either on the right, the centre, or the left of the political spectrum. Messori's comment is only one example of an older and more general negative sentiment that Italian Catholics have held against the so-called American way of life, or what they know of it. Even after the fall of Fascism and the end of the Second World War, when the Americans (then on Italian soil) were the only strong ally and interlocutor against the Communist threat, the Catholic party that would govern Italy for the following fifty years (Democrazia Cristiana) remained suspicious of the American way of life, regardless of its own political allegiance to the United States.

While the Leftist intellectuals had a polymorphous attitude towards U.S. culture, which for them at times represented "freedom," either during Fascism or later on, conservative and Catholic intellectuals could not easily reconcile traditionalism with American liberalism; the cultural discourses were, and still are, very different from the political decisions made by the government.

Mapping the Journey

Although each chapter of this book focuses on different works, the unifying principle is thematic, so the works to be discussed in each section have been chosen according to the particular topic treated therein. I move from the "I"s of *Caro diario* and *Sogni mancini*, who focus on their own displacement and portray America in the process (chapter 1), to the literary and cinematic displacement of America itself in *City*, *Lamerica*, and *Non ci resta che piangere* (chapter 2). Chapters 3 and 4 deal with two voyages to the United States. Unlike the characters of the other works, the protagonists of *L'arcadia americana* and *Treno di panna* travel to America (the protagonist of *Sogni mancini* lives in America) with the ultimate result of reinforcing their cultural identities. The confrontation with the American myth occurs in a geographical space that takes on the contours of their European views. In chapter 3, I draw a comparison between *Treno di panna* and Jean Baudrillard's *Amérique*. My comparison shows how the unchanged subject of *Treno di panna* deploys an old, imperialistic European gaze to shape an image of America ultimately unquestioned by the Italy of the 1980s.

Chapter 5 takes into consideration the shift in perspective that is happening in Italian literature and film with regard to America. History now becomes central to the story of the individual who deals with America. It is a shift that allows artistic productions to reappropriate the phenomenon of the great migration as part of Italian national history. While the American dream remains central to these newer works, as does the individual, those who change are the dreamers: they are now the people who moved to the United States within a specific historical context.

This introduction, while not an exhaustive analysis of any of the topics treated, is meant to clarify how and why my work stands at the intersection of Italian literature and film, the American myth, ethics of the subject, and issues of cultural globalization. It explains why Italian intellectuals are historically in constant displacement, ideal (political) or metaphorical, and why and how this position of displacement makes them individuals constantly working on themselves and negotiating issues of identity and alterity so relevant in globalization for the encounter and cohabitation of different cultures. It also explains how and why these intellectuals need to confront, and ultimately do confront, America in their search for a viable universal ethics that can rely on the individual.

1 Wandering Subjects

The "I" at Wonder in *Caro diario* and *Sogni mancini*

The "I"s of Nanni Moretti's *Caro diario* (1994) and Francesca Duranti's *Sogni mancini* (1996) wander between places and wonder about their identities. Ultimately, they transport and translate their identities, since the sense of moral responsibility with which they invest themselves, as individuals in society, is manifested from a position of constant geographical and ideological displacement. America is central to *Sogni mancini*, while in *Caro diario* it comes in the form of a cultural construct absorbed in the Italian context. In both cases, it represents one of the two horns of the dilemma: is America to be chosen, or not? And if so, why, and how? The two protagonists of *Caro diario* and *Sogni mancini* are Italian leftist intellectuals living in completely different milieux. One is in Rome, the other is in Manhattan. What they share is (a) the way they position themselves vis-à-vis the Italian sociopolitical context, which is an integral part of what they feel is their personal identity, (b) their refusal to join social and political mainstream currents, and (c) their will to be happy only when actively choosing to go elsewhere, physically or ideally. That new place is not America *tout court* for them. Simply embracing the American Dream does not represent a viable solution for them, whether America be central (*Sogni mancini*) or collateral and almost incidental (*Caro diario*) to their discourse.

The Moralizing "I" of Nanni Moretti

What is perhaps most attractive about these Italian theorists and the movements they grow out of is their joyful character.

Michael Hardt

Michael Hardt writes the above in the introduction to *Radical Thought in Italy*, a collection of essays written primarily by Italian leftist intellectuals who are considered the theorists of the extra-parliamentary Left that was a major protagonist of the Italian social and political scene from 1968 to the mid-1980s. Nanni Moretti was politically a child of . that extra-parliamentary Left, and the mark of irony is the unmistakable sign of his work. He never espoused, though, a certain extremist tendency of those years to conceive culture and art as a means of propaganda for an overly confident ideology.[1] Self-irony is essential for Moretti: "I make fun of my own milieu because I think that, when you make fun of yourself, you have more of a right to make fun of others" (Porton and Ellickson 14).

Moretti started off his career as a director in the 1970s, selling his collection of postage stamps to buy a Super8 video camera with which, in February 1973, at the Ostiense train station in Rome, he filmed the arrival of thousands of workers from all over Italy who gathered in the capital for a national rally of protest against their work conditions. Most of his films are informed by his preoccupation with Italian society and politics; he talks about himself in order to talk about Italy. From the beginning, he has been an independent director, never aligning himself with the mainstream of Italian cinema and always refusing the funding of big corporations such as Penta Film[2] (Penta was the Italian distributor for the film *Henry*, which Moretti watches and criticizes in *Caro diario*). His first movie was, in fact, the Super8 *Io sono un autarchico* (I Am an Autarchic, 1977).

Moretti is widely recognized as one of the initiators of the new Italian cinema that developed in the 1980s.[3] Manuela Gieri explains how Moretti belonged to a group of new directors who, regardless of noticeable ideological and artistic differences, "all aimed at retrieving a shared gaze in the present, at staging the crisis of the subject and of its inability to remember, at openly questioning the very notion of identity – personal and collective/national, moved by the need for a new cultural solidarity [...]" ("Landscapes" 42). She continues,

Indeed, Moretti's cinema as a whole can certainly be described as a highly moral and at times even moralistic personal and collective discourse [...]. If it is true that a film is a fragment of reality and an attempt at its representation, it is also unquestionably true that with his cinema Nanni Moretti has constantly witnessed and interpreted the past of an entire generation, even though largely censuring it because of its most controversial moments: that is, terrorism [*sic*]. [...] Moretti contributed to the creation of a new mode of filmmaking and to the definition of an equally new relationship between cinema and history as well as cinema and society. (50)

What Moretti and other directors such as Gianni Amelio and Gabriele Salvatores did was to re-establish that link between cinema and history, since, as Gieri explains, "For the generation of those who came of age in filmmaking in the 1970s, the present was unfortunately the time of removal of the past, and largely an age of celebration of the so-called *edonismo reganiano* in the years of Bettino Craxi's leadership of the country" (42). In order to understand Nanni Moretti's social commitment, it is necessary to have a look at the sociopolitical scenery to which Gieri refers, as it is within the frame of Moretti's commitment that images of America come into play in *Caro diario*.

Edonismo reaganiano (Reagan-era hedonism) is an expression coined in the 1980s by the Italian television editorialist (journalist and writer) Roberto D'Agostino, and it refers to the new Italian lifestyle that emerged in those years. Thanks to a change in the socioeconomic landscape that came about during the years in which the Socialist Bettino Craxi led the Italian government (1983–7), the middle-class Italian was becoming an investor. He was happy and possibly wealthy enough. The new generation was an ambitious one made up of young entrepreneurs devoted to a fast and easy economic and personal success. They were the Italian "Yuppies," dedicated also to a very attentive care of the self, which is the reason why the "lookologo" ("lookologue") D'Agostino created the ironic expression *edonismo reaganiano*. The myth of Wall Street had landed in Italy. The terrorism of the *anni di piombo* (years of lead) had already been forgotten without even having been elaborated at the level of the social conscience. In a satiric and very successful television program called "Quelli della notte" (Those of the Night, 1985), D'Agostino created for himself the figure of the "lookologo," an opinionist of the new generation's looks – in other words, sort of a parodic organic intellectual of that generation itself, for which history and memory of both the past and the present were taboos.

The Italianized America in the background of this scenario is the one of the Reagan era. In the spring of 1988, the songwriter and singer Luca Barbarossa launched "Yuppies," a song that describes perfectly the Italian yuppies and the political and economic milieu in which they emerged. The song compares Italy to America, "this Italy, a bit American," in order to highlight the ridiculous result that was brought about by the adoption of an American model on Italian soil. In *Caro diario* we witness the same sense of ridicule in the portrayal of the mayor of Stromboli, for instance, who wants to make the island into a multicultural enclave by importing palms from Los Angeles and by playing a sound track from a spaghetti Western all day long. Here is part of Barbarossa's song:

sono i figli di quest'Italia / quest'Italia un po' americana / sempre meno contadini / sempre piu' figli di puttana [...] sono i figli di quest'Italia / quest'Italia che sta crescendo / sempre meno contadini / sempre piu' fondi d'investimento [...]. E di politica non ne parlano / evitano il discorso / loro votano solamente / chi gli fa vincere un concorso [...] / quest'Italia che va di corsa / toglie i soldi dal materasso / e li sputtana tutti in borsa / sono i figli di quest'Italia / quest' Italia antifascista / se cerchi casa non c'e' problema / basta conoscere un socialista [...].[4]

[they're the children of today's Italy, / this Italy a bit American, / who are less and less peasants, / and more and more sons of a bitch [...] they're the children of this Italy, / this Italy that's growing: / less and less peasants, / more and more investment funds [...]. And they don't talk about politics, / they avoid it, they just vote for those who help them get a state job [...] / this Italy that is in a hurry / takes the money from under the mattress to throw it all away in the stock exchange / they're the children of this Italy, the antifascist Italy / if you're looking for a house, no problem: all you need is to know a Socialist [...].][5]

The nationwide scandal "Tangentopoli," which exploded in February 1992, changed the scenery that the song describes.

"Tangentopoli" ("Bribe Polis," coined from Paperopoli, Donald Duck's town) referred to the collusion between private industry and the Italian political parties in public building and services – corruption, concussion, and illicit financing of the parties.[6] Fininvest, the investment company belonging then to Silvio Berlusconi, was investigated as well. When Berlusconi won the election for the first time in 1994, his Fininvest was still under investigation. Nanni Moretti recalls that Election Day in the opening scene of *Aprile*, but his political and moral fight against Silvio Berlusconi and the overwhelming power of television began earlier. Among other things, *Caro diario* is an open attack on the banality and, at the same time, on the hypnotic power of modern television. Thierry Jousse writes,

L'irruption de Silvio Berlusconi au pouvoir en Italie est un événement con-
sidérable. Cette menace pour la démocratie se produit justement dans un
pays où le cinema est précisément très affaibli. Reste Nanni Moretti, seule
figure de cinéaste capable de faire front à la télécratie. (62)

[Silvio Berlusconi's rise to power, in Italy, is a considerable event. This
menace to democracy occurs, not surprisingly, in a country where cinema
is, precisely, very weakened. There remains Nanni Moretti, the only figure
of a cineaste able to confront telecracy.][7]

This was the political and social climate, past and present, in which and
against which Nanni Moretti, as well as Gianni Amelio, created their
"cinema of resistance," as Gieri likes to call it ("Landscapes" 52). In
L'unico paese al mondo (The Only Country in the World, 1994), a collection of nine short films that nine "young" Italian directors prepared
against Berlusconi's candidacy for the political elections of 1994, we see
Moretti on his Vespa again, as in Caro diario, still wearing his white hel-
met. This time, instead of wandering through Rome, he drives through
Paris. He addresses his diary again, "Caro diario ... ," to explain how
France, unlike Italy, did not allow Berlusconi to ascend to power in the
French media industry.

Before Caro diario, in Moretti's films, cinema and history and cinema
and society meet in the representation of a subject that is a mirror, a
product and a producer of the ideology of her/his generation. Such is,
for instance, Michele Apicella, the protagonist of several of Moretti's
films up to Palombella rossa (Red Lob, 1989). Moretti himself interprets
Apicella and highlights the juxtaposition between himself and his character by giving Michele his mother's maiden name, Apicella.[8]

With Caro diario, and the subsequent Aprile (1998), Moretti definitively embraces self-representation by abandoning the alias Apicella
and interpreting himself.[9] The barrier between the enunciating and
enunciated subject collapses (Gieri, "Landscapes" 50); the intellectual
who works at representation, Moretti, is now also represented, which
makes the film relevant to my discourse. In Caro diario, the leftist intellectual Moretti represents his position towards history and society as an
individual, displays his role and his morality, and gives guidelines for
the formation of a new ethicality.[10] Gieri explains:

Despite his distaste for the so-called "cinema civile," in the good company
of Gianni Amelio and a few other directors, and even when choosing

different avenues, Nanni Moretti has constantly worked [...] for the creation of a cinema strongly committed to social, political and cultural critique and change, as well as the building of a new and honest *personal* and *collective* identity. ("Landscapes" 52, my emphasis)

Gianni Amelio's *Lamerica* is an instance of such a committed attempt at moral change. For both Amelio and Moretti this is a moral change that entails the rescue of historical memory:

Nanni Moretti's gaze onto the world is forcefully moral as it constantly traverses the ambiguous space between comedy and drama [...]. The same moral stance characterizes Gianni Amelio's entire cinematic production [...]. Both directors refocus their tales, as their gazes move from the mass to the individual, from the panorama to the detail in the attempt to retrieve truth, time, and thus history [...]. Nanni Moretti's and Gianni Amelio's reply to a contemporary interpretation of memory, and thus of time and space, has to do with the retrieval of a form of morality in the face of the world of existence. (Gieri, "Landscapes" 53)

Scholars and cinema experts all seem to agree on Moretti's necessary morality.[11] In a 1989 article devoted to *Palombella rossa*, Serge Toubiana writes,

Nanni Moretti est, dans la nouvelle génération (à 35 ans, après six ou sept films, il porte depuis quatre ou cinq ans sur ses épaules tout le renouveau cinématographique en Italie) le seul à s'inscrire dans la tradition rossellinienne et pasolininenne du *regard moral*. (Toubiana 21)[12]

[In the new generation, Nanni Moretti (at 35, after six or seven movies, he has been bearing on his shoulder all the renewal of the Italian cinema for four or five years) is the only one to inscribe himself in the Rossellinian and Pasolinian tradition of the *moral gaze*.]

We shall find the same moral gaze and equal necessity for the intellectual to remember history in Francesca Duranti's *Sogni mancini*, in Gina Lagorio's *L'arcadia americana*, and in Benigni and Troisi's film *Non ci resta che piangere* – a necessity that, in these artistic productions, indeed clashes with the pursuit of America as a solution. The counterproof to this attitude is in Baricco's *City*, where America becomes the protagonist of a text that builds itself in a space similar to the World Wide Web and that expands in a continuous present, a space in which memory is literary, confined to the world of fictional creation.

Caro diario: The Glue of Irony between Stupor and Stupidity

In *Caro diario* Moretti takes the opportunity to talk about Italy by talking about himself and thus traces the frame of his position and function as an intellectual in society.[13] In the process, some icons of America are targeted and destroyed. This destruction deploys two narrative elements, stupor and stupidity, as well as a device to over-expose them, irony.

   While stupor and stupidity are the two sides of the same coin, as their etymology attests,[14] the irony of *Caro diario* is the means by which it is possible to look at both sides of the coin at the same time and be stupefied by stupidity. In the process, some images of America are targeted as they are woven into the Italian cultural constructs that Moretti attacks. Neither America as a myth nor the United States is central to *Caro diario*. The film critiques the then-current decadence of Italian cinema (and, at the same time, it pays homage to great Italian directors such as Pasolini and Antonioni)[15] and the decadence of other aspects of Italian culture as they relate to the protagonist's identity and his vision of Italy. However, those collateral images of a specifically Italianized American dream become relevant to my study because they are deployed as elements of widely shared knowledge with the audience, in order to carry out a discourse about Italy and dreams of escapism. Before analysing this aspect of the film, I will briefly describe the plot.

   The film is divided into three episodes, "In Vespa" ("On My Vespa"), "Isole" ("Islands"), and "Medici" ("Doctors"). In the first episode, Moretti undertakes his rediscovery of Rome on a Vespa. Wandering through the empty streets of the city on a summer day, Moretti stops at a cinema to watch *Henry* (John McNaughton, 1986), a film that many seemed to like at the time, but one that Moretti considered very bad. Here Moretti takes the chance to tell us what happens to Italian cinemas during the summer – they only show extremely commercial or pornographic films – and what he thinks of a certain cinema altogether. The other film he watches is a fictional one whose few scenes Moretti set up on purpose for *Caro diario*. In this film, Moretti observes, and wants us to observe, a group of friends in their forties talking in a sitting room about how socially and politically engaged they were twenty years before, how middle-class they have become now, and how they have lost any will to fight for any ideals.

Moretti shows us this generation of accommodated men and women to take his distance from them, thus framing his identity and intellectual position. Recalling old rallies, one of the characters in the film declares, "We used to yell horrible things." Moretti replies, on his Vespa, "Voi gridavate cose orrende. Io gridavo solo cose giuste e ora sono uno splendido quarantenne" ("You used to yell horrible things. I yelled only right things and I am now a splendid forty-year-old man"). From this moment on, his drive through the streets of Rome is a voyage through his own passions, dreams, manias, ideas, and fixations. He wonders why Romans have left downtown to live on the periphery; he joins a group of salsa dancers; he talks to Jennifer Beals, whom he meets by chance in the street; he portrays himself as the nightmare of all the film experts who wrote good critiques of *Henry* in a scene where a journalist is trying to sleep while Moretti, sitting by his bed, rereads for him his review of *Henry* in an accusatory tone. The journalist shivers, moans, and cries from an evidently childish sense of guilt. Once again, Moretti's wandering through his own ideas is meant to describe a specific social and intellectual scenario. The hovering presence of his "I," this unchanging focal point, is there to deliver a sociopolitical and cultural discourse. At the end of the episode, Moretti pays tribute to Pier Paolo Pasolini, driving to the place where he was killed. Here, by almost disappearing from the scene, he leaves that space to silence and memory, or the lack of it (that forgotten place in an open field is not celebratory).

In the second episode, "Islands," Moretti travels with a good friend of his to the Aeolian Islands, a group off the Sicilian coast. He is going through a creative crisis and hopes that the trip will help him focus on his work. His friend, a retired professor of literature who, for the past twenty years, has been working exclusively on Joyce's *Ulysses*, has no television and prides himself on never watching TV. During the trip, though, he is bewitched by television and by prime time programs, soap operas, and *telenovelas*. In this episode, Moretti explores the banality of television and its power. More generally, he ironizes several kinds of excesses and extremisms, from the parents on the island of Salina, who live exclusively for their children, mastered by them, to the lascivious lifestyle of the tourists at Panarea; from the moralist hermit of Alicudi, who is extremely disgusted by Italian society, to his friend's new fixation on television. In this episode Moretti states he is happy only in the transit from one island to the next. And it is important to highlight this detail since Moretti's moral gaze on society always comes from a position of conscious and wanted displacement, of non-homologation. In the first episode, "On My Vespa," he declares that he will only ever feel at ease within a minority. The responsibility with which Moretti invests the individual as bearer of moral values cannot be separated from a position of displacement.

The third episode, "Medici" (Doctors), is the tale of Moretti's unfortunate journey from one physician to the next during his illness, a benign tumour, and a recording of the illness's development up to its healing. Seated among the many boxes of medicines that have done nothing for him, he will conclude that the best way to begin each day is to have a glass of clear water: a sign of purification, which takes us back to the first episode. Antonella D'Aquino sees Moretti's enterprise on his Vespa, together with the entire film, as a journey of purification. Purification, in this case, also means to purify oneself of an unfulfilled dream.

Moretti's purification is accomplished through a dénouement of the stupidity of one's stupor, which is operated by irony. In *Caro diario*, stupor and stupidity are the effects generated by the contemplation of a dream. In this regard, I will refer to four scenes from the film: (1) the Italian film that we view with Moretti in a cinema, (2) Moretti's encounter with a man getting out of his car in the neighbourhood of Casalpalocco, (3) the encounter with Jennifer Beals, and (4) the farewell to the mayor of Stromboli.

The film we watch with Moretti in the first episode is "a fake movie that I myself [Moretti] shot in order to mock a certain genre of Italian films, extremely boring, typical of a certain generation" (Saada and Jousse 56).[16] In this parody we see ex-intellectuals and ex-dissenters arguing with each other in a sitting room. They fought for radical leftist ideals in the 1970s but are now completely assimilated into the social and political system, forming the middle- and upper-class social strata. As they themselves declare, their stupor can be defined as "a state of mental stupefaction; apathy or torpor of mind" (*Oxford English Dictionary Online*). This stupor is equated to stupidity by the accumulation of examples and details in their discourse: not even the box of the old and reassuring pain reliever is the same anymore, if compared to the past.

By undermining the ability of the people sitting there to develop a discourse that could eventually make sense, Moretti undermines the value of their old ideals and dreams in the first place, thus destroying the validity of those dreams. By means of exaggeration, Moretti pushes the parabola to its climax, so that the steep slope of descent provokes greater destruction. Visually, we see this process represented in the scene of Moretti's encounter with the Americans on the volcano, in Stromboli.

The same process that undermines one's ability to judge situations clearly is carried out with the man at Casalpalocco, a resident of the neighbourhood whom Moretti approaches in the street to ask him why he chose to live there. The director questions the choice of the residents of Casalpalocco to move to that tranquil neighbourhood thirty years before on the basis of their inability to recognize the beauty of down-town Rome. He gives himself the authority to do so. What gets di-minished in the process is the dream of the residents of Casalpalocco, whom Moretti portrays metonymically, while driving: "I can smell jogging suits, videotapes, watch-dogs in the garden, pizzas in card-board boxes." And slippers, he will add soon after, while talking to the man who is, indeed, wearing slippers (we do not see them, but Moretti gives us the information with a visual sign by simply pointing at them).

It is easy to recognize in Moretti's discourse icons of a modern life that bears the weight of American culture. These are also symptoms of a life too comfortable, lived behind private gates, void of any social or political preoccupation. This is what Moretti criticizes. He asks himself, "Why did they come here thirty years ago?" The answer he receives from the gentleman he meets – "Don't you see how beautiful it is?" – only serves the purpose of reinforcing his critique.

In the encounter with Jennifer Beals, Moretti undermines and de-stroys his own dream to become a dancer. He has always wanted to be a dancer since he saw *Flashdance*. Moretti builds up the stupidity of his dream by holding up a mirror for us that reveals the blind spot of the salsa dancers he meets on his way (he first watches them, then he joins the band to sing). The words of Juan Luis Guerra's song "Buscando VISA para un sueño" ("seeking a VISA for a dream") make a striking contrast to the atmosphere of the carefree and merry scene. The song describes people queuing at the gates of the U.S. embassy in Santo Domingo to obtain a permit to enter the United States.

Once Moretti has established the blindness of his dream, he *meets* his dream, which here reaches its climax. Jennifer Beals is walking in the street with her then-husband, the director Alexander Rockwell, whose *In the Soup* (1992) has been one of the few American films Moretti screens at his cinema theatre, the Nuovo Sacher (New Sacher). Nanni approaches the two and, after having made sure that the woman is really the American actress, he talks about his passion for dancing, about hyper-functional Romagna and how he wishes he had lived there because, if he had done so, he would have certainly learned how to dance and would have had access to a better lifestyle. Emilia Romagna is that historically leftist region of Italy well known for its economic prosperity, its functional social infrastructures, and its tradition of ballroom dancing. Jennifer Beals will draft the descending part of Nanni Moretti's parabola. She will construct Moretti first as a foot-maniac, then as "a bit off," finally as "quasi scemo" ("almost stupid").

Moretti's dream of becoming a dancer has the contours of a utopia, and his representation of Romagna as the place where only better things can happen is also utopian. In his conversation with Jennifer Beals, this utopia is embodied by an American icon, *Flashdance*, which is in turn the representation of the American dream. In the film, in fact, an American subject becomes accomplished, passing from being a Cinderella to being a very lucky woman. She finally marries the owner of the factory where she works and she becomes a dancer.

We now move to the mayor of Stromboli and his idea to transform his island into a new amusement park. The mayor welcomes Moretti and his friend to the island and tries to have them hosted by some of the inhabitants of Stromboli. He is unsuccessful because his citizens hate and mistrust him in reaction to his ideas to give Stromboli a new identity by rebuilding it. Sergio Leone, Vittorio Storaro, and Ennio Morricone are the names that come to the mayor's mind when, in a state of awe, he describes to Moretti and his friend how he would like to transform the island by filling the streets with the music of Ennio Morricone (possibly the sound-track of Leone's spaghetti Western, *The Good, the Bad and the Ugly*) and by illuminating the island with the photographic direction of Storaro. "Tutto nuovo!" he says, "All new!" Moretti and his friend look at him with compassionate sympathy while going aboard the ferry that will take them far from Stromboli and its mayor, who watches the two leave from the dock. And while the boat takes to the sea, the mayor shouts to them, once again, "Tutto nuovo!" in a scene meant to be ironically pathetic. Morricone, Storaro, and Leone are all great names in Italian and American cinema, those who, more than realizing a dream, have produced dreams. The mayor wants to make of Stromboli a new, "naturalized" world in order to give its people an identity that can only be fictional. Moretti flees this artificial landscape and plays out his escape by leaving the mayor in mid-sentence. And again, the dream is made of "America," the fictional America, with the palm trees from Los Angeles and music from the spaghetti Western.

Moretti flees America and tells us that there is no New Land to go to that can magically solve sociopolitical problems and issues of coexistence among cultures. Turning Stromboli into a Disneyland that can create a new identity for its people in order to accommodate issues of diversity is Moretti's nightmare. The same fictional America will be at the decentred centre of *City*. The subjects of the novel, who are themselves icons of America and shreds of its exploded myth, are outcasts in exactly the same way as the dream they represent. Their America will only survive in literature.

Unlike the more radical leftist of years past, Italian leftist intellectuals of today do not feel the need to fight the myth any longer. They just abandon the myth and take on responsibility for this as intellectuals engaged with issues stemming from the necessity of global ethics.

Identities *in absentia* in *Sogni mancini*

Sogni mancini's protagonist is a direct representation of the Italian intellectual I discuss in this book, who is on the Left without joining any political party. Her sociopolitical stance overlaps with the author's. It is important, then, to take a look at Duranti's background to understand how, in the novel, the narrator's voice becomes the representation of the intellectual who stands behind the story, and within it.

Francesca Duranti published her first novel, *La bambina* (The Little Girl, 1976), at age 41. In this autobiographical narrative she gives an account of her life as a child in a large Tuscan villa during the Second World War and soon after. Born into the upper middle class (her mother was the daughter of a Genoese industrialist), she grew up in a leftist environment. Her paternal grandfather was one of the founders of the Italian Socialist party, and her father became a member of Parliament, for the same party, during the first post-war elections. A strong antifascist, her father was kept under strict surveillance during the war. A professor of law at the university of Pisa, he also served as minister of education in the 1950s. In the preface to the Italian edition of *Sogni mancini* (published in 1996 and translated into English in 2000),[17] Duranti observes that the intellectual relationship with her father deeply informed her sense of democracy and respect for alterity. Not so happy was the relationship with her mother, who was a woman with a strong personality but "devoid of maternal qualities, cold and sometimes psychologically cruel" (Kozma).[18]

A successful writer whose work is translated into several languages, Duranti lives now between Lucca and New York, a lifestyle that she shares with the protagonist of *Sogni mancini*, who, at the end of the novel, decides to live between two countries.

Sogni mancini directly engages issues of displacement, the search for an ethical self, and images of America, and it does so in a manner which could be considered exemplary of the generations of authors who matured soon after the 1970s. What Duranti's work also does is to bridge Italy and America in ways that enrich the discourse and cultural phenomenon we call Italian American. I will first give a summary of the plot, then I will move on to analysing issues of self and identity, matters of space, and what place America occupies in the context that the narrator and protagonist of the novel, Martina Satriano, frames for herself as viable and livable.

Martina Satriano, a forty-two-year-old professor of history of European culture at New York University, was born in Southern Italy at the end of the 1950s. Her family moves to Nugola, in Tuscany, when she is only one. After a failed marriage, Martina emigrates to the United States to pursue graduate studies and thus fulfils a dream that the Italian sociopolitical situation prevented her from achieving. Her narrative is a long lecture that she imagines writing for her American students. The chapters' titles refer to specific days of the week followed by the name of the dish she has eaten on that day.[19]

The story begins with her mother's death, a point of crisis in Martina's life, which also corresponds to the moment when she discovers she had probably been born left-handed, but was forced to use her right hand instead. This discovery will bring to the surface her deep, personal identity crisis. Her voyage to Italy to take part in her mother's funeral is the watershed between past and present. From there, the narrative moves back and forth on the line of time (with many metalepses that bring the reader back to the time of the writing, as is typical of a letter) and ends in a hopeful present where the crisis has been resolved. Something else contributes to her crisis – a *luminare* of Italian academia, Professor Cerignola, is interested enough in her work to fly to the United States and invite her to take a position in an Italian university, which, for Martina, would mean going back as a winner to that same country she had to leave because its doors of academia were closed to her. But, in order to do so, she, a self-declared Leftist, would be obliged to work with people ideologically on the Right. The theme that bridges Martina's temporal voyage is her preoccupation with identity, which unfolds on two levels, both personal and academic. The project on which she is working at the beginning of her story is one meant to promote tolerance among human beings: to weaken the boundaries of personal identity by crossing the line between conscious life and dreams. For this purpose, she uses a machine (a Dream Machine, which is, essentially, a tape recorder equipped with automatic, self-hypnotic commands) that should allow her dreams to merge with her daytime life. Her search for an alternative personal identity (her left-handed self) clashes with her research on abating or weakening the concept of identity itself, since alternative identity does not mean no identity at all, or even weak identity. By the end of the story, her obsession with destroying/finding identity will be resolved with the test of life's contingency. A puppy she rescues from the street will erase the tapes of her Dream Machine, and love will change her way of looking at herself and at life – she finds again, in New York, her teenage love Costantino, now renamed Kevin Shell, and renews a relationship with him.

Sogni mancini, then, is a conversation. Not only does it come in the form of a long talk by the narrator to her university students (a lecture that she never delivers, written in a sober and friendly epistolary style), but it is also constructed around conversations. The main and basic conversation is that of the narrator with her self, or more accurately, her possible selves. Hence, in *Sogni mancini*, discourses are based on issues of identity. For my analysis, and without gendering my discussion,[20] I focus on how the individual, in her singularity,[21] negotiates ethics, and the concept of America with it, while looking at herself as a responsible individual – responsible for ethical choices.[22] With regard to this, in the preface to *Sogni mancini* Francesca Duranti writes,

La mia protagonista è una donna come tutte le altre che ripercorre i suoi ricordi, cucina i suoi pasti, arranca nella sua carriera, cura il suo corpo, vive i suoi amori, lava i suoi bucati, affronta le sue tentazioni. Ma intanto cerca di aprire per tutti le porte di quella regione dello spirito che fu di suo padre e del mio, applicando a una macchina per scaldare i croissant una modifica destinata a redimere il mondo dall'intolleranza." ("Prefazione")

[My protagonist is a woman like any other who travels through her memories, cooks her food, strives hard for her career, takes care of her body, lives her romances, does her laundry, and faces her temptations. Meanwhile, she tries to open for all the doors to a specific region of the spirit that was her father's and mine by modifying a machine made to warm up croissants; a modification destined to redeem the world from intolerance.][23]

Here Duranti frames the subject of her novel within Martina's actions, activities with which every woman could identify herself, according to the author. As for the specificity of this subject as an individual (her singularity), Martina Satriano seems to believe that the singularity of the "I" must be ethnically specific. In fact, she says:

"Se abbiamo dentro qualcosa" avrei voluto dire, "una specie di baricentro indivisibile, che non è I think, I doubt, I believe, I vote, I speak, I sit, ma semplicemente I am, debbo supporre, nel mio modesto caso personale, che questo minuscolo granello sia lucano, toscano o newyorkese?" (Sogni mancini 56)

["Because if we have within us something like an invisible centre of gravity, which is not 'I think,' 'I speak,' 'I believe,' 'I vote,' but simply 'I am'; if that's so – as I believe it is – what precisely is this thing in my case? Is this minuscule particle of light from Lucania, or from Tuscany, or from New York?" (Left-Handed Dreams 43)]

In order to define the specificity of her self, Martina is trying to frame her selfhood in terms of cultural identity: in what where and when is that selfhood to be individuated, and what where and when does it individuate in turn? Lucania, Tuscany, or New York? For the time being, in the past, or in a time that has not been, that is to say the time in which she could have been left-handed? "Questa scheggia di identità è destra o è mancina?" (55; "Is this shred of identity right- or left-handed?" 43), she asks.

Martina's project to search for an alternative identity will fail. She will discover that, as Emmanuel Levinas puts it, "no concept corresponds to the I as being."[24] From this realization, Martina will conclude that the specificity of her singularity cannot correspond to any framing of cultural identity. Still, she will need to define the spatial landscape that frames her action – and not her identity, because the piles of adjectives that she uses to define herself will only demonstrate the indefinableness of that self, while space will only frame her action and what she thinks the best settlement for her identity.

The spatial framing of her action entails for Martina a definition of home: Italy or America? Let us begin a closer reading of the text by considering matters of spaces and places. When talking to Professor Cerignola about why she left Italy, Martina says:

> Ero scompagnata. Non avevo amicizie utili, ero figlia di contadini, facevo la cuoca. E benché fossi nata in una famiglia cattolica, ero miscredente. Ed ero una democratica di sinistra con una profonda avversione per il comunismo. (*Sogni mancini* 77)

> [I was unmatched, like a single sock. I didn't have friends high up, I was a farmer's daughter, I was working as a cook. I didn't belong to any of the powerful ideological families: although born Catholic, I was not a believer, and I was a leftist liberal with a great aversion to Communism. (*Left-Handed Dreams* 64)][25]

She was a woman quite out of place in a country where ideological appurtenance was necessary in the 1960s, as much as having someone in the right place to open a career for you, which is often the case still today.

Although Martina chooses the form of a letter to narrate her life menu, this narrative is rather a travelogue, the journal of a voyage back and forth from the past to the future, from Italy to the United States, from one of Martina Satriano's possible identities to the other. The journey can be seen as an enactment of Foucault's "le travail du soi sur soi." What work should one do on oneself? the French historian asked. Martina seeks a pragmatic answer, and she intends her labour on herself as an experiment in the abatement of identity and for the sake of tolerance.

Call me Robinson. "Chiamatemi Robinson," says Martina the traveller at the beginning of her story, and my attention is obviously called to what is excluded, and hence highlighted, in this literary medley – I think of Melville's Ishmael, rather than Defoe's Crusoe, all the more so considering the Dream Machine that Martina has built for her next scholarly project: a machine that attempts to blend dreams with reality, the unconscious with the conscious, so as to bring them together in a flow where the two become indistinguishable, leaving out bad dreams and nightmares.[26] For this reason, my mind comes to rest on Ishmael's young Platonist, who goes aboard a whaler with the *Phaedon*, rather than Bowditch,[27] in his head, and once on the main mast, "lulled into such an opium-like listlessness of vacant, unconscious reverie is this absent-minded youth by the blending cadence of waves with thoughts, that at last he loses his identity [...] in this enchanted mood thy spirit ebbs away to whence it came; becomes diffused through time and space [...]" (*Moby-Dick* 256–7). Martina has programmed her Dream Machine for the same purpose. As she explains to Professor Cerignola, her ultimate goal is "To undermine this damned identity by forcing all the alternative hypothesis to come out of the shadow..." (63). In this way, Duranti says in her preface to the novel, Martina is trying to open the door to that region of the spirit available to all, a space that is outlined for us in that same foreword, when she tries to give a full meaning to the term "parallax":

> Chiesi a papà cosa volesse dire Monarchia e cosa volesse dire Repubblica. [...] le ragioni di entrambe le scelte mi furono esposte senza forzare il mio consenso, senza accentuare né minimizzare la forza degli argomenti a favore o contro. Tanto che alla fine, per sapere cosa avrebbe votato lui, dovetti chiederglielo.
>
> Per me fu come gettare il primo sguardo in quella regione dello spirito che era la sua sola dimora: una regione, allora come ora, malinconicamente disabitata. Imparai a conoscerla meglio in seguito: osservando che la sua amata biblioteca di ateo convinto custodiva la collezione completa del Migne, tutta la Patrologia greca e latina in quattrocento volumi amorosamente letti e annotati [...]. ("Prefazione")

> [I asked daddy what Monarchy and Republic meant. [...] I was given the reasons for both choices without any attempt at persuading me of either, without stressing or minimizing the strength of the arguments pro or con; so much so that, in the end, I had to ask him what he would vote for in order to know it.
>
> For me, it had been like glancing for the first time at the region of the spirit that was his only abode: a region then and now melancholically uninhabited. I learned to know it better later on, by observing his beloved library, the library of a convinced atheist. It held the complete Migne collection, all the Greek and Latin patrology in 400 volumes, all carefully read and glossed in the margin [...].]

This uninhabited region of the spirit becomes a desert island for Martina, who says again, "Chiamatemi Robinson, dunque. Quasi mi piace naufragare per essere costretta a costruirmi la mia capanna sull'isola deserta" (32; "So call me Robinson. I almost like being shipwrecked so that I'll be forced to build myself a hut on a desert island" 23).

Keeping in mind that spiritual region of diversity, we begin to see how the blending of Ishmael and Crusoe, in "Call me Robinson," contains harmoniously Martina's intentions and action. Being open to the unknown and to diversity, both represented by the reference to Ishmael in the "Call me" portion of that statement, is a major theme of *Sogni mancini*, as its "Foreword" highlights; from this point of view that region of the spirit certainly calls to mind the *Pequod* and its crew of *isolatoes*.[28] However, Martina's move to conquer her oneiric world, and to inhabit a New Land of tolerance devoid of all the "monsters" (as she calls nightmares and bad dreams), does not resemble Ishmael's non-conquering and non-ruling desire to explore a world of diversity at sea, and not on land, espousing all that is already there, good and bad. Rather, Martina's desire to conquer her deserted New Atlantis brings her closer to Crusoe.

Martina chooses a world for herself in which, like Ishmael on the *Pequod* and Crusoe on his island, she will always be somehow a foreigner, but still at home within the perimeter of the vital space that she draws for her daily life (Manhattan). Her voluntary displacement is not only geographical, but primarily cultural; it is driven by her attention to the ethics of her choices. Like Ishmael, Martina leaves behind in Italy what makes her unhappy and joins a world of diversity in Manhattan, which she describes as such. Furthermore, we meet her when she herself is a patchwork of diversity, questioning and reaffirming pieces of her cultural background, while looking for possible, alternative identities to the one she knows. However, like Crusoe, she needs her hut on dry land where she can anchor and secure her existence through her daily rites and routines – the repetition of her habits, which she describes in detail.

The individualistic yet universalistic aspect of Martina's agency reflects the historical inclination of Italian intellectuals to raise the moral aspect of the issues at stake in their discussions above national specificities.

Martina's attempt to conquer for humanity "that region of the spirit available to all" is a voyage towards a mythical America intended as space of social and ethical accomplishment. The conquest of that region comes, for Martina, through the abatement of identity, which is in itself a quest for universally viable ethics. The abatement comes through the exploration of what Other she might be, or might have possibly been. In this sense, Martina's efforts echo Giorgio Agamben's position on ethics.

In chapter 11 of *La comunità che viene*, entitled "Etica," Agamben writes:

> Vi è infatti qualcosa che l'uomo è e ha da essere, ma questo qualcosa non è un'essenza, non è, anzi, propriamente una cosa: è il semplice fatto della propria esistenza come possibilità o potenza. Ma appunto per questo tutto si complica, appunto per questo l'etica diventa effettiva. (39)

> [There is in effect something that humans are and have to be, but this something is not an essence or properly a thing: it is the simple fact of one's own existence as possibility or potentiality. But precisely because of this, things become complicated; precisely because of this ethics becomes effective. (*The Coming Community* 43)]

However, until the end of the novel, when some events will change her mind, Martina is not interested in simply conceiving and considering the *possibility* of being the Other; she wants to define what Other resides in herself, thus persisting in seeking cultural coordinates for selfhood, conflating being with agency.[29]

Martina refuses to surrender to the idea of being *tale quale è*, such as she is.[30] Every morning, before going to teach, she plays bridge in all four positions in order to exercise her ability to think differently and to take on other identities: "Il bridge giocato in questo modo, è per me un esercizio non tanto di logica quanto di morale [...]. Un esercizio di dis-identificazione e di immedesimazione nell'identità altrui" (50; "Played this way, bridge is not so much an exercise in logic as in morals [...]. An exercise in deidentification and reidentification as someone else" 40). Here lies the contradiction: she does not really go beyond the concept of identity. Although she deems this movement "beyond" necessary in order to create a space for human tolerance, Martina only moves laterally, or in circles, not beyond. She even tries to confer bounded identity to her dreams, linking together the good ones in an ordinate/ordained sequence, while leaving out the "monsters," as she calls them. In the end, she eventually understands that love, as Agamben says, can only desire its object *tale quale è*.[31] Yet, she will still need to overdetermine spatially that *tale quale è*.

I am on the Left, "Io *sono* di sinistra" (*Sogni mancini* 216), Martina says to Professor Cerignola. She knows where she stands ideologically, but she cannot figure out whether her dexterity was to rely on her left. Was the right right? Is she a repressed lefty, as she herself puts the question? Starting with the title, the novel's rhetorical strategy rests upon a game of parallelisms, political and physiological, that will find no solution. Martina's repressed left-handed side becomes the metaphor for the Leftist she did not want to be while living in Italy; her conversations with Professor Cerignola run on this ironic binary of signification. Yet, the track will lead nowhere. Martina's left-handed dreams are only the reflections – mirrored thoughts – of her right self, meaning the individual she is as opposed to the one that does not exist, if not as a mirrored reflection: *Sogni mancini* are like *tiri mancini*, left-handed blows, which catch you by surprise and knock you down. In fact, Martina's left-handed dreams will turn into a left-handed blow.

The Other in Martina is *étrangère à elle même*, unknown to herself, as Kristeva would put it. More specifically, the Other who haunts Martina is her closest neighbour: the left-handed girl she could have been. This repressed self, as Martina defines it, peeps into her life just when she is playing her identity game with the morning bridge. A few hours after the death of her mother, Martina realizes that she could have been left-handed by observing the way she holds her cards. However, memory will not help her remember, and so she begins her voyage into the past looking for those who could unveil the truth.

The past brings her new life in the form of sudden events for which her daily routine cannot account: a puppy that destroys her scientific project, sexual intercourse with the guy next door, and her old and new love Costantino.

Professor Cerignola brings, instead, a reversed American dream. He offers Martina the chance of a magnificent job in Italy where this time she would be respected and recognized. But she would have to give up her left side for it, and work with those politically on the right. "Io *sono* di sinistra," Martina repeats and so declines the offer, thus renouncing the Italian dream. Professor Cerignola's appearance in her life, just when her mother dies and she can consider reverting to her natural left-handedness, is one of the novel's most obvious ironies.

During her last meeting with Cerignola, she says:

Tutte le identità alternative – quelle dei sogni e tutte le altre che non hanno avuto modo di realizzarsi, a cominciare dal mio Io mancino – avrebbero potuto materializzarsi, è vero. Sono state ad un pelo dal farlo, ma non è accaduto. Quella che esiste realmente è questa, seduta davanti a lei in pantaloni neri e blusa rossa. Non ho neppure riacceso la Macchina, non lo farò più. (*Sogni mancini* 218)

[All the alternative identities – the ones in the dreams and the others that never had the opportunity to come into being, my left-handed self in-cluded – might have been, but they are not. They have been on the verge of existence, but they didn't make it over the verge. The one who made it is sitting here in front of you, in black trousers and red blouse. I haven't even turned the Machine back on. I never will. (*Left-Handed Dreams* 185–6)]

Martina is finally ready to embrace herself *such as she is*. She cannot ac-cept Cerignola's offer, nor does she feel ready to be part of that new political Left whose avatar once made her feel an outcast. Leaving Italy was the right decision, she concludes.

Her last literary gesture is to frame for us, once more, her space that will coincide geographically with Manhattan, which she has instinc-tively called home already, although this geographical coincidence does not mean acceptance of the United States as her only *patria*, and does not frame Martina's vital space:

Non chiamerò i miei figli Dexter, Savile o Kenneth. Non lascerò un bar-bone a morire solo su un marciapiede. Niente potrà convincermi che la pena di morte sia una cosa necessaria. Non crederò mai che il bidet sia un attrezzo sconveniente. Continuerò ad amare questo Paese e continuerò a rimanere in parte estranea. (*Sogni mancini* 224)

[I won't call my children Dexter, Saville, or Kenneth. I won't leave a home-less man to die alone on a sidewalk. Nothing will convince me that capital punishment is necessary. I won't ever believe a bidet is an unbecoming fixture. I'll go on loving this country and I'll go on being in part an out-sider. (*Left-Handed Dreams* 191)]

By saying that she will not call her children Dexter, Saville, or Kenneth, Martina points out that she will not forget her Italian roots as many who immigrated to the States have done to survive in America. Several times in the text she underlines her choice, through which we can certainly see the difference between how "emigrating to America" was perceived in Italian culture up until the mid-1900s and how it is perceived today. America occupies a different position in the life and culture of those who leave Italy for it nowadays. About Martina's identity, Marina Spunta explains how the protagonist leaves "behind her sense of being Italian in America to adopt a more positive Italian-American identity" ("The Food" 233).[32] Martina, though, according to her own words, does not seem to ever leave behind her sense of being Italian in America. In fact, at the end of the novel, she states, "And I will have this dog, this life, and everything else, including Costantino and *my two countries*" (197).

What Martina cannot accept of Italy was left behind when she moved to the United States. She renews her choice, like a vow, when she refuses Professor Cerignola's job offer. There is not a new Italian-American life for her, since she will simply keep on leading the life she had so far, if not for the fact that, having found Costantino again, she is thinking of travelling back and forth between Italy and the United States. In this sense, she is certainly moving towards Italian Americanness, or American Italianness. Martina is ready to accept now her "multifaceted individual identity with a social commitment in a new hybrid society" ("The Food" 244). This attitude, though, cannot be labelled as "Italian American" *tout court*. Martina never refers to herself as Italian American. She never frames her identity as such. The ultimate result of her search for identity is to refuse any frame. Martina's Italian Americanness cannot be taken for granted because it does not automatically ensue from her decision to remain in Manhattan. With regard to this choice, Martina decides to remain on the island of Manhattan specifically – not America at large, but the geographical space that delimits the possibility of her action, and not her identity.

In the preface to *Writing with an Accent*, the Italian-American author and scholar Edvige Giunta (born in Italy) writes:

> However, I regard myself as an Italian American, too, although I am not exactly sure when I became one. It was long before I became an American citizen. I began to call myself Italian American when American English no longer felt clumsy and hard on my tongue; when I stopped shuttling back and forth between Italy and the United States, and did not go back to Italy for five years; when I started feeling kinship and solidarity towards the descendants of earlier Italian immigrants in the United States. In some ways, my choice to call myself Italian American is political, a response to those who claim that I do not fulfill their expectations of Italian Americans [...] what does it mean to be Italian American? Does it mean to be Italian *and* American? A particular kind of Italian? Or a particular kind of American? Either? Neither? (x)

Giunta's problematic self-inscription into Italian-American ethnicity, as explained above, raises several relevant issues. The first of these is that such a definition cannot be simply applied to all the Italians who move to the United States just because they decide to remain. Giunta's questions are a sign of how blurred the confines of ethnic belonging can be, and how different the perceptions of such belonging. In *A Semiotic of Ethnicity*, for instance, Anthony Tamburri defines as "Italian/American"[33] authors and intellectuals such as Luigi Fontanella, who belongs to "a new group of writers" and who, "having arrived in the United States after the economic boom of the 1950s, resides in the United States and writes in the language of her/his own country of origin" (110), which makes Martina Satriano similar to him. Tamburri expands the notion of the Italian-American writer in a way that comprehends that "new group," and thus takes into consideration the metamorphosis that the Italian-American ethnicity is undergoing, thanks to a new type of immigration substantially different from the one before the 1950s, and of which Martina is an example. He nonetheless highlights a crucial difference between the Italian American integrated into the Italian-American community and the expatriates who are not integrated, do not share the same Italian-American background, and do not seem to go in that direction, consciously. Referring to an essay by Paolo Valesio, "The Writer between Two Worlds: The Italian Writer in the United States," and agreeing with him, Tamburri writes, "the writer between two worlds seems to refrain from constructing any direct rapport with the Italian/American community in specifics or in the United States society in general" (117). This brings me back to Giunta. Although her definition of Italian American as applied to herself cannot be taken as *the* definition, it still outlines some substantial traits that Martina lacks: (1) self-inscription, though highly qualified, into the Italian American ethnicity, (2) a self-conscious, chosen kinship with the Italian American community, and (3) distance from Italy, a distance that Martina does not take, since for Costantino's sake she decides to travel back and forth between Italy and America (as did Giunta herself, subsequently).

Let us consider who Costantino is, for a moment (his nominal *costanza* bears the name of an emperor and he has built an empire in the United States). Costantino is now Kevin Shell, a man who did become American by radical choices, and who, like many Italian Americans of the first generation, decided to change his name and to erase his Italianness in order to fully and successfully embrace the American Dream. This man has made a decision to go back to live where his roots are, in Italy, and Martina is part of his roots. For Costantino, and not Kevin, Martina will travel between two countries; she says more than once, to herself and her next-door friend, that nine hours of air travel are nothing.

In one of the notes to her text, Spunta writes, "The first sign of Martina's 'Americanness' and lack of 'Italianness' is her getting to like American coffee" ("The Food" 247). I would like to add that even if getting to like American coffee can be read as a sign of Americanness (and I would not agree), it certainly cannot be read as a sign of lack of Italianness, not even in Martina's case.

All this shows how dangerous and tricky ethnic definitions can be, a major issue for Italian-American scholars. What makes Martina Satriano relevant to my work is exactly her refusal to be either ethnically or nationally framed, her will to live between two worlds. If this condition makes Martina, as a fictional character, or the real people who resemble her, fall under the classification of Italian-American writers, it does not make Martina or those who resemble her Italian American altogether.

Martina's dream of tolerance resides in the rejection of a specific ethnic belonging, and in a so-called weak identity, as Spunta also explains. However, in order to practise tolerance with herself and others, Martina has to give up her grandiose academic project linked to the Dream Machine. In the end, she gives up the idea of revolutionary change. Still addressing her students, she says:

> Lorenzo da Ponte e Mozart hanno narrato una storia d'amore tra una camieriera e un fattore, affianconadoli a un Conte e una Contessa. Era solo una storia […]. E la rivoluzione Francese? Tante teste tagliate e dopo pochi anni Napoleone si faceva ritrarre con la corona in testa e l'ermellino. E allora? Lasciate perdere. Ho perso il filo io stessa. Vi ho raccontato una storia: di più non so fare. (*Sogni mancini* 224)

> [Lorenzo da Ponte and Mozart told a love story about a maid and a butler, and, in parallel, a story about a count and a countess as secondary characters. It's just a story […]. And the French Revolution? A lot of heads cut off and after a few years Napoleon is portrayed wearing a crown and ermine robes. And so? Forget it, I've lost the train of thought myself. I've told you a story; I can't do more than that. (*Left-Handed Dreams* 191–2)]

Martina's universal hopes assume a lower profile while we move towards a private happy ending. Now that she has given up her left-handed dreams, she can finally focus exclusively on the acceptance of her ambiguous self, of her two halves:

> Senza riunificazione. Dio ne scampi. Le due metà le vogliamo sempre lì, in rappresentanza delle quattro del bridge, delle trecentosessantacinque all'anno dei sogni e di tante altre possibili. Entrambe lì, nella loro preziosa duplicità a rappresentare il *Prossimo* di cui vi parlavo nell'ultimo corso, e a proteggerlo dall'intolleranza se una delle due prendesse il sopravvento sull'altra [...]. (*Sogni mancini* 225)

> [But they shouldn't be reunited, though – heaven forbid. We want two halves, standing in for the four bridge hands, for the 365 days' worth of dreams and many other possibilities. And both these, in their valuable duplicity, to represent the Proximum I spoke in one of our most boring class sessions, and to protect him from intolerance if one of the two halves should assume an advantage over the other [...]. (*Left-Handed Dreams* 192–3)][34]

"Lì," she says in the Italian text – the two halves of her identity should remain there. "There" is Robinson's island, of course. Martina needs a space to define the range of her agency. This space is neither Italy nor America as she will always be foreign, somehow, but is simply the place necessary for her self to live in. Yet, she ends up describing herself spatially: she will remain in New York because she knows its *galateo*, she knows where to go and buy good wine at an honest price, right around the corner, and where she can shop in Queens.

While trying to end her tale on a happier, lighter note, Martina moves towards the centre of her space; her discourse goes from "this country," to Manhattan, to her apartment. At home: "And now that that's decided, I turn the key, open the door, smell the basil on my window sill, and I'm home" (197). There she remains, the "democratica di sinistra," the leftist liberal whom America has neither redeemed, nor saved. There she breathes, queen of her basil, imagining a familial future not at all different from the destiny that possibly awaited her former university mates who chanted slogans against the bourgeois family – those she never really wanted to join because of their extremism and intolerance. To be happy, Martina needs her own small piece of land and thus situates her self in that Liberal tradition of historical backyards:

> [...] Pangloss sometimes used to say to Candide: – All events are linked together in the best of possible worlds; for, after all, if you had not been

driven from a fine castle by being kicked in the backside for the love of Miss Cunégonde; if you hadn't been sent before the Inquisition, if you hadn't traveled across America on foot, if you hadn't given a good sword thrust to the baron, if you hadn't lost all your sheep from the good land of Eldorado, you wouldn't be sitting here eating candied citron and pistachios.

– That is very well put, said Candide, but we must cultivate our garden. (Voltaire 75)

Martina ends up cultivating her heterotopian garden when she renounces the pursuit of her cutting-edge research between dreams and reality, and chooses to operate ethically within reach of the things she wants. By surrendering to her contingent self, and by renouncing the factual realization of alternative identities as the basis of her politics of tolerance (the Dream Machine), Martina seems to suggest that *Liberté*, *Egalité*, and *Fraternité* need the land of the *isolato* in order to survive, which is to say that they must rely on subjective ethics, a concept that Francesca Duranti has been suggesting since the preface to this book whose plot unfolds without surprises. Martina's final choice was clear from the beginning, since the alternatives did not seem viable. Entrusting the idea of tolerance to a machine, or to the finding of a multiple identity, could only be a failure. The America that Martina inhabits, and that does not correspond to a complete acceptance of the United States, will not redeem her left-handed dreams.

Duranti's character runs away from those Leftists whom Moretti joined in the 1960s and 1970s, for she is ideologically far removed from Moretti's nostalgia for a "real" Left as enacted in *Aprile* (Moretti, 1998), a sort of thematic sequel to *Caro diario*, where Moretti interprets himself again. The opening scene of *Aprile* will always remain in Italian collective memory.

It is 1994, the year in which Silvio Berlusconi's party won the elections for the first time. On that funereal day for the Italian Left, Moretti, sitting in his kitchen, smokes a gigantic joint while following the progress of the Parliamentary elections on television. His elderly mother is sitting next to him.

That attitude is one of the symbols of an old Left to which Moretti, the protagonist, still clings. He is so disillusioned by the new politics of the "Democratici di Sinistra" that, later in the film, talking to the television screen, he urges the then-secretary of the party, Massimo D'Alema, to "say something leftist," while the man is engaged in an argument with Berlusconi on a television show. Moretti's disillusionment translates into his inability to produce a documentary about the current Italian political landscape, and into a wider preoccupation with his private life. In the end, instead of making a documentary on Italian political life, he will finally make the musical that he was thinking about in *Caro diario*, the story of a Trotskyite pastry chef in 1950s Italy.

While *Aprile*'s Moretti is disappointed with the Democratici di Sinistra, Martina Satriano states that she does not even know them. Both turn away from the Italian Left in different ways, one feeling nostalgia for the past, the other escaping both the past and the present. But while in *Aprile* the "I'''s political disengagement retains the contours of an action of resistance to a frustrating present, Martina's political disengagement is based entirely on the giving up of any active resistance, since she has left Italy. The appurtenance that she declares when saying "Io *sono* di sinistra" reveals nothing more or less than a background of values ascribable to a political tradition recognizable as Left. She recognizes herself as part of this tradition, but she does not seem to believe either in collective action or revolution. Martina has never belonged to the revolutionary Left that would regard the United States as the "dream" to be avoided, but her America is neither victorious nor particularly empowering. It is only part of that space where she can actualize her self, dreaming a dream that is not left-handed anymore, or not handed by the Left. Her self finds the spatial coordinates for its individual agency in displacement.

The America in which Martina lives is the space that frames the possibility of her agency, but not her ethics; in fact, as she clearly states, America is not the myth to be embraced as the land of ethical accomplishment. As a subject of globalization, ready to live between two nations, Martina builds her ethics by rejecting what is for her unacceptable in both. She makes herself the singular bearer of values across nations; thinking of her subjectivity as merely "constituted in and constitutive of the vast network of social labor" (Hardt and Negri, *Labor* 11) downplays the power of abstraction of her individuality. Unless we pay attention to what Levinas calls the *intentum* of the "I" – how it understands itself – we cannot fully envisage a way to a peaceful cohabitation of different cultures. Martina rejects part of U.S. culture for the sake of that cohabitation, as well as part of the historical Left that used to wave the banner against the United States; thus, she appropriates a right to ethical accomplishment, avoids espousing national ideology or cultural appurtenance, and speaks from a perspective of displacement.

Voluntary subjects of ideological displacement, Nanni Moretti and Francesca Duranti show with their works that they belong fully to the Italian literary tradition of selves engaged in humanistic issues that go beyond geopolitical borders. The history of their country, from Fascism to the "years of lead," passing through forty years of government by a Catholic party, has taught them to be on the Left as intellectuals in order to be progressive, but not to obey any extremist dictates. It has also taught them to be politically and ethically responsible individuals. America, in its geopolitical, mythic, and cultural manifestations, is part of their history. To confront America as absorbed by Italian culture, and to confront America as a dream of salvation, is part of their task as intellectuals engaged with humanistic ethics. This confrontation, which implies the role of America in globalization, sees Italian artistic productions once more on the forefront of humanism at an international level. In *Morals and Stories*, Tobin Siebers reminds us that, in Greek, *ēthos* originally meant "to be found somewhere," in addition to signifying "character" and "ethics" (5). No better description could be found for Martina and for the "I" of *Caro diario*, who think of themselves as sites for the formation of ethics. The historically weak Italian national identity, as opposed to the Italian identity, allows the subject to focus on him / herself as a subject of the world, rather than a subject of only one nation, and as a subject who, as an intellectual, feels the moral duty to be actively engaged in the improvement of civil society. This weak national identity seems to strengthen when the individual deals with images of America as the elsewhere to which they run for ethical accomplishment and salvation. Nevertheless, the refractoriness of the Italian subjects / intellectuals to a rigid national identity, and the constant projection of their thought on a humanistic universal plane, allow them to discuss the significance of America far beyond its meaning in national culture.

2 America Ubiqua

Displacing the Continent

Unlike the works explored in the previous chapter, Roberto Benigni and Massimo Troisi's *Non ci resta che piangere* (Nothing Left but to Cry, 1984), Gianni Amelio's *Lamerica* (1994), and Alessandro Baricco's *City* (1999) are not first-person narratives. Their subjects, rather than being individuals in search of identity who narrate a voyage of self-exploration, embody, reflect, or directly discuss icons of the mythic America and so delineate the role that these same images hold in Italian culture and history. All these works have as their central theme the choice between good and bad, where good means a better life for the human beings involved, and bad, or not so good, is the status quo and also the stage at which the actions of the stories begin. While moving from bad, or not so good, to good, or better, these representations of mythic America as such will fail in their search, become outcast, or remain forever in a world of literature. In other words, these stories reveal that the American dream per se, be it represented by Italy for the Albanians (*Lamerica*), or by Walt Disney for Shatzy Shell (*City*), or by Shatzy Shell herself, will not help to find a solution for a better life; on the contrary, on the way to something better, those dreamy icons will be destroyed.

The subjects of *City*, *Non ci resta che piangere*, and *Lamerica* completely embody some aspect of the mythic America woven by and into Italian culture, and they do not question themselves. They are shreds of the American dream, and, as such, they become losers. America, as imaginary, remains in the realm of the imagination, unable to create a viable social ethic. In the formation of a subjective ethic, the role played by America is negative, again, because the American dream espoused by the individual in its idealism, or in its mythic narrative, does not come to represent an alternative to the evils of the modern, globalized world. This time, in the following stories, what is displaced is not simply the subject, but the America that s/he enacts.

In the three works I discuss, America is located in a dimension created by some major suspension and manipulation of the space-time continuum, be it the organization of the artistic space, as in *City*, or the space and time in which the plot unfolds, as in the two films, *Non ci resta che piangere* and *Lamerica*. America in these texts exists elsewhere, in several spaces at the same time, or in a suspended time.

In Baricco's[1] theatrical monologue *Novecento*, the character opens the performance as follows:

Succedeva sempre che a un certo punto uno alzava la testa … e la vedeva. È una cosa difficile da capire. Voglio dire … Ci stavamo in più di mille, su quella nave, tra ricconi in viaggio, e emigranti, e gente strana, e noi … Eppure c'era sempre uno … uno solo, uno che per primo la vedeva […] e gridava (*piano e lentamente*): l'America. Poi rimaneva lì immobile, come se avesse dovuto entrare in una fotografia, con la faccia di uno che l'aveva fatta lui, l'America. […]

Quello che per primo vede l'America. Su ogni nave ce n'è uno. E non bisogna pensare che siano cose che succedono per caso, no … e nemmeno per una questione di diottrie, è il destino, quello. Quella è gente che da sempre c'aveva già quell'istante stampato nella vita. E quando erano bambini, tu potevi guardali negli occhi, e se guardavi bene, già la vedevi, l'America, già lì […] c'era già, in quegli occhi di bambino, tutta, l'America. (11–12)

[It always happened that, at a certain point, somebody would lift his head and see it. It's difficult to understand. I mean … we were more than a thousand on that ship, rich people on a trip, and emigrants, and weird folks, and us … Yet, there was always someone … just one, one who would see it first […] and cry (*softly and slowly*): America. Then he would stand still as if he had to enter a picture, with the face of someone who had made America himself. […]

The one who sees America first. There is one on every ship. And you must not think that such things happen by chance, no … nor by a matter of good sight, that is destiny. Those are people who already had that moment impressed in their lives. And when they were children, you could look into their eyes, and if you looked carefully, you could already see it, America, already there […] it was already there, America, in those young eyes, all of it.][2]

This is a good example of how America can be displaced and replaced by way of singular subjectivity, taking the form of destiny in a suspension of time, a time that has always been in its entirety. In this passage, America is located in at least three different places at the same time: the land that the ship is approaching / but we do not see it; the eyes of the individual who sees it; and the picture he seems ready to enter, in a time dimension that is eternal.

City is not set in America, Baricco says. America is not the scene of *Lamerica*; and in July 1492, the narrative time of *Non ci resta che piangere*, America did not exist yet. Still, its presence is evoked, its cultural space is shaped and made meaningful to specific ends, such as reflecting upon Italy. The three works are set against the background of an America that has always been there, as in the eyes of the one who sees it first.

In these three works, the subjects who evoke and reinvent America are subject to and subjects of a space-time disruption, compression, or dilation into a global dimension where historical time becomes all present and globalized. These subjects, the very voice through which a certain America is shaped, are themselves the sites of the space-time disruption, and they are either insane, or outcasts, or both. In any case, they are set apart from the norm. They are anomalies, and their America, catalyst of their ethicality, will neither empower nor redeem them.

Their atemporal anomaly expresses the end of America as an ethical alternative in history, thus showing the place that the myth holds today in Italian culture.

The Site of *City*: A Global Explosion

In *City* America is deprived of its mythical, salvific distance as an exceptional land of human and social accomplishment, à la Tocqueville, and is made part of the larger West. The novel's subjects, themselves a manifestation of the American dream, are disempowered in society and in history. There are obvious references to U.S. culture on almost every page. The plot is rooted in it, and so the reader imagines that the story is set in a U.S. city; but its author will deny it with, probably, ironic intent. This aspect, however, will be discussed further on.

City is constituted by several stories, as most of its characters are occupied with telling, or thinking, their own tales. We do have two protagonists, though, whose vicissitudes frame what could be called the main plot. One is Gould, a thirteen-year-old prodigy who attends university and lives alone, since his father is in the high ranks of the army and his mother is in a mental institution. Gould is mentally ill. He has two imaginary friends, the giant Diesel and the mute Poomerang, who are constantly with him. Despite his muteness, Poomerang responds to Gould and he himself, together with Diesel, imagines stories while observing the reality around him. Diesel and Poomerang are, indeed, two characters of their own. Gould's imagination goes further than that and has its best creative moments when the boy is in the bathroom. There, Gould elaborates an intricate radio serial about a boxer's life.

The other leading character is Shatzy Shell, a woman in her thirties who works at a publishing house as a telephone pollster, and who also dreams of making a Western; she always carries with her a tape recorder into which she speaks her ideas and stories. At the publishing house, Shatzy collects opinions rather than simply doing her job, which consists of getting the answers needed within thirty seconds and moving on to the next phone call. Shatzy engages in long conversations with her interlocutors, one of which happens to be Gould. At the end of their first phone conversation, Gould invites Shatzy out for dinner, together with his two imaginary friends. The story begins when Shatzy and Gould connect for the first time.

Shatzy is collecting suggestions about the possible endings of a serial publication, the adventures of Balloon Mac, a "supereroe cieco che di giorno faceva il dentista e di notte combatteva il Male grazie ai poteri molto particolari della sua saliva (City 9; "a blind superhero who worked as a dentist by day and at night battled Evil using the special powers of his saliva" City 4), and of his white mother called Mami Jane. The novel begins where real life and fiction meet: "So, Mr. Klauser, should Mami Jane die?" The book, then, starts at that "site" where fiction becomes interactive, as we would say for a hypertext, where the reader enters the story to manipulate it.

More than anything else, City is a novel about representation; it represents representations in many forms, from Balloon Mac's serial to the philosophical abstraction of Professor Bandini explained through analogies, from Shatzy's Westerns to Gould's story about boxing. City is a novel about narration and representation in their exploited and exploded forms.

Shatzy's phone call with Gould is her last at the publishing house. She gets fired; but, immediately after, she agrees to become Gould's governess as she is appalled by the fact that the boy is left to himself. As she leaves the office, she takes with her the two photographs she kept on her desk: one of Walt Disney sitting on a train for children in "Disneyland, Anaheim, California" (28); and one of Eva Braun. The two are oddly connected by Shatzy's idea of happiness. As a child, Shatzy was told that Eva Braun was Hitler's daughter, not his companion, and that if Eva could cope with such a brutal father, then she, Shatzy, could certainly understand her psychologically abusive, alcoholic, and depressed father. Shatzy tried to imagine how Hitler could be tender and affectionate with his daughter. An unhappy child, she found her happiness in Walt Disney's productions:

> Insomma, lui era il più grande. [...]. Un reazionario bestiale, se vuoi, ma ci sapeva fare con la felicità, [...] il più grande noleggiatore di felicità che si sia mai visto, ne aveva per tutte le tasche, [...] non sarà la felicità autentica, l'originale, per così dire, ma quelle erano copie favolose, meglio dell'originale [...]. (28)

> [So he was the biggest [...] a terrible reactionary, if you like, but he was good at happiness [...]. He had happiness for hire, the most ever seen, he had some for every pocket [...] maybe it's not authentic happiness, original, so to speak, but those were fabulous copies, better than the original [...]. (22)]

The reference to Disney and specifically to Anaheim, California (a rare mention of a city in *City*) relates the idea of the prefabrication of happiness to the country that holds the right to pursue it as one of its constitutive elements. Shatzy's discourse about authenticity, which can be read here as the authenticity of the American Dream, is not dissimilar at all to Jean Baudrillard's effort to explain America's authenticity as residing exactly in that socioeconomic effort to construct happiness plastically, so to speak. Although Baricco states that America, in *City*, is absorbed into the larger West, the novel's strong references to U.S. culture, such as Walt Disney in his construction of happiness, speak clearly and loudly to the concept of the New World. With regards to Disney, Neal Gabler writes:

> Obviously Disney's work had universal appeal, but in America, with its almost religious belief in possibilities, his urge to wish fulfillment was especially resonant. [...] in both Disney's imagination and the American imagination perfection was seen as an attainable goal. In a world that was always confusing, dangerous, and even tragic, a world that seemed beyond any

individual's control, Disney and America promised not only dominance, but also improvement [...]. Disneyland was just a modern variant of the old Puritan ideal of a shining City on a Hill. (*Walt Disney* xvii)[3]

Shatzy chooses this idea of happiness to save her present and future life, but to no avail – the American dream, as laid out in *City*, will not save her. She will choose to die, after a car accident leaves her completely paralysed, and before she ever gets to write her Western.

The lack of authenticity Shatzy mentions when talking of happiness is certainly one of the most abused stereotypes of the United States in European literature, including Italian literature, and is also clearly visible in Andrea De Carlo's *Treno di panna* and in Gina Lagorio's *L'arcadia americana*. It torments Alessandro Baricco, however, when fiction infringes upon history glamorously, when it is not possible to distinguish between them any longer. In an editorial written for *La Repubblica* the day after 9/11, Baricco tries to explain his feelings when the tragedy of the Twin Towers reached him through the television. He states:

Arrivo a capire che c'è qualcosa in quello che vedo alla televisione che non quadra, e non sono i morti, la ferocia, la paura [...] provo a dirlo: è tutto troppo bello. C'è un'ipertrofia irragionevole di esattezza simbolica, di purezza del gesto, di spettacolarità [...] c'è troppo Hollywood, c'è troppa fiction. La storia non era mai stata così. Il mondo non ha il tempo di essere così [...] non è il semplice stupore di vedere la finzione diventare realtà: è il terrore di vedere la realtà più seria che ci sia accadere nei modi della finzione. ("Quando la storia si presenta come un film")

[I finally understand that there is something in what I see on television that doesn't fit, and it's not the dead, the ferocity, the fear [...] I try to say it: everything is too beautiful. There is an unreasonable hypertrophy of symbolic exactness, of purity of the gesture, of spectacularity [...] there is too much Hollywood, too much fiction. History had never been like that. The world has no time to be like that [...] it is not the simple stupor of watching fiction become reality: it is the terror of seeing the most serious reality of all happen in the modes of fiction. ("When History Presents Itself as a Film")][4]

City does not bear the signs of his terror towards history happening in the modes of fiction yet; however, the novel is certainly constructed on the blurred confines between fiction and reality, where America lies and is negated at the same time. In the face of evidence and against it, and maybe with irony, Baricco tries to convince his American publisher that *City* is not set in America.

Baricco's *City* is structured on the model of the World Wide Web. Pronounced with an Italian accent, city sounds like "siti," a word that means websites. Like the internet, this novel has no centre and the basic categories of narrative such as time, space, and perspective are exploded: it is all there for us, present at the same time. We have only to click on a link and follow it. For example, if we want to exclusively follow the story about the boxers, we can just follow Gould to the toilet throughout the novel and skip all the rest. If all we are interested in is Shatzy's Western vignettes, then the tape recorder will be there for us throughout the novel, playing the last scene on its own, with no one to turn it on.[5]

One can also imagine *City* as the site of an explosion, a puzzle where pieces will never again fit together, or a mind that has lost its common sense. All the minds in *City* seem to have serious problems adjusting to the world around them. Even the point of view in *City* has no integrity whatsoever. In a narrative, usually one perspective corresponds to one character's point of view. Here we have a split personality with three different points of view, and, consequently, three different paths to follow, if we so desire. Whether we choose to call this insanity or not, we are dealing with a matter of identity. The subject in *City* is not a body in movement through time and space, as in *Caro diario*, but a "sito," or "site." Rather than being born to find our road to travel, Shatzy believes that we all could have been born plazas, or intersections, without moving in any direction. We are not going anywhere; we are places, she declares. Or, as Professor Bandini puts it, we are porches, constantly controlling our inner being from outside, and therefore never being ourselves.

Though the problem of identity as personal integrity – the integrity of the self – is obsessively present in every page of the book, we only have a couple of instances where the narrating voice becomes a first person. This is not surprising, since the novel deals with scattered identities, and denies any possible centre, any possible closure of the circle. In this web, America is nowhere and everywhere. "America," textual America with its myths (its narratives and its films), is no longer a point of reference as it was for the modernist intellectual – no longer a space, in time, with which to confront oneself, a site to reach through a real or metaphorical journey. America is shattered, like all the rest, deprived of its centrality and its distance. America is scattered all over the place, and thus none of its pieces is any more important than another. They are all part of the whole. What *City* does to America is to give it a new dimension, culturally composed of many "sites" among other important "sites."

For the launching of his novel *Senza Sangue* (2002; *Without Blood*, 2004), Baricco chatted with his readers on the publisher Rizzoli's website. On that occasion, I asked him to talk about *City*'s America, and the irony that built it, or was built into it. His reply is subtle with regard to America. Here is what he wrote:

> Una cosa che ti può essere utile per il tuo studio è la seguente: io non ho mai pensato che *City* fosse ambientato in America. Naturalmente ci sono molte cose prettamente americane, ma, anche molte altre che con gli Stati Uniti c'entrano poco (che ne dici della passione di Gould per il soccer?). Per me *City* è ambientato in Occidente, che ormai è un Paese unico, con molte inflessioni statunitensi, ma ricco anche di altre mille cose. Quel che è successo è che l'editore americano ha messo sul risvolto che il libro era ambientato negli Stati Uniti. Ho cercato di far loro capire che non era vero, ma non c'è stato nulla da fare. Forse pensano che in questo modo lo vendono un po' di più. Non so. D'altronde gli americani sono un tantino ego-riferiti, come tu certo sai. Un giorno, a NY, ho incontrato un mio lettore che era andato pazzo per *Silk*, l'aveva letto mille volte e non so che altro, insomma era veramente rapito da quel libro, e sai la cosa che lo ha lasciato veramente secco quando mi ha incontrato? Scoprire che ero ITALIANO: Non gli era mai passato per la mente che io potessi essere uno scrittore NON americano. E' stato un trauma scoprire che *Silk*, in realtà, si intitolava *Seta*. Così. ("*City* e l'America")

[Something that can help you for your study is the following: I have never thought that *City* was set in America. Obviously, there are many things peculiarly American, but also many others that have nothing to do with the United States (what about Gould's passion for soccer?). For me *City* is set in the West that is by now only one country, with many US inflections, but also rich with a thousand other things. What happened is that the U.S. publisher wrote on the flip-side of the dust jacket that the book was set in the United States. I tried to make them understand that this was not true, but there was nothing to be done. Maybe they think that, in this way, the book will sell better, I don't know. On the other hand, Americans are a little bit self-centred, as you certainly know. One day, in NY, I met a reader of mine who was crazy for *Silk*, he had read it thousands of times and who knows what else. In short, he was totally taken by that book, and you know what left him completely astonished when he met me? The discovery that I was ITALIAN: never had it occurred to him that I could be anything but an American writer. It was a shock for him to discover that *Silk* was entitled *Seta*. Just like that.]

Through what I call an act of cultural "revenge," with *City* Baricco is obviously depriving textual America of its identity, the identity that European mythologization has assigned to the country. He is doing so by absorbing that identity into the larger West. His reply to my question about the irony that has built America obviously has its own ironic twist. He tells me of an American who had deprived *Seta* of its Italian identity.

In the web project devoted to *City*, Baricco's answer to my question is reprised with further explanation:

> L'immagine di una metropoli con inflessioni statunitensi è evocata immediatamente già dall'uso della parola inglese "city" nel titolo. L'ambientazione metropolitana stessa, tuttavia, è solo una delle sfaccettature dell'idea di spazio cui allude il titolo e non implica affatto l'univocità del contesto di riferimento. Lo stesso Baricco lega esplicitamente, e ogni volta in cui gli si presenta l'occasione di parlare di *City*, la connotazione spaziale della parola "città" a un'idea della struttura testuale anziché a quella di spazio di ambientazione del romanzo, in linea con le suggestioni ipertestuali che nell'opera affiorano [...]. ("L'impronta di una città qualisasi")

> The image of a city with U.S. traits is immediately evoked already in the use of the word "city" as a title. However, the metropolitan setting is only one facet of the idea of space to which the title refers and does not imply at all the unequivocalness of the referential context. Every time he has an occasion to speak of *City*, Baricco himself explicitly relates the spatial connotation of the word "city" to an idea of textual structure, rather than an idea of space setting in the novel. This is in line with the hypertextual suggestions that surface in the novel [...]. ("The Mark of a Generic City")

City is masterfully structured as a hypertext; however, whether or not the novel is set in the United States, and the author asks us to believe it is not, its pages exude America abundantly. The book is a textual "American" environment. At the same time, Baricco states the impossibility of framing a cultural identity within the space of a specific national culture. He doesn't even frame identity within the limits of self-integrity (sanity). Baricco continues to erode the supremacy of the American myth in *Next: Piccolo libro sulla globalizzazione e sul mondo che verrà* (Next: A Small Book about Globalization and the World to Come, 2002). After drawing the line that links cultural globalization to America (though he never defines globalization), a relationship that in many manifestations he calls cultural colonialism, Baricco closes his small book with an anecdote and a few questions. He describes a scene he watches on the seashore of Reggio·Calabria, a city in Southern Italy.

There is a wedding party on the shore. A photographer is shooting a film of the bride and the groom on the beach and has an idea. The couple boards one of the boats lined up on the shore, the most beautiful one, and poses just like Leonardo Di Caprio and Kate Winslet in *Titanic*. The two stand on the prow, arms wide open; the young man is behind his wife, and both face and breathe the infinite (Sicily is right there, across from them). Relatives and friends all laugh hard at the scene, shouting something in dialect that Baricco does not understand. He comments,

> Ecco riassunto in una domanda quello che non capisco della globalizzazione culturale: ma lì, a Reggio Calabria, in quel momento, *chi stava fregando chi*? Hollywood si stava rubando l'anima di tutti, o Reggio Calabria esorcizzava definitivamente Hollywood, prendendola per i fondelli? Chi esce sconfitto da quell'immagine: *Titanic*, i due sposini, nessuno, tutti quanti? (90)

> [Here's summed up in a question what I don't understand about cultural globalization: but there, in Reggio Calabria, in that moment, *who was tricking whom*? Was Hollywood stealing everyone's soul, or was Reggio Calabria exorcising Hollywood definitively, by mocking it? Who is defeated in that image: *Titanic*, the newlyweds, no one, everyone?]

Like the questions in one of those magazine tests where, we feel, neither a, nor b, nor c, nor d is the right answer, who is defeated is hard to say, but reading *City*, one has no doubt about who is exorcising what, and Baricco's denial of the overwhelming presence of America in his novel is the greatest self-ironic exorcism of the entire story.

The Ethical Space of *City*'s Subjects

City's characters and their identities can be read as sites rather than as bodies moving through time and space. Despite their being places, these exceptional characters are, paradoxically, and by their own exceptionalism, out of place if cast against the social panorama that the novel sketches for us in the background. In other words, *City*'s personae are outcasts. They are either mentally disturbed (Gould, his mother, Professor Kilroy), living on the margin of their lives (Shatzy), characterized as losers of some sort (Professor Bandini), or physically handicapped (Diesel is a giant, Poomerang is mute; although the two are only projections of Gould's fantasy, they are characters). *City*, then, does not deal with matters of displacement. There is no concept of "displacement" in this website, and there is no other place for *City*'s characters to be. Their being sites out of place constitutes *City*, and their being out of place is only a consequence of the contrast with a social normality adumbrated in the background. This is not a minor detail, since the shadow of that normality gives us to understand that these characters, as social subjects, are weak and disempowered. They have no valuable ethical agency within the limits of the accepted social norms, and the images of America they project are as much outcasts as they are.

Professor Bandini gives us a clear instance of the process I have just outlined.

> L'Anomalia del *porch* – continuò il prof. Bandini – è evidentemente quella di essere, al contempo, un luogo dentro e un luogo fuori. In certo modo, esso rappresenta una soglia prolungata, in cui la casa non è più, e tuttavia ancora non si è estinta nella minaccia del fuori. È una zona franca in cui l'idea di luogo protetto [...] si sporge oltre la propria definizione [...]. E non è escluso che proprio questa sua identità debole concorra al suo fascino, essendo incline, l'uomo, ad amare i luoghi che sembrano incarnare la propria precarietà, il proprio essere creatura allo scoperto e di confine.
>
> In privato, il prof. Bandini riasumeva quetso suo ragionamento con un'espressione che riteneva imprudente usare in pubblico, ma che considerava felicemente sintetica. "Gli uomini *hanno* case, ma *sono* verande." Una volta aveva provato ad enunciarla alla moglie, e la moglie aveva riso fino a starne male. La cosa l'aveva piuttosto colpito. In seguito la moglie l'aveva lasciato per andare a vivere con una traduttrice di ventidue anni più vecchia di lei. (153)

["The anomaly of the porch," continued Prof. Bandini, "is, obviously, that it is inside and outside at the same time. In a sense, it represents an extended threshold, where the house no longer exists, but has not yet vanished into the threat of the outside. It's a no man's land where the idea of a protected place [...] expands beyond its own definition and rises up again, undefended [...] and it's not impossible that its identity as weakness contributes to its attraction, since man tends to love places that seem to incarnate his own precariousness, the fact that he is exposed, a creature of the borderland."

In private, Prof. Bandini summed up his argument with an expression that he considered it imprudent to use in public, but which he regarded as a happy synthesis. "Men *have* houses: but they *are* porches." He had once tried saying it to his wife, and his wife had laughed until she was sick. That had rather wounded him. She later left him for a translator, a woman twenty-two years her senior. (153)[6]]

In Bandini's discourse, everything is "out." The individual is projected outside of him/herself in order to defend an entity, the self, of which s/he does not really have any knowledge:

Lui pensava, davvero, che gli uomini stanno stanno sulla veranda della propria vita (esuli quindi da se stessi) e che questo è l'unico modo possibile, per loro, di difendere la propria vita dal mondo. (154)

[He [Bandini] thought, indeed, that men are on the porch of their own life (and therefore in exile from themselves) and that this is the only possible way for them to defend their life from the world. (154)]

As far as the narrative strategy is concerned, Bandini's discourse loses power and credibility because of his wife's offensive reaction; the brief tale of the end of his marriage is a detail whose only purpose in the plot is to make a loser of Bandini. We do not know anything else about Bandini, nor are we reminded of him or his marriage again. However, the mind goes to another literary Bandini, Arturo, the protagonist of four semi-autobiographical novels by John Fante. This is yet another example of how hypertextual *City* hyper-relates itself to textual "America." In his introduction to the 2004 Italian edition of Fante's *Chiedi alla polvere* (*Ask the Dust*, 1939), Baricco recalls the conversation between the old, ill Fante and Charles Bukowski at the Motion Picture Hospital (*Chiedi alla polvere* xi). Bukowski asked Fante what happened to Camilla, the Mexican waitress with whom Arturo Bandini is deeply in love in *Ask the Dust*, and who disappears in the desert at the end of the novel. Fante replied that "the bitch turned out to be a lesbian" (Sounes 189).[7] In case we had missed the nominal connection between Baricco's character and Fante's protagonist, we find in this extra / hyper / textual turn of fate one more link between the two Bandinis.

Already evoking America with his last name, Baricco's Bandini uses an American icon to metaphorically describe his idea about men constantly sitting outside of themselves, an image that seems to have popped out of one of Shatzy's Westerns: a man on a porch, sitting on a rocking chair, caressing a gun in his lap while watching the horizon. Bandini's creed takes the shape of "America," and is finally rejected by his "normalized" world (his wife). His America is a narrative, as much as Shatzy's America (the Westerns), and Gould's America (the boxers' story), in which the self finds refuge and recuperates some sort of idyllic integrity. America here delineates the space of the utopian realization of the self, which is denied to the subjects of *City* within the limits of their normal, social lives. The ethics of these subjects lose any value within the social contract, and their power of subversion is nullified. Gould's attaching chewing gum onto the keyboards of ATMs has no relevant consequences for the customers who try to obtain cash – they will eventually get their money. Professor Kilroy's six theses on intellectual dishonesty find no better place on which to be written than the brochure of a porn-video booth, and the brochure gets lost in the end. Shatzy ends up narrating her Western stories in an asylum. Furthermore, the only voice that is a first-person narrator – the only "I" allowed to speak with its own voice – is the one recognized as insane by society's criteria, Gould's mother. The outcasts of this *City* all choose exile in "America." Here America, real or ideal, is no longer the place of tangible salvation that it once was for authors such as Vittorini or Pavese, or for the emigrants who sought survival, but it is only the textual realization of an individual's anomaly. This realization is cast out of the normal, social panorama, and so America itself is cast out. In the end, the realization of an individual's anomalous state is an icon of the American dream itself. America is here twice an outcast, redeemed only by the aesthetic perfection of Baricco's pages in which the Western and the boxers' story unfold.

Once again, it is Professor Bandini's discourse about porches and houses that gives us an idea of the individualism that is targeted through America:

In definitiva – proseguì il prof. Bandini – quell'uomo e quel *porch*, insieme, costituiscono un'icona laica, eppure sacra, in cui si celebra il diritto dell'umano al possesso di un luogo suo proprio, sottratto all'indistinto essere del semplicemente esistente. Di più: quell'icona celebra la pretesa dell'umano a essere in grado di difendere quale luogo, con le armi di una metodica viltà (il basculare della sedia a dondolo) o di un attrezzato coraggio (il fucile carico). Tuttavia, la condizione umana è riassunta in quell'immagine. (153–4)

["Finally," continued Prof. Bandini, "the man and the porch together constitute an icon, secular, and yet sacred, too, which celebrates the human being's right to defend that place of his own, removed from the vague state of simply existing. Further: the icon celebrates the human being's right to defend that place, using the weapons of cowardice (the rocking of the rocking chair) or of a well-equipped courage (the loaded gun). The entire human condition is summed up in that image. (154)]

This is an image destined to be consigned to the realm of literature, and that is at the opposite end of *City*'s human geography, where no one belongs anywhere, and everyone is basically engaged in a monologue. The anomalous subjects of *City*, all intent on dealing with their American dream, are individuals who, although rejecting the social norm and its politics, cannot propose an alternative to the ethics that they refuse. They are not selves who are working on themselves, as in *Caro diario* and *Sogni mancini*. Instead, they pursue individual projects that exclude this labour – Bandini's defensive American self on the porch – and do not produce a viable ethic in a global context that needs, instead, a self-questioning approach to the Other. In *City*, the American dream is consigned altogether to the realm of literature. The novel positions itself at the greatest possible distance from the "land to which we turn with the same hope [...] of whoever has decided to defend at the price of pains and error the dignity of the human condition" (Pintor 244–5).

Non ci resta che piangere: The Counter-Enterprise

In Benigni and Troisi's *Non ci resta che piangere*, America as imagined and described by one of its protagonists, Saverio, serves the purpose of attacking Italian politics and social habits. Here too, as in *City*, the displaced subjects of the narrative do not question themselves. Rather, they are profoundly convinced of their ideals and their mission: to prevent the discovery of America for the sake of humanity. While setting up the counter-enterprise to Columbus's voyage, they ironically take on an ideal individualism that never doubts itself, and they subvert and ridicule it. The America belonging to Saverio's cultural baggage is a set of stereotypes that overexposes his superficial education. America is used to discuss Italy and even though the myth of its negativity comes in the form of an unacceptable stereotype, the film redeems neither America nor the subjects who, in an effort to reproduce the enterprise, are blind to themselves and to history.

Roberto Benigni is known in the United States as an actor and director, thanks to the three Oscars he won in 1999 with *La vita è bella*, 1997 (*Life Is Beautiful*), and to films such as *Down by Law*, 1986 (J. Jarmusch); *Son of the Pink Panther*, 1993 (B. Edwards); *Il piccolo diavolo*, 1988 (*The Little Devil*, R. Benigni); and *Johnny Stecchino*, 1991 (R. Benigni). His affiliation with the Italian Left is well known, if for nothing else than the public kisses he reserved for more than one leftist politician in his film *Berlinguer ti voglio bene*, directed by Giuseppe Bertolucci, for which Benigni also wrote the screenplay. Enrico Berlinguer was the national secretary of the Italian Communist Party from 1972 until his premature death in 1984. He was the man who changed the Communist Party in Italy to make it more democratic, and he initiated the so-called "compromesso storico" (historical compromise) with the governing Catholic party, Democrazia Cristiana. This was a new, collaborative dialogue meant to help the governability of the country. In June 1983, when Benigni finally met Berlinguer at a party rally, at the end of his intervention and while still on stage, Benigni carried Berlinguer off in his arms. As a son of Tuscan peasants, born in a region that was a bastion of Italian Communism, Benigni began his career in his home town as an actor at the Festa dell'Unità, the annual festival of the Partito Comunista Italiano held in most Italian towns and cities by the local branches of the party. He was raised a Communist. About his Leftism, Stefano Masi writes:

The "marginal" Benigni, who at the time was a provocative regular on an offbeat TV show hosted by Renzo Arbore, is today a blockbuster who has raked in billions of lire at the Christmas box office, in a progressive Italy led by an equally modern left-wing government. With Kommunism no more [...] the most Communist comic in all Italy is today plastered across the *Wall Street Journal*'s front pages – making his rounds as he shakes hands with America's motion-picture tycoons in California, the powerful Jewish "clique" in Hollywood. (Masi 14)

Masi probably finds Benigni's American success to be a contradiction to the actor's Communist beliefs.

Less known than Benigni is Massimo Troisi, co-protagonist and co-director of *Non ci resta che piangere*. The United States knows Troisi for *The Postman* (M. Radford, 1994), which won several Oscars in 1996 and provoked the criticism of several historians who accused the film of being unfaithful to the facts and of treating Neruda as a victim of the Chilean regime rather than a worshipper of Stalinism. Troisi died of a heart attack the day after the shooting of the film concluded.

Born in San Giorgio a Cremano, Naples, in 1953, Troisi became a comedian in the tradition of the Neapolitan theatre established by Antonio Petito and the De Filippo family at the end of the nineteenth century and into the twentieth. His beginning as an artist of leftist tendencies started in a way that recalls the terrible fights between Peppone and Don Camillo, Communist mayor and priest of an un-named small, post–Second World War Italian town, best enemies born from the humoristic pen of the Italian writer Giovannino Guareschi. In 1971, with his friend Peppe Borrelli, Troisi wrote a vanguard text entitled *Crocefissioni d'oggi* (Today's Crucifixions). The text tells about the workers' struggle, about feminism, abortion, and the emigration of peasants to Northern Italy. Since he and his friends had no other place in which to perform than in the open space at the local church of Sant'Anna, they had to submit the script to the parish priest for approval. To avoid censorship, the writers submitted an incomplete script, but staged the complete version. The first night of the show, the clever priest switched on the lights in the theatre in the middle of the performance, and threw out the actors.[8]

Troisi and his friends founded the *Centro Teatro Spazio* (Theatre Space Centre), still famous today as a workshop for new artists, and the first texts that they staged out of the Centro were performed at the Feste dell'Unità in the towns around Naples.

Troisi was, and is still, deeply loved in Italy. He and Benigni had be-come close friends when they decided to collaborate on a film script and direct it together. Matilde Hochkofler writes:

> In realtà insieme si divertono. "Finché una sera," ricorda Benigni, "mentre Troisi stava preparando un piatto di spaghetti alla napoletana, ci è venuto in mente di chiederci cosa sarebbe accaduto se in quella cucina ci fosse stato anche Leonardo da Vinci." È così che cominciano un'avventura che li porta nel 1492. (133)

[Actually, they have fun together. "Until one night," recalls Benigni, "while Troisi was cooking spaghetti alla napoletana, we wondered what would have happened if Leonardo da Vinci had been in that kitchen." This is how they begin an adventure that takes them to 1492.]

In the film, the two actually meet Leonardo da Vinci.

In *Non ci resta che piangere*, the iconic idea and meaning of America relies mainly on Saverio (Benigni). America will be stereotypically depicted through negative images that will only overexpose Saverio's blind idealism. His attempt to stop Columbus points out that setting out for America – either to reach it, or to prevent its discovery – does not lead to any effective and valuable consequence for the subject involved.

Saverio is a schoolteacher who is unable to cope with reality. His sister Gabriellina is seriously depressed from unrequited love, and Saverio cannot come to terms with the fact that Gabriellina's fiancé, Fred, had left her three years earlier. When he finds himself back in the year 1492, he decides to stop Columbus from discovering America to prevent the birth of Fred, among more important reasons, thus delivering the world from the effects of the discovery. Saverio is a man of enduring hope who does not give up, especially in the face of reality. When he reaches Palos, he cannot believe that Columbus has already left, and persists in calling to him out loud from the sea shore, while repeating to Mario (Troisi): "Maybe we can still make it."

Non ci resta che piangere is a witty satire that uses the counter-movement to the enterprise of the "Italiano," Columbus, in order to attack the stereotype of Italy as the country that gave birth to a great tradition of poets, artists, and navigators, a tradition celebrated mythically by the liberal, post-unification Italian historiography whose modes of narrative persisted in Italian schools until the 1970s.

From the very beginning of the film, Saverio and Mario remind us that Columbus's route to the Indies proved to be problematic. The two friends, sitting in Saverio's car, tired of waiting at a train crossing, discuss a change of route. Mario suggests a country road that goes in a direction different from the known road, but that might constitute a way around the obstacle. That road will take them to 1492.

More generally, *Non ci resta che piangere* attacks the side effects of that sort of idealism which renders man blind to his historical reality and, therefore, unable to contribute to the well-being of humanity. To this effect, the quixotic counter-enterprise of Saverio and Mario targets the

Italian ethos from the cultural underpinnings of commonplaces and stereotypes that the poorly educated and highly idealistic schoolteacher
administers to his friend Mario, janitor of the school where he teaches,
as sacraments of knowledge. Once the two Italians (part of that people
known in history books as a people of great discoverers and poets) meet
history, they show themselves ignorant of any practical knowledge:
Mario and Saverio sadly realize that they do not know how to build a
toilet. Rather than writing songs or poetry for his new Renaissance love,
Mario sings the Beatles and the Italian national anthem. In this counter-
tale of Italianism, *Non ci resta che piangere* attacks the inability of the
Italian social strata, and of Western civilized man in general, to live up
to their present and their history – man does not know the reality
in which he lives, which translates into Mario and Saverio's inability to
reproduce the mechanics of a toilet.

The accusation of social blindness reaches its apex in the exasperated
inability of Italian bureaucracy to deal with everyday life. When Mario
and Saverio on their carriage pass a frontier line (many such borders
existed in Italy around 1492), they pay their dues three times only because they lose a bag immediately before crossing the line, and they
have to cross it twice more to retrieve their belongings. The man who
sits at the customs table asks them to pay for each crossing, and does so
in a mechanical way that repeats every time exactly the same sequence
of actions, and exactly the same sequence of words and questions that
do not require an answer.

In this mock-heroic frame, Italian America displays its iconic role in
the most dramatic scene, when the heroic ideals of Saverio meet the
mocking Italianism of Mario, who leaves his new fiancée to join his
friend on the way to Spain. Here is the scene.

It is indeed 1492, and Saverio feels the need to save the world from
the discovery. He packs and catches up with Mario, who is singing for
Pia in her courtyard. Elegantly dressed in deep blue, the colour of the
Italian national soccer team, and with a ball under his right arm, Mario
appears to have popped out of a Renaissance painting. He is singing
"Volare," one of the songs that signify the success of modern Italian
music in the world. Pia asks for one more song, and Mario sings the
national anthem. Right in the middle of his performance, Saverio calls
him back to his duty as a citizen: they must stop Columbus. Mario is
not too easily convinced, so Saverio has to remind him what America
means and he scrolls down his list of topical reasons: slaughter of the
natives, slavery, the electric chair, and, furthermore, the lack of any

good American in culture, art, sports, or gastronomy. With a touch à la Raynal, Saverio condemns Americans for their barbarity.[9] Mario tries to react and reminds Saverio of Cassius Clay. "Imported," is the answer. He is not American, he is black (African American). But it is not until Saverio touches the issue of national pride that Mario decides to go, "For the people, for Italy."

It is worthwhile to reproduce here part of Saverio's discourse against America to review the metonymic process by which he moves from one idea to the next. The fabulistic mode of narration and the linguistic non sequiturs all show the level of naïve ignorance to which the authors of the film, Benigni and Troisi, point. Saverio is only looking for a good excuse; his truest interest is indeed private – to prevent the birth of Fred:

Ma come! Gli indiani! Non si vede più un indiano a pagarlo oro da nessuna parte del mondo! Li hanno ammazzati tutti! Hanno fatto finta d'essere arrivati prima gli americani e hanno detto agli indiani: "E voi che ci fate qui?" "Noi ci siamo sempre stati." "Sempre stati?" TRA – Secchi tutti! Gli indiani che avevano scoperto l'America, altro che Colombo! Eh! Gli indiani stavano già lì. Se non si trovava nessuno, l'aveva scoperta lui, ma c'erano già gli indiani. Come se io adesso vado in Puglia e dico: "Eh! La Puglia!" Sono duemila anni che i pugliesi stanno lì! L'indiano è stato sterminato. Non c'è un Americano buono in nessuna parte del mondo, né nella cultura, né nelle arti, né nello sport. (*Non ci resta che piangere*)

[Come on! The Indians! You can't see a single Indian in the world any longer! They killed all of them! Americans pretended they arrived first! They saw the Indians and said: "And you, what are you doing here?" "We've always been here!" "Always been here?!" And BANG, they did 'em all in! Indians discovered America, not Columbus! If he hadn't found anyone, then he could say he had discovered it. But there were Indians first! It's like I go to Apulia and say, "Hey, Apulia!" So what? Apulia's people have been there for two thousand years! The Indians have been exterminated! There is no good American in any part of the world, not in culture, not in the arts, not in sports.]

The weakness of Saverio's line of reasoning takes away credibility from him and his enterprise, and the friend that he succeeds in convincing is not the best example of his cause. Mario, representing the national soccer team in blue, with a ball under his arm, singing popular songs, and mainly occupied with his amorous relationship, is definitely an Italian version of Sancho Panza.

It is not out of place to mention here how much of this discourse is pointing out the blindness of a certain political ideology to which, historically, the Italian Left has not been immune. I recalled in the introduction the episode of the public argument that occurred in the 1950s between Elio Vittorini, writer of *Americana* and director of the Communist magazine *Il Politecnico*, and Palmiro Togliatti, leader of the Communist Party. Togliatti was disappointed with Vittorini because his interests in literature and the arts did not directly pursue the goal of the Party to convert the nation to Communism. Vittorini's independence, as well as that of other intellectuals, clashed with the Party hierarchy and priorities, and Ward reminds us that the history of Italian intellectuals is also the story of a defeat in trying to build a bridge between high culture and the masses. The Communist intellectual was expected to obey the Party. Blind obedience was not the hallmark of Italian intellectuals. Saverio is not only the product of atavistic school curricula, he is also the symptom of a Left that, in the 1970s, was still dogmatic. On this character rests the construction of America in the film: an individual who is displaced, an anomaly in a time that is not his own, and whose naïve ethics are as noble as they are unrealistic and powerless. Saverio's cultural construct, America, serves the purpose of displaying his vision of the world; it is against the background of America that the ironic discussion of ignorance and ideology is played out.

As for the title, *Non ci resta che piangere*, it is a reference to the fact that Mario and Saverio cannot return to the twentieth century, that it is impossible to change the ethos of a people, and that the world cannot be saved from America.

Lamerica

As we have seen in chapter 1, film experts and scholars consider Gianni Amelio one of the initiators of the new Italian cinema, together with Nanni Moretti, Gabriele Salvatores, and other filmmakers who "all [aim] at retrieving a shared gaze in the present, at staging the crisis of the subject and of its inability to remember, at openly questioning the very notion of identity – personal and collective/national, moved by the need for a new cultural solidarity" (Gieri, "Landscapes" 42). Gianni Amelio partakes in that shared gaze in the present with films that Emanuela Martini sees as *favole*, fairytales, that "siano tessute sulle immagini e la scansione del nostro tempo, [...] favole che vivono del senso di colpa per come si è ridotto il mondo. Non 'dalla parte dei bambini,' ma ripiegate sulle responsabilità collettive che, se son tali, devono essere anche individuali, di ciascuno di noi (*Gianni Amelio* 10; "[fairytales that] are woven into the images and the scansion of our times, [...] fairytales that live off the sense of guilt for what the world has become, not 'on the children's side,' but pointing at collective responsibilities that, being such, must be also individual, concern each of us"). As in Moretti, but with a completely different style, in Amelio collective history meets the individual and focuses on her / his (mis)adventures. Martini sees in this focus the thread that constitutes Amelio's cinema, starting from his first film *La fine del gioco* (The End of the Game, 1970) (*Gianni Amelio* 9–10).

Amelio's *Lamerica* exemplifies Donald Heiney's claim, already cited, that for Italian intellectuals to talk about America has always meant to reflect upon Italy, upon themselves and their social function.[10] In fact, in his conversation with Amelio about the film, the journalist and writer Goffredo Fofi says:

> *Lamerica* mette sotto accusa il nostro modo di essere oggi in Italia, ciò che siamo diventati: nello stesso tempo il tuo film è specificamente italiano, ma sposa un'Italia che non c'è più e dice che quest'Italia che non c'è più, c'è forse in altre parti del mondo e che noi abbiamo dei doveri verso di essa, perché abbiamo dei doveri verso i nostri padri e il nostro passato. Lamerica, che tu lo voglia o no, ti pone in una situazione che non è solo quella del regista, in una situazione delicata: che tu lo voglia o no, ti si chiederà di essere portavoce di altro che non solo il film. (Amelio and Fofi, *Amelio secondo il cinema* 5)

> [*Lamerica* is an accusation against our way of being today in Italy, against what we have become; at the same time, the film is peculiarly Italian, extremely Italian, but it espouses an Italy that does not exist any longer, that might exist elsewhere in the world, and to which we are somewhat responsible, since we have some responsibilities to our fathers and our past. *Lamerica*, whether you like it or not, puts you in a situation that does not involve you only as a director, a delicate situation. Whether you like it or not, you will be asked to be a spokesman of something else than just the film.]

In *Lamerica, film e storia del film*, Amelio himself traces the link with the past and the sense of historical responsibility to which Fofi refers above:

All'inizio, nei primi incontri di sceneggiatura, il titolo era semplicemente L'America, con l'apostrofo [...]. È rimasto così per tanto tempo. Poi un giorno ho detto che, sí, il suono era bello ma il significato non mi piaceva. E ho proposto di togliere l'apostrofo, di scriverlo come l'avrebbe scritto un emigrato. Mesi dopo, un mio amico di Ostia, un ragazzo cresciuto senza cultura, ma a cui piace molto leggere, è venuto da me con La storia della Morante, l'ultimo libro che gli avevo prestato e ha aperto il romanzo alla pagina in cui Nino dice a Useppe: "Un bel giorno sai che famo noi due? Ci imbarchiamo su una nave transoceanica e partiamo per l'America." Useppe, che è piccolino e sta imparando a parlare, ripete stupito "La LAMERICA?," scritto cosí nel testo, proprio come l'avevo pensato io, senza apostrofo. Avevo letto La storia tanto tempo prima, ma questo particolare davvero non lo ricordavo. O forse si era sedimentato nel mio inconscio e, senza neppure rendermene conto, è riaffiorato con il tempo. Il mio punto di riferimento, in realtà, erano le molte lettere di emigranti dall'ortografia incerta che, nel corso della vita, mi è capitato di leggere. Per questo il film avrei anche potuto chiamarlo "La MERICA." (3)

[In the beginning, during the first meetings for the film script, the title was simply L'America, with the apostrophe [...]. But one day I said that, yes, the sound was beautiful, but I didn't like the meaning. And so I proposed to take off the apostrophe, and write the title as an emigrant would have. Several months later, a friend of mine from Ostia, a boy raised without an education, but who likes reading very much, came to me with Morante's La Storia, the latest book I had lent him, and opened the novel to the page in which Nino says to Useppe: "You know what we're gonna do, the two of us, one of these days? We go onboard a transoceanic ship and leave for America." Useppe, who's a little child and is just learning to speak, repeats surprised "La LAMERICA?" Written like this in the text, just like I had thought of it, without the apostrophe. I had read Morante's La storia long before, but I honestly didn't remember this detail. Or, maybe, it was buried in my unconscious, and it emerged with time, without my awareness. Honestly, my reference points were the many letters of emigrants, with an uncertain orthography, that I happened to read in the course of my life. That's why I could have just as well called the film La MERICA.]

But he did not. He chose the link with one of the greatest Italian modern writers, Elsa Morante, and inserted his film into the discourse of the cultural tradition discussed so far. The passage above sets the tone of the film, in which present and past merge in a space that is neither

America nor Italy, but Albania, and conflate in the mind of Spiro, the mentally ill co-protagonist of the film.

Amelio's past contributes to the film as well. His father and uncle left for Argentina when Gianni was less than two years old. They returned years later, first his father and then his uncle, who by that time had a wife and five children. Remembering the arrival of his uncle's family, Amelio says:

> sono arrivati al paese con gli abiti leggeri dell'estate di Buenos Aires e da noi era inverno, un gelo terribile. Mi è sembrato di rivederli tra gli albanesi sbarcati a Bari, senza nemmeno una valigia da poveri, accolti come sappiamo. (*Lamerica: film e storia del film* 14)

> [They arrived in town with the light dresses of the summer in Buenos Aires, and it was winter in Italy, freezing cold. I thought to see them again among the Albanians disembarked in Bari, without even a poor suitcase.]

As mentioned above, personal and collective history will merge in the film through the director's strong appeal to memory. In "Albanitaliamerica" Antonio Vitti writes:

> Infatti, oltre ai motivi personali il film è stato realizzato per gli italiani che oggi hanno una memoria corta, una crisi della memoria [...] secondo il regista, per quanto molti nomi siano cambiati, dagli anni ottanta è uscita una generazione che è ancora al potere e non ricorda il passato di miseria che molti italiani hanno vissuto. (250–1)

> [In fact, besides the personal reasons, the film has been made for those Italians who, today, have a short memory, a crisis of the memory [...] according to the director, even though many names have changed, the 1980s have created a generation that is still in power and does not remember the past of misery that many Italians lived.]

Italo Calvino describes the superficiality of this generation in his presentation of Andrea De Carlo's *Treno di panna*, a novel that is in itself a product and a display of that will to forget history. In *L'arcadia americana*, Gina Lagorio, as much as Nanni Moretti in *Caro diario*, insists on the necessity of reviving historical memory for the sake of humanity. *Lamerica* does not speak only to Italians and their forgetfulness. Vitti writes, "Fra le grandi questioni della nostra epoca l'esodo dei popoli in cerca di benessere è uno dei più grandi e difficili da affrontare" (249; "Among the big issues of our epoch the exodus of peoples seeking well-being is one of the greatest and most difficult to face"). For the Italian intellectuals committed to an ethical solution of human issues, the human cannot be separated from the global, and the individual cannot be separated from the collective and the political, national, and supranational.

Like Lagorio, Moretti, Benigni, and Duranti, Amelio has a keen sense of what ethics can mean and how it assumes a universal aspect once it relies on the responsibility of the individual. In an interview released to *Cineaste* in 2002 for his film *Così ridevamo* (*The Way We Laughed*, 1998), when talking about the sociopolitical "illness" of a rightist Italy, he refers to it as a national problem;[11] but what is right, wrong, or fundamental in his discourse is universally so.

> Yet, there should be a foundation of any political behaviour, an ethic that we have lost in this country as a result of the advent of the right. This lack of ethics is also the result of an illness that began, in my opinion, about twenty years ago, an illness that went untreated and became very serious. This illness is the indifference towards the fundamental issue of living in a society – the respect that I as a citizen, must have for you as a fellow citizen, regardless of your ideas [...]. The problem, then, is not with a particular party, but with an attitude that is morally dirty and wrong (Crowdus 18).

"I" and "you" are the subjects of the universal, and on the global stage where the "I"s and "you"s operate, it can happen that history makes Italy another America, and Albania another Italy.

At the time of the film's shooting, Albania was a country that in many aspects resembled post-war Italy, poor and underdeveloped. In 1991, the massive migration of Albanians to Italy – more than ten thousand – created an explosive situation, since the country was not ready to host so many foreigners; the crisis lasted for years. Italy asked the Albanian government to stop the huge wave of illegal emigration with the promise of economic help. Among the many forms of economic help were the mainly failed investments of Italian capital in Albania's modern industry that was yet to be built.

The two protagonists of the film, Fiore and Gino, go to Albania to build a shoe factory that should employ Albanian workers. Fiore's plan is to declare bankruptcy after cashing the sum that the Italian government will give him to start production. He declares that he has done so already in Africa, with Gino's father as a partner.

The film begins with scenes from one of the Fascist propaganda documentaries about the success of Mussolini in Albania after the occupation of 1939. The Duce, according to the documentary, transformed the poor and underdeveloped Albania into a modern country, and the Albanians for their part seemed to be happy with it, celebrating Italy for the rebirth of their economy. In Durazzo, 1991, where the scene moves soon after, we still see Albanians celebrating Italy: "Italy, Italy, you are the world," the crowd shouts. The dramatic paradox of the film – Italy as the saviour that cannot save Albania from the consequences of a Fascist or a Communist regime – is set into an immediate contrast of past and present; but that paradox never becomes parodic. Amelio does not allow us to laugh.

At the end of the 1980s, Albanians knew Italy only through television. Albania had been cut off from the rest of the world by the Communist regime, until its dictator Enver Hoxha died in 1985 and his successor allowed people to watch television programs broadcast by nearby countries, such as Italy. Albanians learned to speak Italian mainly through television; yet, Amelio says to *Cineaste*: "Although Italy is very close to Albania geographically, in terms of their culture the two nations are as far apart as Italy was from the United States fifty years ago" (Porton and Crowdus 7).

In order to develop his plot, Fiore needs a straw man to serve as the president of the phony company. This man is Spiro Tozai, alias Michele Talarico, an Italian soldier whom the Communist regime had interned in an asylum for dissidents and soldiers left there by the withdrawing Italian army. Spiro has lost his sanity and is convinced he is still at war. He flees from Gino because he wants to go back home to Sicily. Gino recaptures him and convinces him that the best he can do is to work as the president of the new factory, cashing money by just putting signatures where necessary.

While chasing Spiro, Gino is obliged to follow the route of illegal Albanian emigrants to Tirana, using their means of transportation because his car's tires have been stolen. The bus he rides with the fugitives is stopped by the police, so he is obliged to travel on an open truck loaded with human cargo, one of whom dies.

It is at this point that we clearly see Spiro as the representation of unyielding and unfulfilled hope. The old man does not understand that the young man sitting next to him has died, not even when everyone around says so, and he tries to wake him up by giving him a piece of bread. Spiro tries to alleviate people's suffering on the ship to Italy with that same small piece of bread, basic nourishment, and symbol of universal communion and equality. To share bread is an integral part of the Christian tradition, where bread means and gives life to all. Spiro, arriving too late with his bread, or not having enough bread, symbolizes a betrayal of humanity towards itself, its inability to rise to its own potential and to fulfil its purpose. That small piece of bread on a truck and a ship filled with so many people is also a sign that Italy will not work any miracle for the Albanians who are trying to reach the country. The fugitives ask Gino about Italy, whether they can find a job there, or possibly marry an Italian woman. Gino tries to explain to them the harshness of the situation and says, "the best that can happen to you in Italy is to find a job as waiters." The answer he gets back is, "Better being a waiter in Italy, than dead in Albania."

When everything seems to be settled, Fiore, from Italy, tells Gino that the business has come to nothing. Now Gino has two problems: he is without a job, and responsible for a man he cannot help. He tries to leave Spiro in a boarding house, giving money to the proprietors so that they can take care of him. But Spiro runs away, yet again.

The descending parabola of Gino's fortune lands him in jail for bribing a public officer. He is lucky enough to be set free, but without his passport. Stripped of his citizenship, Gino is equal to any other Albanian fugitive, as the head of the police reminds him, and he has to embark upon an old ship with thousands of others to cross the Adriatic in danger, thirst, and hunger. On the ship, Gino sees Spiro again. The old man sitting on the deck is trying to feed someone next to him, yet again, with another small piece of bread. Spiro, without any trace of resentment for having been abandoned, invites Gino to sit next to him: "Paisa'! I'm so happy to see you again! Don't be sad, we have been unlucky, both of us."

At this point, the film conflates past and present. Spiro, in a close-up, begins to talk about America, because he is convinced that he is going there. He tells how he will send for his wife and child once he is there. He asks Gino whether he can speak English. Still in a close-up where the deep wrinkles on his face become the image of an old hope left unfulfilled, he says: "I am tired, but I want to be awake when we reach New York." The camera then pans to some of the other faces on the ship, resting for a few seconds on each. They are the faces of adults and children; "you could look into their eyes, and if you looked carefully, you could already see it, America, already there [...] it was already there, America, in those young eyes, all of it" (Baricco, *Novecento*).

Albania is Italy, and Italy is America in the mind of Spiro, whose un-yielding hope suggests his comic counterpart Saverio, in *Non ci resta che piangere*. Spiro tries to awaken the young man from the dead by giving him bread, and Saverio tries to call back Columbus by yelling at the ocean and repeating, "Maybe we can still make it." "America," the promised land, becomes the background against which unfulfilled hopes are measured, in *City* as well as in *Lamerica* and *Non ci resta che piangere*. It seems almost unavoidable that Italy should confront itself with the American dream once again, in order to find for it a more ad-equate displacement in globalization.

The three narratives dismiss the viability of the American myth as a social, economic, ethical, or political path to salvation. The subjects who set out for America remain wanderers in their utopias, and their agency is disempowered. What emerges from these three works produced by Italian leftist intellectuals is that setting out for "America," as myth, as ideal, as imaginary, will not present any solution for the ethical prob-lems raised by globalization; there is no land of all possibilities for hu-man accomplishment to run to anymore. The "here" in history remains the only space for effective agency; this seems to be the claim and the call put forth by Baricco, Benigni and Troisi, and Amelio. Those subjects who engage America without questioning themselves and their ethics – without working on themselves – can only be victims of a utopia that undermines their agency. Moretti, Duranti, Amelio, Benigni and Troisi, and Baricco do not seem to believe in any possible effective ethical role for America on a sociopolitical level; rather, they suggest that the myth should be abandoned entirely. In doing so, they confront themselves, as intellectuals, with the death of a myth, and they take on the task of stag-ing and communicating this same death.

In the next two chapters, the protagonists of Andrea De Carlo's *Treno di panna* and Gina Lagorio's *L'arcadia americana*, although unwilling to really question themselves, will show a different aspect from the sub-jects of the narratives discussed here: they travel to America, and whether following the American Dream (*Treno di panna*), or just observ-ing it (*L'arcadia americana*), they will obstinately cling to their own cul-tural identity, closing the possibility of a fair dialogue with American culture. Their discourse on America is set against their cultural back-ground, and their obstinacy is not open, but subtly built on the rhetori-cal strategies of their narratives. Although belonging to two different generations and having developed as writers in very different social contexts, De Carlo's and Lagorio's discourses about America will arrive at the same conclusions. We shall see which ones.

3 On a Trip to America: The "I" Travels

Setting Out for the Self

What does it mean to go to America? The two "I"s of Andrea De Carlo's *Treno di panna* and Gina Lagorio's *L'arcadia americana* rediscover America as geographical location. Unlike Moretti, who meets America in Italy, or Benigni and Troisi, who never get there, the two narrators of the novels under examination in this chapter and the next do go to the United States of America on a voyage that is, supposedly, a voyage of self-discovery, but turns out to be a voyage of self-defence: defence of a well-established cultural identity that prevents the "I" from engaging with America on a deeper level of understanding, where the connection could eventually affect the traveller. Hence, also in the case of these two novels, America will not redeem the subjects who approach her with their defences up.

Treno di panna and *L'arcadia americana* are two clear examples of how setting out for America epitomizes setting out for the self. Yet, the subjects engaged in the quest for the self will ultimately not get to an America that could possibly be the stage for their renewal. The America that the subjects reach (and shape) is nothing more than what their gaze is willing to see and engage with, a vision which often corresponds to a series of stereotypes that the protagonists do not really question or confront. We are not dealing with subjects negotiating America (*Sogni mancini*), or displacing and subverting it (*Lamerica*, *Non ci resta che piangere*), or enacting it (*City*). Nor are we dealing here with subjects who either directly or ironically attack Italian political and social habits by deploying images of America. What we do have here are two subjects who shape their cultural identity against the (un)making of stereotyped images of America which they themselves (re)produce, and they do so without ever questioning themselves. America, in the end, will have left them unchanged. Moreover, not only will the subjects of *Treno di panna* and *L'arcadia americana* remain unchanged, but their European identity, displayed against the background of their America, will be reinforced. To reveal this rhetorical strategy, I shall juxtapose *Treno di panna* and Jean Baudrillard's *Amérique*.

Amérique is a text that obliged European culture to face itself while gazing at America, a text that is, thus, more a theatrical display of Europe than a display of America. I use the word "theatrical" deliberately, for this expression is dear to Baudrillard in his *Amérique* and brings him ultimately to compare the Italian staging of its culture (what seems to Baudrillard the utmost theatrical exposition) to the American staging of its (un)culture (I am borrowing the word *inculture* from *Amérique*). Baudrillard writes:

> For the European, even today, America represents something akin to exile, a fantasy of emigration and, therefore, a form of interiorization of his or her own culture. At the same time, it corresponds to a violent extraversion and therefore to the zero degree of that same culture. No other country embodies to the same extent both this function of disincarnation and, at the same time, the functions of exacerbation and radicalization of the elements of our European cultures ... It is by an act of force or *coup de théâtre* – the geographical exile of the Founding Fathers of the seventeenth [sic!][1] century adding itself to the voluntary exile of man within his own consciousness – that what in Europe had remained a critical and religious esotericism became transformed on the New Continent into a pragmatic exotericism. (*America* 75)

We see from this passage how in Baudrillard's discursive practice America is conceived and explained in comparison to Europe. Yet, and paradoxically enough, the author asks Europe to understand America without judging it according to European canons: an America vertiginously free from any European sense of history and culture. In "Jean Baudrillard's *America*" Mario Klarel defines Baudrillard's discursive mode as "associative and aphoristic" (227). When the moment comes for Baudrillard to discuss the staging of signs in American (un)culture, to understand those signs as the consequences of the historical *coup de théâtre*, he cannot avoid comparing the American stage to the Italian stage that stands at the opposite end of the semantic continuum culture / (un)culture.

Baudrillard thinks that the Italian staging of cultural signs is hyper-signification, the utmost degree of connotation and saturation of cultural reference: an artificial paradise, as artificial and theatrical as the American paradise. In Baudrillard's view, Italy epitomizes European sophistication at its highest degree and so stands exactly at one end of the spectrum that is the staging-of-culture/(un)culture, and he cannot read America without setting it against the other end of that axis. This means that he is sketching an America defined by that axis: it is indeed the old look of Europe that drafts his exasperated America.

Baudrillard's discursive strategy is identical to the strategy that underlies the narrative technique in *Treno di panna*, on which a comparison with *Amérique* casts full light, thus allowing us to better understand how, indeed, the narrator of *Treno di panna* (as well as the narrator of *L'arcadia americana*), while crossing America, remains an armoured bearer of unrelenting European identity.

Treno di panna, a Train That Goes Nowhere

Andrea De Carlo's North American narratives (*Treno di Panna*, 1981; *Uccelli da gabbia e da voliera*, 1982) are, if not autobiographical, certainly autofictional.[2] *Treno di Panna*, our writer's *opera prima*, is based extensively on De Carlo's experience in Los Angeles, and was partly written there first in English, then finalized in Italian, and published in Italian.[3] This overlapping of life and fiction – a first-person narrative, in this case – is relevant when one considers the impact of America on the individual and the role that Italian intellectuals have had in the shaping of popular images of the United States in Italian society from the 1980s to the beginning of the new millennium.

Like many authors who preceded him, before writing about California, Los Angeles, and Hollywood, and before going there, De Carlo was under the spell of American culture: the blues, the novels, Bob Dylan, the movies, Pop Art. He travelled for a few years across the United States, all over Europe, and to Australia.

In this respect, De Carlo became the symbol of a generation that wanted to live and travel widely, and his debut in the world of fiction meant the birth of a new phase for Italian narrative.[4] The one who best understood the value of De Carlo's writing was his discoverer, Italo Calvino. In a blurb for the dust-jacket of the work's first edition (1981), Calvino pointed out two main characteristics of the novel that distinguished it from its literary antecedents. First, the protagonist's extremely superficial way of dealing with the world around him, which Calvino called "la superficie della coscienza che sfiora un mondo tutto in superficie" ("the surface of conscience that brushes against a world all made of surface"). Second, the particular void that probably lies beneath the surface, at which De Carlo courageously points, but which he does not explore.

To begin with the first characteristic, brushing against the surface of the world was a liberating attitude of the emergent generation of the 1980s; on the other hand, in the novel, the possible void behind the surface is not exclusively inherent to the world that *Treno di panna*'s protagonist explores (Los Angeles). That superficial world is created by the "I"'s lack of a deeper engagement with it, which means that the images of America filtered and reproduced for us by the "I" narrator in *Treno di panna* are generated through a gaze that does not really engage with America. Thus, for the protagonist, America will have no relevant weight in the development of his ethic, despite the fact that he gets caught in the American dream.

Unlike the journalist in *L'arcadia americana*, Giovanni, the young photographer protagonist of *Treno di panna*, lands in the United States apparently without any sort of expectations or prejudices. At the opening of his story, he describes the surface of what he sees as light shapes it, and the sensations he perceives from this surface:

> Alle undici e venti di sera guardavo Los Angeles dall'alto: il reticolo infinito di punti luminosi [...]. Alla fine siamo arrivati in basso, quasi sopra le case. Siamo rollati sulla pista. Attraverso il vetro spesso ho visto la pioggia sull'aereoporto, luci di altri aerei nell'acqua. (*Treno di panna* 9)

> [At 11:20 pm I was looking down on Los Angeles: an endless mesh of bright points [...]. At last we got down, almost grazing the rooftops. We taxied along the runway. Through the thick window-glass I could see rain over the airport, other aircraft lights through the wet. (*The Cream Train* 1)]

Another description of Los Angeles as a city made by the light will close the circle of the story at the end of the novel.

The motif of light is the *leitmotif* of the "I"'s narrative technique. Through light, mainly artificial and deceptive, our protagonist surfs his American experience with his senses, without ever weaving his feelings into the plot of an inner life's narrative. Far from being a bildungsroman, *Treno di panna* leaves us in the dark with regard to the emotional growth of its protagonist, his ethical values, and his relationship to the United States. While artificially shaping surfaces, light ends up illuminating the moral vacuum beyond the surface of things and beings, which gives the American dream a specific function. Neither good nor bad, the American dream does nothing for the protagonist, who slides unchanged through his story and disappears from our sight like one of the rays that Los Angeles absorbs in the darkness of its nights:

> Ho guardato in basso, e di colpo c'era la città come un immenso lago nero pieno di plancton luminoso, esteso fino ai margini dell'orizzonte. Ho guardato i punti di luce che vibravano nella distanza: quelli che formavano un'armatura sottile di paesaggio, fragile, tremante; quelli in movimento lungo percorsi ondulati, lungo traiettorie semicircolari, lungo linee intersecate. C'erano punti che lasciavano tracce filanti, bave di luce liquida; punti che si aggregavano in concentrazioni intense, fino a disegnare i contorni di un frammento di città e poi scomporli di nuovo, per separarsi e allontanarsi e perdersi sempre più nel buio. Li guardavo solcare gli spazi del tutto neri che colmavano inerti il vuoto, in attesa di assorbire qualche riflesso nella notte umida. (*Treno di panna* 188)

> [I looked below me, and suddenly, there was the town, like an immense black lake full of luminous plankton, stretching as far as the horizon's edges. I looked at the points of light that glimmered in the distance: the ones that formed a flimsy framework of landscape, frail and trembling; the ones in motion along undulating pathways, along semi-circular trajectories, along intersecting lines. There were points that left trails behind them, dribbles of liquid light; points that clustered together in intense concentrations, so as to trace the outline of a fragment of the town and then shatter it once more, dispersing and receding and vanishing ever more into the darkness. I watched them slice through the dead, solid black spaces that made up the void, waiting to absorb some gleam in the moist night. (*The Cream Train* 184)]

It is here, on the last page of the novel, that we find the protagonist looking at Los Angeles, again, in precisely the same way he looked at it while landing in California, on the first page.

There is certainly a story in *Treno di panna*, organized in a plot that follows the timeline of the events. The events unfold at the end of the 1970s, while the writing is taking place presumably two years after the conclusion of the story. This two-year gap between the time of the events and the time of the narration will not produce any narrative detachment of the "I" from the story he tells. The "I" never creates a discursive distance from his past to place it within the larger picture of his life experience, or to comment upon it; rather, he resituates himself in that past and describes it. Giuliano Manacorda synthesizes Giovanni's narrative technique as follows:

> Un'ottica ravvicinatissima e meticolosa che non tralscia alcun particolare è lo strumento con cui De Carlo segue punto per punto lo svolgersi tutto in superfice di itinerari senza approdi, registrati nel martellante tempo presente di una cronaca in prima persona. (909)

> [An extremely close and meticulous look that does not skip any detail is the means by which De Carlo follows step by step the unravelling of superficial itineraries with no final destination, recorded with the hammering present tense [sic] of a first-person chronicle.]

This story is a chronicle of events.

The young protagonist of *Treno di panna* goes to California to visit Ron and Tracy, a couple he had met in Greece the previous summer. Giovanni has been on holiday for the entire year, or so it seems. His job as a photographer (we do not know what sort of photography he does, nor do we know for whom he works) seems more of an excuse to travel than the real pursuit of a profession. Living with Ron and Tracy in Los Angeles, since he is soon broke, he will first find a job as a sandwich boy, then as a waiter; afterwards, he will move up the ladder by teaching Italian in Beverly Hills and Santa Monica.

In order to find employment, Giovanni has to make up references for his résumé. He has never been either a waiter or a teacher before. We do not know what he has done exactly in the realm of work history until that moment, but he moves deftly behind the identities he creates for himself. In Beverly Hills, he becomes the Italian teacher of a famous actress who goes by the captivating name of Marsha Mellows. Meeting Marsha is an exultation of puffy whiteness, a rejoicing of sugar – Marsha Mellows was the protagonist of one of Giovanni's favourite films, *Treno di panna*, literally whipped-cream train.[5] In this encounter, the inflated flimisiness of whipped cream adds up to that of the marshmallows, creating an image of pampered pleasure. Meeting Marsha Mellows is the only event that excites Giovanni's senses. She will open the gates of Beverly Hills' villas for him. In the meantime, Giovanni has bought a car, lived with a girlfriend, and moved into his own house on the beach after breaking up with his companion. By the end of the novel, where we find Giovanni watching Los Angeles again (from atop Beverly Hills this time, rather than from a plane), we do not know if or why he has decided to settle in Los Angeles, why he had previously decided to live with a woman for whom he did not care and who certainly had not touched him beyond the surface of his humanity, whether his sojourn in California has changed him or put his life on a different path. The very matter of weaving any plot of human growth beyond the perception of his senses is absent from the "I"'s care. The same can be said for his social advancement.

Giovanni has no plan for his future, so he passes from job to job out of inertia: when he is tired of one, he moves on to the next, but the criteria by which he chooses them seem to enter his consciousness unclearly and to remain obscure in his mind. Giovanni is neither assertively ambitious nor an active social climber, or at least he never confesses to being one. Here is how he describes his daily life after buying a car that he uses to drive through Beverly Hills and Bel Air to observe the luxurious houses, gardens, and cars:

> La mia vita quotidiana mi pareva una sorta di filtro opalino, attraverso cui osservare una catena infinita di possibilità inespresse. Vedevo decine di immagini di me stesso a Los Angeles, in ruoli diversi ma comunque dall'altra parte delle siepi e cancelletti che andavo a guardare ogni giorno. (*Treno di panna* 104)

> [My everyday life appeared to me like a sort of opaline filter through which I was able to observe an infinite chain of unexpressed possibilities. I visualized dozens of images of myself in Los Angeles, playing different roles, but always on the other side of the hedges and front gates that I went to gaze at every day. (*The Cream Train* 99)]

There is a distance between Giovanni and his own life. The way he participates in it never completely involves him, just as the narration of the events leaves him almost emotionless. Giovanni is a spectator of the world that surrounds him and sees him acting in it only to a limited extent. Narratively, this distancing game is played through the use of light that wraps things up, creating a distance between the protagonist and the world around him. As already noted, Los Angeles is artificially created by light in Giovanni's tale.

Giovanni also creates a second degree of distance from what happens to him by the very mode of his narrative, which is almost emotionally unparticipative. One could attribute the protagonist's attitude to the lapse of time occurring between the events and their narration, were it not for the fact that the narrating voice insistently points at his distance from the events in the very moment they occurred, as, for example, in this case:

> Jill [the woman with whom he lives for a while] si è seccata quando le ho detto che non saremmo più riusciti a mangiare insieme. Ha detto "Cristo, cosí non ci vediamo più." Si stava sfilando i calzoni, in piedi sulla porta del bagno. Le ho detto che mi dispiaceva [...]. Sono stato in bagno dieci minuti a litigare con lei: appoggiato di schiena al lavandino, con le mani in tasca. Gridavamo tutti e due, in competizione con il rumore della doccia che scrosciava. La vedevo come una silhouette rosa zigrinata attraverso il vetro scherma-acqua: con un braccio alzato, mentre si passava il sapone sotto l'ascella. (*Treno di panna* 134)

> [Jill was annoyed when I told her we wouldn't manage to eat together any more. "Christ," she said, "this way we won't be seeing each other anymore." She was getting out of her trousers, standing in the doorway to the bathroom. I told her I was sorry [...]. I spent ten minutes arguing with her in the bathroom: leaning back against the wash-stand with my hands in my pockets. We were both yelling against the splashing of the shower. I could see her as a marbled pink silhouette through the glass screen: one arm raised as she soaped her armpit. (*The Cream Train* 130)]

The argument between the two is pushed to the background by Giovanni's involvement with the surface of the event – the woman taking a shower. Not only does Giovanni step back from the pathos of the fight in the very moment it happens, but he also chooses to describe the event by emphasizing that same distance and making it central to his narration. The detailed, analytical look that he gives to the surface of the world around him conversely lengthens that emotional distance. Things and beings described from such a doubled distance appear morally diminished and grotesque, when not insignificant or irrelevant. This is not to say that *Treno di panna* suffers from its narrator's apparent lack of depth; rather, the novel is built exactly on that apparent absence of engagement, which carries with it a strong moral judgment about people's lives and habits in Los Angeles, and about the Hollywood dream.

Filippo La Porta is convinced that De Carlo's analysis of life in Los Angeles neither judges nor condemns, but the result of De Carlo's narrative technique differs markedly from his conclusions. If it is true that description is not the "ancilla narrationis," secondary to narration, as Genette defined it, but rather generates the plot, we have a clear example of this in *Treno di panna*, where the mere description of the events' surfaces becomes the novel itself. As such, the description, then, does carry with it a moral stance, although inexplicit, that concerns the American dream as lived in Los Angeles and Hollywood.

Giovanni's entire American experience is based on this superficial modality of approach (meant as approach to surfaces, although extremely detailed), and if on the narrative level we have a twenty-five-year-old man exclusively absorbed by what he sees / saw, on the level of the writing we have an author constantly pointing at what silently transpires for the reader from Giovanni's descriptions of surfaces: disengagement from a deeper human and social connection, and absence of historical conscience.

Giovanni himself is certainly judgmental. While narrating from his own distance, he points at that same form of disengagement in the people he meets. Here is Giovanni's description of Ron:

La prima volta che ho visto Ron e Tracy erano seduti in un bar all'aperto: adagiati all'indietro su sedie bianche. Ron parlava con un ibizano ubriaco, a due tavoli di distanza. Mi ricordo bene il loro modo di essere; il loro modo di essere vestiti. Si muovevano con la più incredibile naturalezza, come se conoscessero il posto da sempre, nelle piccole sfumature.

Ron parlava uno spagnolo grottesco, che più tardi mi ha detto di aver imparato durante una vacanza di venti giorni in Messico. Conosceva pochi termini chiave; li prnonunciava male senza riflettere. L'ibizano era ostile; sconnesso, oscillante. Ricorreva a piccoli trucchi per tirare la conversazione dalla sua. Legava le parole due a due, le accentuva in modo da venarle di ridicolo; giocava sugli accostamenti per creare altri significati.

Ron era impermeabile a queste sottigliezze: gli scivolavano addosso come piccole frecce senza punta. Raccolglieva a caso pochi elementi della conversazione e li ricomponeva secondo un ordine lineare [...]. Alla fine l'ibizano si è messo a bestemmiare per la frustrazione; si è alzato in piedi gridando. Ron è riuscito a cambiare anche il senso di questo scatto, lo ha interpretato come una manifestazione di giovilità rozza. Si è alzato anche lui, con un bicchiere di Madeira in mano; ha gridato parole a caso. (*Treno di panna* 18)

[The first time I saw Ron and Tracy, they were sitting outside a bar: reclining on white armchairs. Ron was talking to a tipsy Ibizan two tables away. I remember very well the way they were; and the way they were dressed. They behaved with the most incredible ease, as if they'd always known the place, its subtle overtones.

Ron spoke grotesque Spanish, which he later told me he'd learnt during a three-week holiday he'd spent in Mexico. He knew a few keywords; mispronounced them unthinkingly. The Ibizan was hostile; disjointed, unsteady. He used little ploys to turn the conversation his way. He linked words together in pairs, stressed them in such a way as to lace them with mockery; played on their juxtaposition to give rise to ulterior meanings.

Ron was impervious to these subtleties: they slid off him like tiny untipped darts. He haphazardly picked up bits and pieces of the conversation and reassembled them in linear fashion [...]. Finally, the Ibizan was reduced to blaspheming out of frustration; he rose to his feet, yelling. Ron even managed to transform the point of this outburst, took it as an expression of rough-and-ready joviality. He also got to his feet, a glass of Madeira in his hand; he mouthed some words at random. (*The Cream Train* 10)]

In this passage, what resonates for the reader is Ron's extreme simple-mindedness, which uncovers one of the worst stereotypes about Americans that the distant gaze of Europe could produce through the centuries. Giovanni's gaze is pitiless, besides being stereotypical itself.

Ron also seems to lack talent as a writer in search of success. If we think that he is supposed to be the New York intellectual on whom his girlfriend Tracy looks with admiration, his ways of communicating with others become even more grotesque, as in one of his letters to Giovanni:

giovanni ciao le macchine passano sopra la mia testa in una catena senza fine di movimento & scuotono la casa & le girano attorno in anelli di energia che si trasmette dall pareti della casa alla mia schiena & poi lungo il braccio fino alla punta della mano che tiene questa penna con cui ti sto scrivendo. ho quasi finito il soggetto per il film più incredibile dela storia del cinema & l'idea mi comunica strane sensazioni & forse un senso di panico & vedremo se la via verso la gloria sarà liscia & facile da percorrere o invece irta di ostacoli & difficoltà. tu folle italiano sognatore sei nel sole & nel blu assurdo di oahu a far l'amore con invitanti danzatrici di hula mentre noi siamo racchiusi sotto questa cupola di nevrosi in questo ranch di talenti in attesa [...]. vorrei essere distaccato come te & quasi ascetico

nel disprezzo del successo & del denaro & avere tutta quella profondità
inperscrutabile dell'europa antica e misteriosa che forse ti dà altre moti-
vazioni & ti permette di goderti la vita alle hawaii mentre noi ce la avvele-
niamo ogni giorno alla ricerca di un attimo di gloria [...] (*Treno di panna* 22)

[ciao giovanni the automobiles are shooting overhead in an endless chain
of motion & shaking the house & encircling it in energy rings which are
transmitted from the house walls to my back and then down my arm right
down to the fingertips of my arms with which i'm holding the pen i'm using to write to you. I've almost finished the script for the most incredible
film in screen history & the idea gives me a strange feeling & perhaps a
sense of panic & we'll see if the path to glory is going to be smooth & easy
or bristling with obstacles & difficulties. you crazy italian dreamer are sitting in the sunshine & the absurd blue of oahu making love to appealing
hula dancers while we're cooped up inside this dome of neurosis on this
talent-ranch waiting [...]. i'd like to be detached like you & almost ascetic
in my contempt for success & money & to have all that inscrutable profun-
dity of ancient mysterious europe which maybe gives you different kinds
of motivation & enables you to enjoy living in hawaii while we poison our
lives day by day striving for an instant of glory [...] (*The Cream Train* 14)]

Exoticism works both ways; if Giovanni has his own say on American
simplicity, Ron is not immune to stereotyped icons of Europe (we never
learn what Giovanni's other profound motivations can be, and he does
not seem to have any). However, the game of the stereotypes is unbal-
anced in *Treno di Panna*. The first-person narrator gains credibility
through the exclusiveness of his viewpoint, while the other characters'
perspectives only come to the reader filtered through Giovanni's eyes
and his own judgmental disengagement. We only have Giovanni to
trust and a couple of letters that support his opinions of Ron and Tracy.
  Giovanni describes Ron and Tracy as extremely self-centred, convinced that he is smarter and more sensitive than they are (or than he
deems them to be). Ironically, Giovanni trusts himself and his ways
of approaching the world with the same unquestioned degree of self-
confidence. This is not a matter of political correctness, nor am I questioning the psychology of three bi-dimensional characters. The question
involves the eye of the beholder: who puts into play and overexposes a
set of stereotypical icons of America? A narrator unable to engage himself beyond surface, and who remains caught in the same dream Ron
and Tracy are pursuing. His distant mode of participating in the events,

and of narrating them, does not make him more capable of revealing truths of any sort about America; rather, it unveils his own inability to engage with America on a deeper level.

Distance (physical, temporal, emotional, or moral) does not produce a clearer view of events; instead, it gives one the possibility of elaborating and repackaging them in a way that better suits the flow of one's own experience, or historical understanding. Distance only produces a different sort of narrative, not a clearer understanding of what happened; it only generates a different discourse that, apparently, empowers the distant speaker who exerts control over the events.

In the case of Giovanni's narrative, no human growth comes out of his engagement with America. Whatever the distance produces, the narrative lacks depth, at any point in time. Even though by the end of the novel the reader is lured into concluding that there is nothing to engage with, since Los Angeles is only made of artificial light (with all that this metaphorically suggests), one must still take into account who is arriving at this conclusion, and in what sort of narrative it has been generated.

Treno di panna is a narrative of distance. In the case of Giovanni one lacks even the flow of personal history and the larger picture that would absorb the distance into a different function. What we have is a self-centred, analytical look at events that relies only on itself to narrate the story. Giovanni's disengagement empowers his voice, but it is precisely this same disengagement that makes him somehow unreliable. The "I" of *Treno di panna* (un)makes American stereotypes by (1) reproducing them from a distance that overdetermines the content of the American icons he shapes, since he looks at America with the culturally conditioned eye of a European, disguised as a "new" traveller; and by (2) emptying those American icons by pointing at the void behind them. The Italy of the 1980s, though, was not very receptive to this aspect of the novel – the emptiness beyond the icon – and appropriated those icons as symbols of hope and of a better future soon to come. Yet, there was nothing new in *Treno di panna* as far as its European America was concerned.

Baudrillard's *Amérique* and Giovanni's America: The Desert Explained and Exposed

Five years after the publication of *Treno di Panna*, the book that decreed the perennial realization of the American Utopia and the death of the hegemony of European culture appeared: *Amérique*. Calling into question the hyper-culturalized European look upon America (which he himself had of the country), Jean Baudrillard described in a most passionate way what De Carlo had depicted with his sidereal, photographic eye: the dizzying emptiness of an America without hope.

About *Amérique*, Mario Klarel writes,

> Baudrillard stands at the end of a long tradition of French evaluations of America, starting with eighteenth-century visitors who considered America as the forerunner of their own revolution. For Crèvecoeur, Condorcet and Volney, America became an image for what France might become in the future. The climax of French scrutiny was provoked after 1830 by the prospect of another French Republic. Alexis de Tocqueville's *Democracy in America* (1835) has been by far the best received book on America by a French author. With Baudrillard – more than 150 years after Tocqueville's *Democracy in America* – America again turned into a fictional space onto which French avant-garde theories or ideologies tried to inscribe themselves. (227)

There seems to be an analogy between Baudrillard's *America* as described and inscribed by Klarel in the French tradition, and the meaning of America in Italian literary discursive practices. European countries do share specific images and conceptions of America. Because of the book's success and importance, Martino Marazzi feels the need to introduce Baudrillard's *Amérique* in his *Little America*, which is a compendium of the Italian authors who have written about America. Marazzi writes:

> Si tratta di un testo [*America*] irritante e irrinunciabile, volutamente provocatorio e paradossale, che si presta senza difficoltà a stroncature feroci, per il credito eccessivo concesso ai luoghi comuni più triti e superficiali [...] (178)

> [It is an irritating and irremissible text [*America*], purposely provocative and paradoxical, which lends itself easily to ferocious destructive criticism for the excessive credit given to the most trite and superficial commonplaces [...]]

It is because of the "credit given to the most trite and superficial commonplaces" that I want to compare Baudrillard's analytical and involved discussion of America with *Treno di panna*, in order to show how Giovanni's look at America, supposedly non-judgmental because of his emotional detachment from his own experience, represents, in fact, the imperial and presumptuous view of old Europe. Baudrillard's definition of America as a desert without hope (without hope because America is a utopia already realized; a desert, because detached from any sort of historical consciousness and culture as intended in Europe) casts light back on Giovanni's perspective on America, unmasking it as extremely traditional and often stereotyped. The narrator of *Treno di panna* describes America from the same perspective that the writer of *Amérique* will adopt later, with a difference: the subject of *Amérique* is consciously self-reflexive, displaying his own fundamentally European perspective while critiquing it. The "I" of *Treno di panna*, in contrast, is completely acritical of himself, engaged in an extreme defence of his identity, as La Porta points out:

> Il viaggio americano del perdigiorno Giovanni del *Treno di panna* (che si può simbolicamente assumere come decollo di una generazione di narratori), apparentemente capriccioso e svagato [...] si rivela una macchina da guerra incaricata di difendere la propria identità tutt'altro che fluttuante: il soffice treno di panna con cui ci si era illusi di giocare si è rivelato, a distanza, un vagone blindato. (29)

> [The American voyage of *Treno di panna*'s idle Giovanni (which can be assumed symbolically as the take-off of a generation of narrators), apparently capricious and thoughtless [...] reveals itself as a war machine in charge of defending its own identity that is all but fluctuating: the soft cream train we deluded ourselves to be dealing with turns out to be, in the long run, an armoured wagon.]

Giovanni remains unchanged by his Californian adventure.

Staging the Insignificant

Discussing America's artificiality, Baudrillard writes:

> Il y a un sorte de miracle dans la fadeur des paradis artificiels, pourvu qu'ils atteignent à la grandeur de toute une (in)culture. En Amérique l'espace donne une envergure même à la fadeur des *suburbs* et des *funky towns*. Le désert est partout et sauve l'insignifiance. [...]

Miracle Italien: celui de la scène.
Miracle américain: celui de l'obscène.
La luxure du sens contre les déserts de l'insignifiance. (*Amérique* 23)

[There is a sort of miracle in the insipidity of *artificial paradises*, so long
as they achieve the greatness of an entire (un)culture. In America, space
lends a sense of grandeur even to the insipidity of the suburbs and "funky
towns". The desert is everywhere preserving insignificance. [...]
  The Italian miracle: that of stage and scene.
  The American miracle: that of the obscene.
  The profusion of sense, as against the deserts of meaninglessness.
(*America* 8)]

For Baudrillard, Italy and America are two artificial paradises, the former achieving the greatness of its culture by staging all its signs, and
the second that of its un-culture by preserving its insignificance, instead, where for insignificance we must understand "the transparency
of all functions in space" (*America* 8). The realization of such an opposition is to be found in Giovanni's narrative technique. The characters, closely observed in their habits, movements, physical postures,
and emotional reactions, recall the amplification of gestures necessary
on a theatrical stage. At the same time, Giovanni's emotional distance
creates a sort of desert of signification by depriving those same movements and postures of any relevant significance that is not their immediate function in that space-time narrative moment, as in the scene
quoted above, when Jill and Giovanni argue in the bathroom. Here the
narrator not only silences the content of what is supposed to be a very
animated discussion between Jill and Giovanni but also takes away the
centre of the scene from the reader's view by focusing on Jill washing
her armpit. We are forced to abandon the scene while the argument is
taking place, and we have the clear sensation that whatever was said
in that fight signified nothing concrete for either the protagonist of the
story, or for Jill herself. The ultimate insignificance of any performance
is certainly well dramatized in *Treno di panna*. Giovanni's dry carica-
ture of his experience at Alfredo's, an Italian restaurant populated by
Mexican waiters, although extremely theatrical in its exaggerated me-
ticulousness, does not involve the reader sympathetically in what happens at any moment.

At Alfredo's, the reader finds no occasion to empathize with any of
the human or spatial elements of the scene. At the end of Giovanni's

first night as a waiter at Alfredo's, his final comment on the waiter who had been his first coach summarizes the atmosphere that had enveloped the scene from the beginning:

> Ho guardato Cormàl mentre contava le sue mance: nascosto dietro un attaccapanni, di profilo. Si bagnava l'indice in punta di lingua e lo passava veloce sul bordo dei biglietti. Muoveva la bocca nel contare, ma senza emettere suoni. Interrompeva il conteggio ogni volta che un altro cameriere si avvicinava, o quando sentiva nuovi passi sulle scale. Quando si è accorto che lo stavo guardando ha avuto un cenno irritato. Era detestabile anche lui: piccolo e patetico, con tutti i difetti degli altri. (*Treno di panna* 56)

> [I watched Cormàl counting up his tip money: hiding behind a clothes-stand, side on to me. He moistened his forefinger with the tip of his tongue and ran it swiftly over the edge of the bills. His mouth moved as he counted, soundlessly. He stopped counting every time another waiter came near him or when he could hear someone else ascending the stairs. When he realized I was watching him, he jerked his head with irritation. He too was loathsome: small and pathetic, with all the same shortcomings as the rest of them. (*The Cream Train* 50)]

Making things small and pathetic is exactly the effect that Giovanni's narration has on the entirety of whatever he sees and describes, giving the reader a final sense of emptiness. In his account, we observe the clash between European and American cultures as Baudrillard drafts them here:

> Ce qui est volatilisé n'est pas seulement l'esthétique du décor [...] mais celle des corps et du langage, de tout ce qui fait l'habitus mental et social de l'Européen, surtout latin, cette *commedia dell'arte* continuelle, pathos e rhétorique de la relation sociale [...]. Notre univers n'est jamais désertique, toujours théâtral. (*Amérique* 242–3)

> [It is not just the aesthetics of décor [...] that vanishes into thin air, but the aesthetics of bodies and language, of everything that forms the European's – especially the Latin European's – mental and social habitus, that continual *commedia dell'arte*, the pathos and rhetoric of social relations [...]. Our universe is never desert-like, always theatrical. (*America* 124)]

Giovanni's descriptions of his adventures (the accounts of his nights at Alfredo's and his lessons with Marsha Mellows) can be viewed as a sequence of scenes from the *commedia dell'arte*; but here the commedia has lost its lively character, its sense of exalted humanity. Even in the case of Giovanni's encounters with Marsha Mellows, where the narrative becomes self-ironic and the pitiless eye of the observer moves his dry, judgmental look from the other onto himself, even in this case, where Giovanni ridicules his own fascination with the actress, the *commedia* remains superficial, and the irony loses the connection to its very source: the depths of the human drama.

There is no empathy for the human scenario in *Treno di panna*, not even any deep unsympathetic feeling that could guide a morally engaged photographic eye as in Swift. In *Treno di panna* the narrating "I" – blind to himself – attributes implicitly the desert-like quality to the object "America" as inherent to it, while his own inability to detect other forms of seduction, or points of deeper engagement with America, is part of the image of America that his narrative creates. La Porta is right: this cream train is an extreme defence of identity, rather than a discovery of the Other. Giovanni's infatuation with Marsha Mellows has little to do with Marsha herself, and a lot to do with Giovanni's stupefaction as a young man and with his exaggerated perception of Marsha.

Giovanni is not interested in establishing any empathetic contact with America. His pitiless look on the country, which Italy had welcomed as "new " both narratively and socially, turns out to be no novelty, at least as far as the images of America portrayed in the book are concerned. The Italy that welcomes *Treno di panna* seems indifferent to this detail, all keen on praising the new way of narrative that De Carlo had opened up. But De Carlo, despite his stylistic departure, had only changed the vestments of the same old European traveller. We find a confirmation of this in *Amérique*, where Baudrillard tries to awaken Europeans to their blindness towards America, but, at the same time, finds himself impotent when trying to define America without comparing it to European standards of culture and history (a sort of failure, for this is exactly the intent of his book). Baudrillard writes:

> Pas de charme, pas de séduction dans tout cela. La séduction est ailleurs, en Italie, dans certains paysages devenues peintures, aussi culturalisés et raffinés dans leur dessin que les villes et les musées qui les enferment. Espaces circonscrits […] de haute séduction, où le sens, à ce point luxueux, est enfin devenu parure. C'est exactement l'inverse ici: pas de séduction, mais une fascination absolue, celle même de la disparition de toute forme critique et esthétique da la vie […]. Celle du désert: immobilité sans désir. (*Amérique* 242)

[No charm, no seduction in all this. Seduction is elsewhere, in Italy, in certain landscapes that have become paintings, as culturalized and refined in their design as the cities and museums that house them. Circumscribed [...] highly seductive spaces where meaning, at these heights of luxury, has finally become adornment. It is exactly the reverse here: there is no seduction, but there is an absolute fascination – the fascination of the very disappearance of all aesthetic and critical forms of life [...]. The fascination of the desert: immobility without desire. (*America* 124)]

Absence of seduction, immobility without desire, is exactly what Giovanni portrays for us when describing Tracy, for instance (but not only):

Tracy era perduta nella contemplazione di Ron; nella cura di se stessa di fronte all'estate spagnola. Stava appoggiata sul gomito sinistro, così da allungare la gamba discosto al tavolino: dorata, lucida. Aveva un vestito di cotone bianco in stile Roma antica, stretto in vita da una cintura marocchina. Il colore dei suoi seni abbronzati filtrava attraverso la trama del tessuto, emergeva alle punte dei capezzoli.
   Anche così non era attraente: priva di eleganza, poco sensibile. Ma la sua sicurezza mi colpiva, il suo modo di muoversi attorno come se non potesse sbagliare in ogni caso. (*Treno di panna* 19)

[Tracy was lost in contemplating Ron, in the care of her body in the Spanish summer. She was leaning on her left elbow so as to stretch her leg away from the table: a gleaming, golden leg. She wore a white cotton dress in ancient Roman style, fastened around the waist by a Moroccan belt. The color of her sun-tanned breasts came through the fabric, more boldly at the nipples.
   Even so, she still didn't look attractive: she lacked elegance and sensitivity. But I was struck by her assurance, her way of moving about as if, whatever happened, she couldn't put a foot wrong. (*The Cream Train* 10–11)]

Giovanni is surprised by the fact that, regardless of her lack of elegance and sensibility – the elements which are implicitly defined by his Italian / European cultural background – Jill is extremely self-confident. This self-confidence and homogeneity, which are completely detached from the roots of a European sense of aesthetic, is what Baudrillard calls the desert as a realized utopia when he refers to America; however, he does so while actively critiquing Europe's cultural constructs – which Giovanni does not.

Even though Baudrillard critiques those European cultural constructs, he cannot bypass them when he describes America, because he cannot find a way to talk about America without comparing America to Europe. In this sense, the contradiction of his rhetorical strategy seems hopeless – destined to remain unresolved. To resolve that contradiction, that tension on which his discourse is built, would mean to realize America as he wishes us to see it. And in fact he writes:

> Ce pays est sans espoir.
>
> Pour nous les fanatiques de l'esthétique e du sens, de la culture, de la saveur et de la séduction […] pour nous qui sommes indéfectiblement liés aux prestiges du sens critique et de la transcendance, pour nous c'est un choc mental et un dégagement inouï de découvrir la fascination du nonsens, de cette déconnection vertigineuse également souvraine dans les déserts et dans les villes. Découvrir qu'on peut jouir de la liquidation de toute culture et s'exalter du sacré de l'indifférence. (*Amérique* 240–1)

> [This country is without hope.
>
> We fanatics of aesthetics and meaning, of culture, of flavor and seduction […] we who are unfailingly attached to the wonders of critical sense and transcendence find it a mental shock and a unique release to discover the fascination of nonsense and of this vertiginous disconnection, as sovereign in the cities as in the deserts. To discover that one can exult in the liquidation of all culture and rejoice in the consecration of in-difference. (*America* 123)]

Baudrillard, who knows himself to be "unfailingly attached to the wonders of critical sense," is trapped in his contradictory discourse that can be resolved, or dissolved, only in the "liquidation of all culture," in his collision with America, so to speak. Hence, the "disconnection" from Europe becomes "vertiginous." Baudrillard also knows that very rarely would a European rejoice in the consecration of indifference. The protagonist of *L'arcadia americana*, for instance, another fanatic of culture, will proceed in the narrative of his story by continuously remarking on differences between America and Europe.

Amérique's novelty is its critique of Europe's old sense of culture, but it does not give us any new vision of America. If anything, it casts light back on *Treno di panna* where the same stereotyped images of America are dramatized. *Treno di panna*'s novelty is its voice's narrative mode, certainly not in what it says about America. If we look at both Giovanni's look on America and Baudrillard's parameters of European culture, we discover that they are dictated by a strong sense of national ethos ·that had not been obliged yet to come to terms with greatly increased problems of immigration, global fluxes of people, and cohabitation of different cultures. Giovanni, the free-spirit idler of the 1980s, could not care less about sympathizing with the Mexican waiters of Alfredo's; neither was he really interested in analysing that specific ethnic aspect of America. In the same way, Baudrillard is not interested in any other America than the one pertaining to European mythology. In other words, while describing America, what Giovanni and Baudrillard are really doing is unveiling themselves and focusing on their own perspectives: an old European cultural trick. Their incapacity to abandon European standards of aesthetics brings each of them to look at American bodies, for example, in the same puzzled, surprised way. Baudrillard: "Ce qui est saisissant, c'est [...] l'absence vertigineuse d'affect et de caractère dans le visages et dans les corps. Beaux, fluids, souple, ou *cool*, ou d'une obésité étrange [...]" (*Amérique* 243; "What is arresting here is [...] the dizzying absence of emotion and character in the faces and bodies. Handsome, fluid, supple, or cool, or grotesquely obese [...]" *America* 125). And Giovanni:

> Mi ricordo di averla [Tracy] osservata nuda sulla spiaggia dove io lei e Ron ci eravamo consociuti. C'era un'omogeneità peculiare nel suo modo di essere fatta, una tessitura di luci che la rendeva del tutto impermeabile alla nudità. Era densa, più che grassa: composta di un unico materiale, solido, elastico. La guardavo entrare in acqua e il suo sedere era una semplice continuazione funzionale della schiena. Avrebbe potuto essere una foca, o un'ampia lontra marina. (*Treno di panna* 12)

> [I remember viewing her naked on the beach, where she, Ron, and I had met. There was a peculiar homogeneity about the way she was made, an intertwining of light that made her totally impermeable to nudity. She was solid, rather than fat: constituted of a single material, compact, elastic. I would watch her enter the water, and her backside was just a functional continuation of her back. She might have been a seal, or a generously proportioned sea-otter. (*The Cream Train* 3–4)]

Giovanni uses his European parameters of beauty to judge Tracy with an act of cultural identity self-defence. Tracy's body, as described by

Giovanni, could be one of those to which Baudrillard refers as being devoid of "emotion and character."

Treno di panna is altogether an act of identity self-defence; but, in contradiction to this founding feature of De Carlo's novel, the Italy that rejoices at the book in 1981 looks at *Treno di panna* as the horizon of a new world for a new, changed generation. Italy appropriates the image of America that Giovanni produces without noticing its vacuity, and overwrites that vacuity to other ends. Here we leave Baudrillard and his juxtaposition of America and Italy to see what effect the desert-like image of America depicted in *Treno di panna* had on the Italian stage.

When De Carlo appeared on the literary scene, he was not only the new writer, but also the symbol of the emergent Italian generation. The resonance that De Carlo had with that particular moment of Italian social history is wonderfully and ironically explained by the journalist and writer Gianni Riotta in "La strategia della distensione" ("The Strategy of Distension"), which is the foreword to the *Corriere della sera*'s 2003 special edition of *Treno di panna*. Riotta explains the success of De Carlo's novel, recalling its effect on the generation that was living through the period of terrorism called "anni di piombo" (years of lead). The title of his piece, "The Strategy of Distension," counterpoints the expression "strategy of tension" used to define a conspiracy theory very popular in Italy during the "years of lead." The conspiracy theory pointed at some corrupted branches of Italian government intelligence as the real perpetrators of the acts of violence attributed to the terrorists. These acts of violence (murders, explosions, and massacres) were to keep a constant state of fear and tension in the country. Riotta writes:

> Chi fu giovane durante gli anni di piombo li ricorderà per sempre, "gambizzato" nella coscienza come le vittime dei brigatisti, sotto casa. Non si era mai del tutto felici, anche innamorati, mai veramente lontani, anche nuotando al mare, mai interamente concentrati, anche studiando. Ogni attimo si sapeva che il nemico terrorista stava tramando [...] Volevamo essere ragazzi, liberi, anticonformisti. La guerra fredda era invece una guerra, e non lo sapevamo. Peggio di noi stavano i coetanei sotto il tallone tardostalinista in Russia, i coetanei sotto le giunte militari in America latina. Noi avevamo la nostra guerra civile fasulla, ma i morti erano veri. Nel 1981 arrivò, come un lampo di felicità, *Treno di panna* di Andrea De Carlo. (7–8)

> [Those who were young during the years of lead will remember them forever, "kneecapped" in their consciousness like the victims of the Brigades,

right out of their homes. We were never completely happy, not even when in love; never completely far away, not even when at the seaside; never really focused, not even when studying. In every moment we knew that the enemy terrorist was plotting something [...]. We wanted to be young, free, and anti-conformist. The Cold War was a real war, instead; but we did not know it. In worse conditions than ours were our coevals under the late Stalinist's heel, and our contemporaries under the Latin-American military dictatorships. We had our fake civil war, but the dead were real. In 1981, Andrea De Carlo's *Treno di panna* arrived as a bolt of happiness.]

Beyond the historical background that Riotta recalls, it is important to notice how he describes the plot of the novel, which, between the lines, tells more about how the book was received:

La storia di Giovanni, un ragazzo italiano qualunque che se ne va in America a guardare la vita. Insegna un po', divide la casa con Ron e Tracy, sazi, ignari, californiani dimentichi delle ideologie e della guerriglia velenosa che rovinava casa nostra. Bagni di mare, corse in autostrada verso l'insipida Jill, il furto di due bottiglie di champagne. Poi l'amicizia con l'attrice Marsha Mellows e il tuffo collettivo in piscina tra le stelle di Hollywood, "morbide" perfino nella vera vita, fuori da cinema e tv [...]. Basta con l'ossessione dell'Italia piegata. Un volo altrove, un passaggio edonista nel mondo che andava avanti, e di lì a poco avrebbe impugnato i personal computer non le rivoltelle Nagant dei brigatisti. (8)

[The story of Giovanni, an ordinary Italian young man who goes to America to see life. He teaches a little, shares a house with Ron and Tracy, who are satisfied, unaware Californians, unaware of the ideologies and the venomous guerrilla that was ruining our home. Sea swims, runs on the highways towards the dull Jill, a theft of two bottles of champagne. Then the friendship with the actress Marsha Mellows and a collective dive in the swimming pool, among the Hollywood stars, "soft" even in real life, outside of cinema and TV [...]. Enough with our obsession of a broken Italy. A flight elsewhere, a hedonistic passage in the world that was going ahead, and would have handled personal computers in a while, not the Nagant revolvers of the Brigades.]

In Riotta's description of the plot, Jill is dull by her own nature, not in Giovanni's eye. Ron and Tracy are ignorant of the Italian social scenario, as if they were supposed to be mindful of it, and the detail seems to have nothing to do with Giovanni's silence about it. Giovanni's America is a given and remains unquestioned, but its image becomes the future, once again. As ironic counterpoint, I think of Moretti walking downhill on the volcano, in *Caro diario*, to reach the Americans who certainly knew the plot of *The Bold and the Beautiful*'s future episodes, since there, in the United States, "they are always ahead." For the generation that faced the beginning of the 1980s, America's icon becomes an image of hope, just like the Italy of *Lamerica*, just like the Disneyfied island of Stromboli's mayor. The description that Riotta gives of *Treno di panna* contrasts with the emptiness that the reader perceives in the novel, and with the ineffectiveness that America has on Giovanni's life.

Riotta continues describing the revivifying effects of De Carlo's language on Italian narrative and its meaning within the European literary tradition:

> Tornare alla tradizione democratica della letteratura e dell'arte, che da Sofocle a Mozart non componeva per l'aristocrazia, ma si sforzava di parlare al cuore e alla ragione degli uomini. Il Novecento europeo, dilaniato dalla sua lunga guerra civile 1914–1989, aveva perduto questa virtù. La solennità commossa con cui i giganti dell'Ottocento, da Manzoni e Tolstoj a Beethoven e Verdi, sapevano parlare s'era perduta. Anche le vette più alte del secolo appena chiuso, da Beckett a Borges, Joyce e Kafka, narravano della fine della parola, della storia, dell'angoscia finale, dell'afasia. Ma sulla morte, la paura, la solitudine e il silenzio non si costruisce un futuro. E così, quando alzammo gli occhi dietro i sacchi di sabbia della nostra gioventù, vedemmo il sole della California e le luci intermittenti di Los Angeles, il futuro narrato da Andrea. (9)

> [To return to the democratic tradition of literature and art, which from Sophocles to Mozart was not composed for the aristocracy, but was meant to speak to people's hearts and minds. The European twentieth century, lacerated by its long civil war of 1914–1989, had lost this virtue. The deep solemnity through which the giants of the nineteenth century could talk, from Manzoni and Tolstoy to Beethoven and Verdi, was lost. Even the highest heights of the last century, from Beckett to Borges, Joyce and Kafka, foretold the end of the word and history, of the final anguish, of aphasia. But no future can be built on death, fear, solitude, and silence. And so, when we lifted our eyes from behind the bags of sand of our youth, we saw the Californian sun and Los Angeles' intermittent lights. The future told by Andrea.]

Elio Vittorini, Giaime Pintor, and Cesare Pavese had already exalted the value of America for an Italy brought to its knees by two wars and twenty years of Fascism. Riotta reproduces that cry of hope for an Italy morally destroyed by terrorism. He does not see any pause in the tragedies that have crossed the country from 1914 to the fall of the Berlin Wall.

What Riotta does not say, or does not see, is that California as depicted in *Treno di panna*, and Giovanni's American experience, did nothing for the human growth of the novel's protagonist, did not engage his social consciousness more than was needed to surf the surface of life, and did not outline any particularly hopeful idea of the future.

What Italians decided to do with *Treno di panna*, to what extent they saw their hopes and dreams reflected in the novel, did not correspond to the content of the novel itself that showed the vacuum which the cream train was crossing, an emptiness depending to a great extent on the unwillingness of the beholder to engage with America on a deeper level of human, social, and historical consciousness and understanding.

The moral level on which Italy has engaged images of the United States has always concerned its volatile hopes and desires (hopes and desires created by looking far from oneself, from one's own present, historical moment), and the subsequent disillusionment with them. Within this context, Moretti's critique of the Italian tendency to look elsewhere for the best (which in *Caro diario* finds its apotheosis in the mayor of Stromboli's Disneyfied dream) becomes more poignant.

The Italy that acclaimed *Treno di panna* was looking at an image of its own hopes, once again called "America." What De Carlo was saying, and what Italy did not grasp at the time, was that America did not exist. In order to say this, the author of *Treno di panna* struck right at the heart of his protagonist's beloved American icon: Marsha Mellows. Once Giovanni embraces the American dream and becomes the Italian teacher of Marsha Mellows, he also becomes as ridiculous as the other characters of the story and shows it in the way he thinks of, talks to, and acts around the actress. Here is part of Giovanni's reaction when he learns he will teach Italian to Marsha Mellows:

> Pensavo a quante riviste mi era capitato di vedere con la faccia di Marsha Mellows in copertina [...]. In questi primi piani la vedevo muovere le labbra e ripetere "Sono Marsha Mellows." Non imamginavo il suono delle parole: immagionavo di leggerle sulle sue labbra, metre venivano pronunciate. "Marsha Mellows," perdeva la sua natura di nome e cognome di persona; diventava un sostantivo, come "mela" o "gelato." (*Treno di panna* 115)

[I thought of the quantity of magazines I'd happened to see carrying Marsha Mellows' face on the front cover [...]. In these close-ups I'd see her lips move and say, "I'm Marsha Mellows." I didn't imagine the sound of the words: I imagined myself reading them on her lips as they were uttered. "Marsha Mellows", it lost the nature of a person's name and surname; it turned into a common noun, like "apple" or "ice-cream." (*The Cream Train* 110)]

The marshmallows turn into an apple, then into an ice-cream, and the more Giovanni filters the woman's features through the distortions of his fantasy, the more he exposes his American dream, the more ridiculous he becomes. The same happens when Moretti meets Jennifer Beals in *Caro diario*. Once confronted with the reality of his dream represented by the actress herself, Moretti becomes "quasi scemo." Unlike Moretti, the "I" of *Treno di panna* is not openly self-ironic for intellectual purposes. His discourse does not entail any reflection on the possibility for the subject to let go of America meant as the dream to be realized elsewhere, as in the case of *Caro diario*. Giovanni's irony is much more subtle because of our young protagonist's unwillingness to initiate any serious discourse about America, which gave Italian readers, at the beginning of the 1980s, the chance to overlook what De Carlo was pointing at through Giovanni – the vacuity of the dream, the flimsiness of both the cream and the marshmallows. Italian readers, then, caught the salvific train, salvific only for Italian literature and its tradition of narratives of the self.

As far as ethical, sociopolitical engagement is concerned, the protagonist of *L'arcadia americana* is at the opposite end of Giovanni's carelessness, just as its author, Gina Lagorio, has lived in a completely different world from the one inhabited by the much younger De Carlo. Their narratives are informed by very diverse personal experiences: the world of Fascism and Resistance is not part of De Carlo's background. Gina Lagorio is a daughter of Italian anti-Fascist history, and an Italian Leftist intellectual. Her book about America in 1999, after the first Gulf War and the United States' intervention in the Kosovar war, had a very different flavour and scope from a book about California in 1981, when Italians were trying to forget "the years of lead."

4 American Arcadia[1]

An "I" on Intellectual and Civil Engagement

Gina Lagorio decided to write *L'arcadia americana* after a voyage she made to the United States at the invitation of the American Association of Italian Studies, in the spring of 1999. About the writing of the novel, when thinking of her next literary project, she said to the journalist Grazia Casagrande, "Bisognerà che mi punga, mi urga qualcosa dentro come mi è successo per *L'arcadia americana* che non ho potuto fare a meno di scrivere [...]" (Casagrande; "Something inside will need to urge me, to prick me, as it happened for *L'arcadia americana* that I couldn't help but write [...]").[2] Reading the novel, one realizes that *L'arcadia americana* shows the author's urgency to convey something about America and, more generally, about the lack of moral responsibility of the new generations confronting, in Europe as in America, the evils of the world. In her story, American academia, and often the United States at large, become a utopian space like Arcadia, to a great extent removed from the world's events.

L'arcadia americana (1999) draws extensively from the myth of classical Arcadia, specifically from the "Et in Arcadia Ego" theme. The first-person narrator is an Italian photographer on a trip to the United States to report from American campuses. He compares these campuses to Arcadia, and in the mythical image he is sketching, he situates himself as the Ego reminder of death, of the passing of time, and of historical memory. His gaze on the United States is heavily shaped by his European cultural heritage. The narrator, although travelling through American university campuses, never leaves Europe, but reaches instead the wobbling heights of cultural snobbism, thus defeating his ideal of possible global ethics grounded in historical memory.

It must be recalled that Gina Lagorio[3] fought for the ideals of democracy since the Second World War, and, for at least the last fifteen years of her life, she was disillusioned by politics and by the lack of, or the superficiality of, engagement of intellectuals in civil society.[4] Her narrator reflects such disillusionment; like the author, he strongly believes in the importance of historical memory as a remedy to social apathy.[5] In this novel, the narrating voice consistently conveys the authorial perspective, feeling the moral responsibility to participate ethically in the development of civil society on a global scale. Nonetheless, he is unable to face the United States on a level of intellectual equality and equanimity. Although he intends to advocate concepts of historical memory and humanism that should serve on a universal scale, the protagonist is mainly in conversation with himself, on a quest for the self, and he shapes an implied reader unmistakably Italian.

The narrator's discursive mode reproduces stereotypes, or simply icons immediately recognizable by people who share his cultural background. In so doing, he fails to bring the level of his discourse beyond the cultural boundaries that determine his language and his mode of confrontation with America. Ultimately, he talks *about* America, never *with* it. America, as a concept, is the pretext with which the narrator engages to resolve his dilemmas; it is also the pre-text he carries with him from the past, made of literary, cinematographic, and musical images that have accompanied his youth and growth. The United States, on the other hand, is the battlefield on which the protagonist confronts himself and his American icons in a struggle to recuperate and redefine his moral and civil commitment to the world. However, the photographer never engages in a dialogue with America that goes beyond his iconization of the nation. This inability must not be regarded only as a psychological feature of the character, or simply as a flaw in the narrative structure, although it is a major cause of this novel's mediocre result. The narrator and his author, well visible behind him, share an attitude – they indulge in a towering position from which their gaze may be wider, but is incapable of exploring in depth the cultural surroundings of what they call American Arcadia.

Alter Ego: The Narrator

The plot is simple: our photographer, in his forties, goes to the United States for the second time. During his first trip, he had visited only big cities. This time, he is facing a life crisis and hopes that this voyage to America will restore his peace of mind and bring him back to himself.

Angry and disillusioned, he leaves behind the war in Kosovo[6] in which he was a correspondent and about which he has published a photographic bestseller (in the ex-Yugoslavia he had volunteered to set up a school with some friends). He also leaves behind an important love story that ended in betrayal. He finds in the United States a new love that will give him renewed hope.

The space opened up by the linearity of the plot is filled with the narrator's comments about the America he discovers and his reflections on contemporary Western life that ensue from his quest. The "I" also confronts himself and looks nostalgically back at the American myths that he shared with the generation growing up in the 1960s. He moves back and forth between the America that he carries with him in his mythological, literary, and political baggage, and the America that he gazes at while roaming from campus to campus, which is a space not less iconic than his memories, or than the images captured in his photographs.

His narrative entails a past that builds up and brings to the foreground the content of his ethics at play in the story, a moral legacy that precedes, supports, and defines all his actions. In an interview with the *Giornale di Brescia*, when questioned about the importance of ethics in *L'arcadia americana*, Gina Lagorio answers, "Credo che nessun essere umano sufficientemente dotato di ragione possa vivere senza seguire una linea di condotta di solito ereditata dall'ambiente in cui è nato (è quel che chiamiamo etica)[…]" (Oberti 5; "I believe that no human being sufficiently endowed with reason can live without following a line of conduct usually inherited from the environment where he or she was born. This is what we call ethics […]"). In the case of *L'arcadia*'s protagonist, this line of conduct is constantly exposed.[7]

Clothed in his morality, our narrator bumps against the American lifestyle, jumping back to himself after each clash. But he seems to be equipped with an airbag of indulgence that protects him, facilitates his going back to himself, and allows him to engage in the clash over and over again – the narrator has the habit of questioning himself and his judgments on America in so far as that questioning gives him the little elasticity necessary to increase his resistance against the American environment. On his arrival in the United States, the photographer is hosted by his old friend Pietro, whose partner, Tom, seems unwilling to contribute to a conversation on the ex-Yugoslavia. The photographer gauges his silence:

> Tom è innocente, è un americano che non sa, che ignora come quasi tutti, democratico convinto, che con Clinton si è risentito solo per la noia che gli

ha causato occuparsi di una nullità come Monica [...]. non ha la più vaga
idea di doversi porre esami di coscienza. A meno che ... a meno che non
sia io a peccare di superficilaità, da latino supponente e sempre pronto a
blaterare col suo prossimo delle cose che gli stanno a cuore. Forse Tom
appartiene alla schiera foltissima di quegli anglosassoni che si chiudono
nel riserbo, un po' per educazione e un po' perché si seccano di confessare
a uno straniero che le stelle e strisce troppo avide di sventolare in tanti
cieli li mettono a disagio. (12–13)

[Tom is innocent, an American who doesn't know, a convinced Democrat
who ignores things, like almost all of the others, who is disappointed with
Clinton only for the trouble caused by dealing with a nonentity such as
Monica [...] he hasn't the slightest idea that he should examine his conscience. Unless ... unless it is I who am guilty of superficiality, as a presumptuous Latino and always ready to blabber with his neighbour of the
things he cares for. Maybe Tom belongs to that crowded group of Anglo-
Saxons who choose self-restraint, partly out of politeness, and partly because it bothers them to confess to a stranger that the stars and stripes, too
eager to wave in many skies, make them feel uncomfortable.]

These opinions about Tom's naïveté are among the preconceptions
with which the protagonist lands in the country, and his allowing for
doubts, with regard to that innocence, sounds like a necessary but fu-
tile exercise in political correctness, which only supports and reiterates
his negative attitude towards America. In fact, at the end of his adventure, he will declare his dislike for the politically correct: "In America
come in Europa: ci si omologa, si slitta, si agisce e la legge di comporta-
mento, la sola novità, è la stessa: il politically correct" (99; "In America,
as in Europe, one agrees, goes along, acts, and the behavioural law, the
only originality, is the same: the politically correct").

Towards the end of the novel, the photographer will equate political
correctness with intellectual apathy: "Ecco, non sarò mai politically
correct: sono ancora troppo pieno di ambizioni, intuizioni, fantasie. E
troppo arreso alle parole" (103; "There you go, I will never be *politically
correct*: I am still too full of ambitions, intuitions, and fantasies. And I
surrendered to words too much"). When faced with this hitch to "PC,"
one finds it difficult to see the narrator's efforts to mitigate his judgmental outbursts as anything other than a touch of balm to soothe his
unyielding soul.

We never know whether Tom is as naïve as the protagonist thinks
him to be, or just reserved, or anything that is not the narrator's idea of

Tom – Tom never speaks. He is there just so that the "I" can spin out his idea of American innocence and measure himself against it. And the narrator goes far beyond expressing his idea. He makes of himself the bearer of the political and historical awareness that "innocent" America is lacking about itself. Here is the scene where America becomes Arcadia, at Pietro's place, while the narrator is drinking a cup of coffee,

> davanti alla vetrata che guarda il giardino nella casa dei miei ospiti sono di nuovo trasecolato vedendo sfrecciare un leprotto a orecchie ritte. Intorno, tutto un becchettio un trillare un gorgheggiare uno svolazzare di uccelli allegrissimi. Ero ancora in accappatoio e ho chiesto ai due che facevano colazione con me: "E questa sarebbe l'America? Ma questa è l'Arcadia!" (11)

> [facing the glass wall that opens on the garden, in the house of my hosts, I was astounded again when I saw a young hare flashing by, ears straight up. All around merry birds pecking, trilling, and warbling were flying here and there. I was still in my bathrobe, and I asked the two who were with me: "And this might be America? But this is Arcadia!"]

Through the window that separates him from the scenery he is looking at, the narrator casts his own idea of America on the landscape. He seems to rename America according to what he sees in the glass pane, the "vetrata," which is a reflection of his own intellectual elaborations and cultural identity, Arcadia, not necessarily America. The space imagistically recreated as Arcadia is one extremely peculiar to the protagonist's European literary and artistic tradition; it is a space that brings America back into the tradition of utopian creations. It seems that America, as a concept, cannot be saved from its destiny as Utopia – realized or not, the destiny that Europe assigned to it from Columbus on, if not prior to Columbus. Europe, as Baudrillard reminded us in *Amérique*, cannot avoid looking at America as a utopian space that eventually disillusioned many for not being the Utopia they expected, and the narrator of *L'arcadia americana* reflects this paradigm. Our photographer never really leaves Europe to visit America, and what he describes of it is the reflection of his own intellectual constructs. His narrative "photographs" are exposures in the light of that reflection. The narrator's questioning of his own viewpoint is only a rhetorical move that supports and reinforces his critique of America by giving it elasticity; he never really confronts America on an even level of authenticity and moral validity. For example, it does not matter that our protagonist likes American coffee and so becomes a convert to American breakfast, as he says. What is noticeable is that his idea of what a cup of coffee should be does not change, despite the conversion: "E l'indomani mattina, sorbendo il caffè in un tazzone da camomilla (mi è piaciuto e ora sono un convertito al breakfast Americano) [...]" (11; "And the morning after, while sipping coffee from a big camomile cup (I liked it and now I am a convert to American breakfast) [...]").

This is how we learn that Americans drink coffee in camomile cups, which in turns tells us what a coffee cup should be like (smaller, evidently), what a camomile cup is like, and that, although agreeable to the point of converting the narrator, the use of that cup is somehow inappropriate. It does not occur to the narrator that his way of labelling cups only works within the parameters of what a cup of coffee and a coffee cup are for Italians. The narrator is talking to his Italian narratees. He is reiterating the contents of his own culture while re-proposing old images of America already well grounded in Italian culture. He does not say that American coffee is served in cups that are the same size as those Italians use for camomile tea. Not at all. He is saying that Americans use camomile cups for coffee; we face here an attitude reminiscent of cultural presumptuousness, and the protagonist's conversion to American coffee does not change this. If this big but minor cup of coffee does not allow for any claim of cultural snobbism (we have no memorial madeleine to dignify this literary cup), maybe the following situation does. The protagonist is at Berkeley, complaining once again about students' lack of knowledge about Kosovo. But something happens, this time, outside of what he believes to be the ordinary. A couple of young people watching television are pretty enthusiastic at the appearance of Bill Bradley on the screen, Democratic candidate for the next presidential elections. A young woman makes a positive remark about the candidate, saying that one can also judge a man by seeing who is standing at his side. According to her, Bradley's wife has written a wonderful book. The protagonist asks why:

> La prego di dirmi perché e lei si appassiona a raccontarmi la storia di una donna che insegna all'università, che è guarita da un cancro e non sopporta l'arroganza degli intellettuali del suo paese di origine. E ascolto stupito il nome di Günter Grass, che non amo, e quello del mio prediletto Böll. Guarda guarda ... questa proprio non me l'aspettavo e mi annoto il titolo che mi sembra promettere bene, *Il linguaggio del silenzio*. (98)

[I beg her to tell me why, and she gets passionate in telling me the story of a woman who teaches at the university, who has recovered from cancer, and who cannot stand the arrogance of the intellectuals in her country of origin. And, astonished, I listen to the names of Günter Grass, whom I do not love, and Böll, my favourite. Surprising ... I really did not expect anything like this. And I take note of the title that sounds promising, *The Language of Silence*.]

The narrator did not expect an American student to mention European intellectuals such as Grass, or Böll. He justifies the unexpected event with a historical reason: the Youth Revolution of '68 began there, at Berkeley, in the United States, so probably "C'è in questi ragazzi quell che c'era in me" (98; "there is in these young people what there was in me"), he says, but he admits that he does not really believe it. This episode certainly has a stronger flavour of cultural snobbism than the previous cup of coffee, but both highlight the same presumptuous attitude in the narrator. Cultural snobbism is certainly not a novelty for European intellectuals, in this case Italian ones, and the narrator's attitude is a symptom and a reflection of a cultural sense of superiority that Beniamino Placido describes in his essay "L'invenzione dell'America":

Ma l'idea che l'America "non ha cultura," l'idea che "loro" sono grandi e grossi e la cultura però (quella vera), ce l'abbiamo noi – questa idea è rimasta. E rimarrà, perché non è un'idea: è parte di un meccanismo di compensazione al quale non sappiamo rinunciare. (Eco, Ceserani, and Placido 93)

[But the idea that America "has no culture," the idea that "they" are big and powerful, but we have culture though (true culture) – this idea persists and will remain, because it is not just an idea: it is part of a mechanism of compensation that we cannot give up.]

Almost twenty years after the publication of this essay (1984), another intellectual who is visiting important American universities – our narrator – cannot avoid taking that same presumptuous stance towards American culture. The mechanism of compensation to which Placido refers works so strongly on *L'arcadia americana*'s narrator as to affect his ability to appreciate American culture. The protagonist is inclined to move away from events he does not like, expect, or understand by taking refuge in one of the American icons from the past that he carries with him and cherishes, as in the case of the 1968 Youth Revolution. But his internal fight with America does not allow him to really enjoy such memories:

> Mi ferisce il ricordo recentissimo, dell'ora assolutamente beata, quasi astratta dal tempo, pura, che ho goduto a Rochester in una libreria immense, la Barnes and Noble, dove ho trovato due dischi del Duca che cercavo da anni, dove ho sorseggiato caffè ascoltandoli e ho sfogliato vecchi copioni hollywoodiani [...] ... libero e solo [...] per un'ora la vita è scivolata su binari di gomma [...]. (98)

> [It hurts me to remember an absolutely blissful hour, pure, almost abstract from time, that I recently enjoyed in Rochester, in an immense bookstore, Barnes and Noble, where I found two records by the Duke that I had sought for years, where I sipped my coffee listening to them, and leafed through some old Hollywood scripts [...] ... alone and free [...] for an hour life ran smoothly on rubber tracks [...].]

This hurtful memory strikes the narrator immediately after he asks himself whether or not he is politically correct, as if it were almost a sin to concede to a moment of bliss and forgetfulness of the present.[8] This reaction connects the narrator intimately to his author, Lagorio, for whom abstraction from time, in other words absence of memory, produces lemurs, not human beings. Memory plays a fundamental role for both. About memory, Lagorio states:

> Se non abbiamo memoria siamo zombie, siamo lemuri, siamo alghe che galleggiano sul mare [...]. Ricordare significa soprattutto questo: analizzare, mettere in chiaro, cercare le cause [...]. (Casagrande)

> [If we had no memory, we'd be zombies, we'd be lemurs, we'd be seaweeds floating on the sea [...]. To remember means, above all, this: to analyse, to clarify, and to look for the causes [...].]

With the same sense of moral urgency, the protagonist of L'arcadia states towards the end of his American voyage:

> Se un ciclone verrà – dal cielo o sulla terra [...] – che ci faccia fuori tutti o quasi, i superstiti ricominceranno a chiedersi perché e che cosa [...]. Dovranno chiederselo i salvati e noi dovremmo pregare fin da subito

perché il padrenostro che è nei cieli non ci induca nella più temibile delle tentazioni: dimenticare chi siamo stati e chi siamo, ogni giorno un po' di più, ogni giorno un po' più in fretta. (104)

[If a tornado comes – from the sky, or on earth […] – that does us all in, or almost all, the survivors will begin again asking themselves why and what […]. The survivors will have to ask themselves, and we should start praying from this very moment so that our father who is in heaven will not lead us into the most dreadful among temptations: to forget who we were and who we are, every day a little more, every day a little faster.]

This is one of the several moments in the novel where the voice of the narrator and the perspective of the author become one. The author and her protagonist also share a demanding urgency to live in history. To believe that the narrator of *L'arcadia americana* is ready to forgive either Tom or the American students for their "innocence" – read, lack of historical memory and ethical sense of present time – does not seem to be an appropriate interpretation of the protagonist's indulgence towards America, which, again, ends up being only a rhetorical device.

The more the protagonist proceeds in his trip, the more severe and rigid he becomes towards America, until he reaches the climax of his rage (before arriving at Berkeley) and he can no longer allow for any pretentious doubts. He voices his rage against America while visiting Oregon with his new friend, and future love, Cecilia. The two are taking a driving tour towards the ocean; once in sight, it scares the narrator, who, again, feels the need to grasp some literary images as a lifebuoy: "Terribile e Scoraggiante. Capsico, ricordo Conrad e Melville e tutta l'epica marinara, ma corro con l'anima al mio Mediterraneo, domestico come la mamma, […] il Pacifico non fa per me" (68; "Terrible and discouraging. I understand. I recall Conrad and Melville and all the sea epics, but my soul runs to my Mediterranean, as domestic as mum, […] the Pacific doesn't suit me"). The "I" is investing the Pacific with his own feelings of near-despair, and the beauty of Oregon, which he compares in turn to Italy and Switzerland, does nothing for his soul. And in fact, while eating an ice-cream, he finally bursts out:

"Dovessi vivere qui, divento matto": comincio così, e non mi fermo più. Parlo e m'ingozzo di panna e di pistacchio, di cioccolato e di nocciola, devo essere nauseante, a guardarmi, lo so […] sgretolo l'America con furia, la sbriciolo, ci metto dentro tutto il vuoto della storia, il Kosovo, la democrazia ingessata, il razzismo, il puritanesimo, la sessuofobia, Cecilia tace, le leggo in faccia che mi trova patetico e disgustoso.

Finisco quando la zuppiera è vuota […]. Mi arriva la sua voce, non più amabile del sibilo di un serpente a sonagli:

"Ma tu, cosa ci sei venuto a fare?" (71–2)

["Should I live here, I would go mad": I begin like this, and I can't stop it. I speak while I gulp down cream and pistachio, chocolate and walnuts. I must look nauseating, and I know it […] I shatter America with fury, I crumble it, I put in it all the historical void, Kosovo, the whitewashed democracy, racism, Puritanism, and the sex phobia. Cecilia is silent. I read on her face that she finds me pathetic and disgusting.

I give it up when the bowl is empty […]. Her voice reaches me, not more amiable than the hiss of a rattlesnake:

"What did you come here for, then?"]

From this question on, the conversation focuses on the reporter's life, on his reasons for going to the United States, and on his need to clear up his mind about the dilemmas inherent to his job as a war correspondent. There is no discussion between the two about America; the protagonist's soliloquy remains the rough draft of a conversation that does not take place. The only America sketched is the one that emerges from the gap between the narrator's mythical icons and the images of his narrative of the present. For the reporter, then, America – literary, mythical, and present – remains a pretext for discussing his life and moral choices.

Et in Arcadia Ego

Returning to the quotation above, "Ma questa è l'Arcadia!" (*L'arcadia americana* 11), suddenly we face an "I" in Arcadia, one more Ego to add to the literary and artistic tradition of the "Et in Arcadia Ego" theme. What calls for the comparison of the novel with the Arcadian myth is not only its title and the narrator's reference to a specific American reality as Arcadia (life on university campuses, although the idea is continuously extended to America in general), but even more so, the position that the "I" assumes, as an intellectual, in this Arcadia.

Two significant paintings illustrate the existence of death in this idyllic place, Francesco Guercino's painting of 1621–3 usually referred to as "Et in Arcadia Ego," and Nicolas Poussin's *Les bergers d'Arcadie* (The

Arcadian Shepherds). The inscription in the two paintings, "Et in Arcadia Ego," gives voice to death in the bucolic picture; the sentence appears on a stone surmounted by a skull in Guercino's painting and on a tombstone in Poussin's. Like the Ego of that *memento mori*, the narrator of the novel brings a moralizing reminder of death and history to the American Arcadia's innocent inhabitants. The narrating "I" of *L'arcadia americana*, full of nostalgia for an American past, both real and mythological, displays emphatic and moralizing references to death in at least three forms: the recalling of the war in Kosovo, the dramatically painful realization of social and political disengagement, and the contemplation of a past that is never to happen again.

Guercino's painting (in the Galleria Corsini, Rome) was the first visual work of art to reproduce the theme of death in Arcadia. Here we find for the first time the inscription "Et in Arcadia Ego." Two Arcadian shepherds, while walking in a wood, find a skull placed on a piece of masonry on which the Latin sentence is incised. In his famous essay *"Et in Arcadia Ego: Poussin and the Elegiac Tradition,"*[9] Erwin Panofsky states that it is death itself that speaks the words.[10]

From Poussin's second version of *Les bergers d'Arcadie* onward, Panofsky explains, "Et in Arcadia Ego" was not a *memento mori* any longer, but the sign of a nostalgic contemplation of things past. Poussin's second painting marked the passage from the moralizing intent of death's presence to the less dramatic nostalgia and pensiveness evoked by the presence of a tomb.[11] The skull is no longer in the picture, and the shepherds looking at the inscription on the tomb have a less intense facial expression.

Lagorio's *L'arcadia americana* seems to cross both traditions, retaining the elements of the dramatic medieval *memento mori* (the Kosovar war) and the more tranquil nostalgia for the past (memories of old films, American literature, and jazz). The novel's Arcadia is certainly influenced by what Arthur Lovejoy and George Boas call the idea of "soft" primitivism in antiquity, as Panofsky reminds us, an idea that "conceives of primitive life as a golden age of plenty, innocence and happiness" (297). This tradition was further idealized by Virgil in the *Eclogues*:

> [...] not only did he emphasize the virtues that the real Arcady had (including the all-prevailing sound of song and flutes [...]); he also added charms which the real Arcady had never possessed: luxuriant vegetation, eternal spring, and inexhaustible leisure for love. In so doing [...] he

transformed two realities into one Utopia [...] It was then, in the imagination of Virgil, and of Virgil alone, that the concept of Arcady as we know it, was born – that a bleak and chilly district of Greece came to be transfigured into an imaginary realm of perfect bliss. (Panofsky 299–300)

Lagorio's Arcadia bears more than just the traces of Virgil's "imaginary realm of perfect bliss." The author does not want us to forget that the realm is imaginary. In an interview with the Italian daily *Giornale di Brescia* she states:

L'America, come dice l'epigrafe del libro assunta da Wallace Stevens, è un Paese enorme, felice nel suo stile, la cui apparente felicità è guardata come un mito da troppe folle, tanto consapevoli quanto disperate. (Oberti)

[America, as described in the epigraph taken from Wallace Stevens, is a huge country, happy in its way, whose apparent happiness is looked upon as a myth by too many crowds who are as aware as they are desperate.]

The novel's epigraph, taken from Stevens, reads: "Un paese grande latente nell'ombra, / Una nazione enorme felice nel suo stile / Ogni cosa tanto irreale quanto può esserlo il reale" ("A great town hanging pendent in a shade / An enormous nation happy in a style / Everything as unreal as real can be"). One can say that the depiction echoes Arcadia. Stevens' verses come from the poem "An Ordinary Evening in New Haven," V (1950), in the collection *The Auroras of Autumn*. Stevens' two tercets preceding the verses just quoted remind us of the protagonist's state of mind when he is facing the windowpane in Princeton:

Inescapable romance, inescapable choice
Of dreams, disillusion as the last illusion,
Reality as a thing seen by the mind,
Not that which is but that which is apprehended,
A mirror, a lake of reflections in a room
A glassy ocean lying at the door (479–80)

The photographer re-elaborates the woods as Arcadia – "Not that which is but that which is apprehended," through a glass window. More re-elaboration comes in the novel. In the chapter devoted to a visit to Oregon, the narrator describes the magnificent beauty of nature, and tends to superimpose European images on this Arcadia:

Ci inoltriamo tra conifere stupende, acque impetuose, cascate e fiumi, felci prati e boschi [...]. Un senso di straniamento mi accompagna e mi sembra naturale la domanda di Cecilia: "Qual è la meta? Vallombrosa?" Le rispondo: "Si va a Camaldoli." (68)

[We advance through marvellous coniferae, impetuous waters, waterfalls, fern and rivers, meadows and woods [...]. I'm accompanied by a sense of estrangement, and Cecilia's question sounds natural to me: "What is the destination? Vallombrosa?" I answer: "We're going to Camaldoli."]

From here on, the woods of Oregon fantastically become part of Switzerland, then almost the Italian Versilia. In a mode that has already been observed, the narrator cannot avoid grasping images of Europe to feel safe in this beautiful land of the unknown. And he has previously explained why. When in Rochester, he joins a family of Italian origin for dinner. On leaving their house and the hostess in particular (she has satellite television and wanted to watch the Italian news about the Kosovar war before dinner), he thinks to himself:

Mi fa malinconia pensare di lasciare questa donna tanto ricca di vita [...]: mi chiedo che cosa la sorregga, nella sua palese nostalgia della giovinezza italiana, in questo vuoto di storia bello sì, arioso sì, ordinato sì, ma vivo per i daini e per gli scoiattoli più che per gli uomini [...]. (52)

[It makes me melancholic to think of leaving this woman so full of life [...]: I wonder what is supporting her, with her patent nostalgia for her Italian youth, in this historical void that is beautiful yes, spacious yes, tidy yes, but alive more for the deer and squirrels than for man [...].]

This Arcadia is beautiful, yes, but unfit for human life, where for "life" we have to understand the sense of history and intellectual engagement of individuals in the world around them. This unfitness of Arcadia for human beings, as deplored by the protagonist, certainly constitutes a stereotyped icon of the United States, an image of historical void and civil disengagement on an intellectual level. The narrator is revisiting an old topos in disguise; the real Arcadians could sing and play beautifully, but they were, otherwise, "also famous for their utter ignorance and low standards of living" (Panofsky 297). The author, who has titled her book "American Arcadia," must have been well aware of this, and her narrator makes no mystery of his disappointment with the lack of information and civil engagement that he finds on American campuses, of which the silence about Kosovo becomes an emblem. In this American Arcadia, where we have already seen the innocent, shepherd-like Tom, at Rutgers we also have the innocent, beautiful musicians (who do not talk about Kosovo, of course). At Rutgers, the narrator is positively surprised to discover a very efficient university system, important scholars, and very well prepared graduate students. He remembers he should have done his undergraduate studies there, long before. But:

> E ancora mi riprende il pensiero di un'America arcadica, dopo essere stata per il primo scorcio di secolo un'isola libera per chi mal respirava fascismo […]. Un suono di chitarra mi ferma […] alla finestra d'una camera a piano terra: dentro, tre ragazzi e una ragazza, a gambe incrociate, sono stretti a cerchio sulla stuoia intorno a un piccoletto che suona. Da Dio, e mi accuccio davanti alla finestra […]. (30)

> [And yet again I'm caught by the thought of an Arcadian America, after having been a free island for those who could not breathe Fascism during the first half of the century […]. The sound of a guitar stops me at the window of a room on the ground floor. Inside, three boys and a girl on a rug, sitting cross-legged, form a circle around a short one who is playing, like a god. And I squat down behind the window […].]

The narrator feels happy for these youths who live in such a naturally beautiful place. "Fortunati come pochi," he says, comparing theirs to his own youth in college, which was precarious, made up of rallies, university occupations, "joints," and exams given every once in a while. He was socially and politically engaged, which these few lucky ones are not. They live in Arcadia.

The painful realization of social and political disengagement is expressed through a sense of death as well. To die, this time, are not the children of Kosovo but a past that has left a perennial void, represented by the ideals of Woodstock and by the Beat Generation. From the beginning of the story, the narrator recalls the American myths that have marked his youth and history in general. He begins with what he considers the two greatest icons – he is at Niagara Falls and has just bought a poster of Marilyn:

> Sarò un sedotto della femminilità, ma […] ero persuaso che Marilyn ha dato più luce alle fantasie rattrappite del mondo che non il suo Kennedy. Certamente sì, povera figlia, che se proprio devo paragonarla a qualche

altro simbolo o totem o mito americano, l'avvicino soltanto alla statua che levava alta la fiaccola per i disperati nel secolo scorso. Forse la leva anche oggi, ma meno liberatrice, se i disperati sono quelli che ci hanno mostarto i registi più tosti e i poeti, dalla Beat Generation in poi. (10)

[I may be seduced by femininity, but [...] I was persuaded that Marilyn cast more light upon the shrunken fantasies of the world than her Kennedy. Of course yes, poor girl, that if I have to compare her at all costs to some other symbol, totem, or American myth, I can match her only with the Statue that lifted up high the torch for the desperate of the last century. Maybe the Statue still lifts it nowadays, but it is less liberating if the desperate are those whom the toughest film directors and the poets, from the Beat Generation onward, showed us.]

The narrator's iconic heritage of America and what he thinks about America are condensed in these few lines. Imagery unfolds in the narrative in the form of nostalgia for much of what American culture exported to Europe during the 1940s, 1950s, and 1960s (music, literature, and film), and for what this meant at the time – assertion of freedom and cultural revolution, both values now dead.

In *L'arcadia americana*, though, the conveyance of the Death in Arcadia theme relies on only one perspective: the Arcadian Ego's. The innocent shepherds do not partake of the picture either with their surprised and intense looks or with their mellow contemplation, as depicted in the paintings discussed above. It is for the Ego to be constantly, dramatically surprised, or contemplative, while the shepherds do not seem to notice the presence of death and history around them. In a postmodern pastiche, a remake of Guercino's or Poussin's painting based on *L'arcadia americana* would probably depict four happy Arcadians engaged in daily activities around a tomb that does not attract their attention, but is just part of the landscape. Over the sarcophagus, a skull would probably watch them astonished at not being properly acknowledged, and the inscription would read "Et in Arcadia Ego!!!"

To recapitulate, this American Arcadia is made of beautiful university campuses, surrounded by a luxuriant nature (and when it is not a beautiful campus, then it is a town such as New Brunswick where the narrator expects to see Louisa May Alcott's girls coming out of small, neat houses at any moment), oases of peace and knowledge, where some adults do serious scholarly work, but, in the end, almost all their inhabitants are far removed from real life in the real world and do not engage with it. They do not examine their consciences. The narrator, estranged by such unreal reality (as the epigraph to the book calls it), feels constantly the need to refer his thoughts and discourses back to Europe. Indeed, he has never really left Europe, not while roaming through the streets of New York, recalling European cathedrals; not while travelling in Oregon; not when seeing in the Berkeley students sparks of the political feelings that inflamed his youth.

Love and Endings in Arcadia

Even though, strategically, towards the end of the novel the narrative brings us back to the beginning where we find the narrator looking at the photos of his trip as we found him on the first page, the novel is open-ended. The very last one-and-one-half-page chapter is devoted to the narrator's reunion with Cecilia at JFK airport in New York, where he will spend his last American days with her. This is the clear beginning of a new love affair, but we will never know what becomes of it, if anything at all. The curtain of the story comes down on their embrace at the airport that seals the narrator's reconciliation with himself, rather than anything else. Cecilia, a graduate student who lives in the Unites States, is no co-protagonist of the novel. Like all the other characters of the story, who are there to fill a background of extras and situations through which our narrator passes, Cecilia is little more than a minor character necessary to the development of the protagonist and his story. She is very far from the full female characters of Lagorio's other novels, protagonists at all levels.[12]

The final embrace between the photographer and Cecilia, who engages the narrator's more immediate emotional side, who is the key to his spontaneity, to his humanity, and to his ability to be compassionate with himself, only tells us that the narrator has finally embraced his heart and is no longer angry with himself. The fact that the key to the narrator's feelings is Italian should not be interpreted as a further sign of rejection of America, since Cecilia lives and works happily in the United States. This love happens, and is fresh and restorative for the protagonist because it exists far from ideology or extreme intellectualism, and it seems even more refreshing if we compare this American Arcadia with an Italian "Arcadia" which Lagorio wrote about in 1982.

This is a short story about the end of a love relationship worn out by time. The two protagonists are advancing towards their maturity, still playing the same old psychological games of tension between them as during their youth, but aware of the end, of an entropic process that cannot be stopped. They spend a summer holiday in the same old house on the lake. That house and the woods around the lake compose the scenery of what, one evening, the man calls "Arcadia" – a sudden reawakening of passion between them. Arcadia is for the woman the beautiful natural setting around the house. However, a renewed, romantic Arcadia is not enough for her. At the end of the story, she unveils the truth. One night, back from a walk to the lake, she enters the dark house and when switching the light on, "Alla luce fredda del neon l'Arcadia le mostrò la sua realtà di deserto regno di morti sconsociuti" ("Arcadia" 126; "By the cold neon light, Arcadia showed its reality, a deserted realm of unknown dead" *13th Moon* 189).

The Arcadia that was the theatre of the protagonists' lifelong love has now become a desert. *L'arcadia americana* will probably not rescue romantic love, as a concept, from its end. As far as romance is concerned, in *L'arcadia americana* the adjective "americana" only means "new" (especially if love is compared with its older Italian Arcadian counterpart), and "new" is an old connotation for America, as old as America itself in its European semiotic construction. The newness of love in this American Arcadia will not rescue any romantic relationship from aging irreparably. The male protagonist of "Arcadia" regards aging as obscene:

> [...] esiste solo il singolo, se esiste: niente è più vuoto di senso del numero due, doveva averlo detto un grande, ma chissà chi era, la memoria, la memoria, è questo il dramma [...] la vecchiaia oscena che striscia e ti accorgi che c'è, acquattata ma vigile, e adesso è un nome che non riesci a ricordare. [...] (106)

> [[...] only the single person exists, if he exists. Nothing is more meaningless than the word two, someone famous must have said that, but who knows who it was, memory, memory, that's the drama [...] obscene old age that slithers by and you become aware that she's there, crouched but alert, and now it's a name that you can't remember. [...] (177–8)]

Almost twenty years after the publication of "Arcadia," as in the passage above, old age still lords it over love, Arcadian or not; it is still deterioration that awaits beings, ideas, and hope. Before leaving for New York, where he will meet Cecilia for the last time in the plot, just before the embrace that will close the story, the protagonist of *L'arcadia americana* takes a picture of an old lady sitting in his hotel lobby. He is thinking of Cecilia, and, for no better-specified reason, he turns around, sees the old lady sitting across from him, and immortalizes her. Once he is back in Italy and is ready to narrate his story (to this initial moment he goes back at the end of the novel), he says:

> Mi colpì e scattai. Ora nella Polaroid che ha la funzione di prima didascalia, quasi un titolo, la sto guardando e capisco meglio il perché del mio click [...]. Quegli zigomi quasi cancellati dal tempo che reggevano un giorno i muscoli che ora sono caduti [...]. (102)

> [She struck me and I took the shot. Now, in the picture that will function as a first caption, almost as a title, I'm looking at her and I understand better the reasons for my click [...] Those cheeks almost erased by time once used to hold the muscles that are now collapsed [...].]

The picture of the old lady becomes the symbol of an America that is no longer the one he grew up with, made of jazz and later the Beat Generation. Such a closure, which recalls the opening of the novel, does not leave much room for us to think that the "new" love is really "new," or will blissfully keep its novelty forever. Just like America, that love is only a passing dream, a reconciliation of the protagonist with the immediate spirit of life. Once home, in his reportage, America is represented by that old lady on whom he casts his judgmental look by admitting "non sarò mai politically correct" (103; "I will never be politically correct"). Cecilia is lost somewhere, and probably the author does not need to write a finale for this love story since she already did so almost twenty years before in "Arcadia." Whether or not our protagonist will go back to America, or whether or not he has signed an armistice with it, we do not know. And it does not seem to matter. This open ending only shows us, once more, that the narrator of the text, behind whom his author is badly disguised, just wanted to tell us something about "America," and ended up telling us something about the position of the intellectual, and the subject in general, in civil society – or, at least, about what that position should be: sociopolitical commitment, together with the necessity to act responsibly against the world's evils.

This position entails the rejection of a certain image of America – America as a mythical concept, as the land of unlimited possibilities for human social and ethical accomplishment. With *L'arcadia americana*, Gina Lagorio took on the task of exposing the myth and declaring it dead. By doing so within the consolidated tradition of Italian narratives of the self,[13] she walked the path of self-reflection, which in turn led her to the continuation of another consolidated tradition, the one that Donald Heiney interpreted as a cultural habit when he wrote that for Italian intellectuals to discuss America has always meant to discuss themselves.[14] While escaping the confrontation with the United States is impossible for the intellectual who wishes to express her / himself about issues of global civil engagement, the use of pre-textual, iconized America to engage in that confrontation undermines any productive dialogue.

Arcadia Responds

"Ava Gardner's Brother-in-Law" represents an open confrontation between a Sicilian man who, without leaving his island, dreams the American dream while remaining voluntarily oblivious to American social and economic history, and an American citizen, an Italian American, who presents himself as the bearer of a more realistic view of the United States. With his realism, he tries to shake the Sicilian's utopian ideas about America. He is the "I" of this first-person narrative and, like the narrator of *L'arcadia americana*, will propose history as a remedy for the American myth and as a path to the formation of viable, universal ethics. This subject's point of view, though, comes from across the pond.

Ben Morreale wrote "Ava Gardner's Brother-in-Law: A Word Play in Sicily" in 1986.[15] The short piece is a dialogue between the Sicilian, Turidru[16] Sinatra, and his Italian American interlocutor, who narrates the introduction and conclusion, and who appears simply as "I." Like Ben Morreale, this I[17] is of Sicilian origin. Every now and then, he goes back to Racalmuto, the writer's place of birth, because he finds it "restful after America" (125). This time he is back to take care of an old aunt's business. The work crosses at least three literary genres. It is partly a narrative, partly a play containing stage directions, such as *"[And here Turidru puts his two forefingers together as if joining a seam]"* (134), and partly a philosophical dialogue. The narrative structure reflects Turidru's personality; according to both his description of himself and the narrator's, the Sicilian protagonist, in his late fifties and unemployed, is a Pirandellian character inclined to philosophical reflections and abstractions about the nature of man and life, who walks the streets of his small village, Racalmuto, as if on stage, and does so in the hope of running into some intelligent man to talk to:

I Turi, you sound like a character out of a Pirandello play.

TURIDRU Where do you think Pirandello found his characters? Right here in the piazza, listening to the likes of me. Men who could not live their meager lives without imagining they were gods in search of believers [...] In the morning I have a bowl of milk with a spot of coffee. My head is thick with reading I did the night before. I pick up the few lira my mother has left me on the table, and I walk avoiding the twenty-four imbeciles I must meet before I encounter one intelligent man. At noon I return to my mother's house, and there I have a plate of escarole and bread and cheese [...]. In the evening a bowl of milk and leftover bread, after which I walk in the piazza hoping once again to find an intelligent man. (136)

Turidru Sinatra, as the narrator explains at the beginning of the story, "is a wiry man [...] He speaks French, some English, and sarcastically calls himself the pique-assiette of the Western world" (125). Turidru lives off the little money his mother gives him every morning. In his youth, he gave up law school after attending for three years. He also gave up on a teaching certificate that would have allowed him to join the ranks of the middle class. The narrator continues:

For a while, he was called, with some Sicilian irony, the lawyer Sinatra, until he wrote to Frank Sinatra, that is, who he was convinced was a cousin. Frank Sinatra did not answer, but he did send Turidru packages which arrived regularly every three months for two years. It was the sort of thing a relative from America would do. It was understandable then, if when Frank Sinatra married Ava Gardner, he became known as *lu cugnatu di* Ava Gardner, Ava Gardner's brother-in-law. (125)

"Ava Gardner's Brother-in-Law" epitomizes the Italian American dream in a subject, Turidru, whose existence is "a long complaining desire" (127) for a way of life he could not actualize in Sicily, and will never be able to actualize in America: "I would like to come home to an elegant apartment filled with white furniture, and a phone would ring as soon as I come home" (129). On the opposite end, the other character of the play represents the individual who did become accomplished in the United States and who reminds Turidru of the hardship and sacrifices Italian immigrants had to face when they moved to America. He now obliges Turidru to face the dreamlike quality of his expectations about America:

I You speak of America like a priest speaks to a child about heaven. Turi, America too is in your head.

TURIDRU Excuse me, in many ways I am a fool, if not I wouldn't be in my present condition – approaching sixty – my life a long complaining desire [...] America has a language; it speaks to me. Heaven has no language. America speaks to me in John O'Hara, Melville, in Hemingway, Mary McCarthy. America is a reality, my friend.

I It is your America, Turi.

The I's role is not only to remind Turidru of his America as a spectral construct of his imagination, while describing for him aspects of the United States' culture and economy with which the Sicilian is not familiar. The interlocutor also demands that Turidru explain his disengagement from the socioeconomical injustice he faces in Sicily and on a larger scale, at a more general level of abstraction: "I How comfortable. The lazy and the rich always say, 'Life is unfair.' [...] It is not enough to say life is unfair. What are you going to do about the unfairness?" (129). Turidru is not going to do anything about the unfairness, which he thinks connatural to life. He wishes he could be like Frank Sinatra, be a genius (since he believes Sinatra is a genius), have as wonderful a voice, and lead as rich and magnificent a life among the women of the chorus line at the Sands, in Las Vegas. He would very much like to live in America.

The two characters begin a conversation about gender roles, in particular about the familiar and social roles of women. Turidru blames gender roles for the stagnation of Sicilian culture, founded on a rigid separation between male and female functions in society, a stasis that creates in humanity a perennial state of expectation where change never breaks in, where men think of themselves as gods and women oblige those same men to play the role of gods. "A fine excuse for a system that serves you well" (127), protests Turidru's interlocutor. And Turidru: "Sure, I am the example of a man well served. I'd rather belong to Sinatra's happy America, where women don't serve men and love is made freely. If love were made freely, there would be less warfare, less violence, let me tell you" (127). The narrator's protests against Turidru's theory will not convince Turidru of being wrong:

I [irritated] There is more rape in Los Angeles than in all of Sicily. More murder in Phoenix or Dallas than in Palermo. More women battered, not to speak of the violence we perpetrate on others – the Indian, the Asian, the Latin American. We have our need to be roosters. And it makes for a great deal of violence and not much happiness [...] The violence of Frank Sinatra is institutionalized violence – power telling women to dance culo di fora [bareassed], to jump through sexual hoops. (128)

But Turidru cannot give up his American dream and concludes: "In a word, the same old vices, but they would be American. That is, the wealth and the women / men relationship would be in circulation. Not as it is here, where the wealth and women are just held onto and nothing grows" (129).

The dialogues about the ethical issues implied in the two different characters' world-views become tighter:

TURIDRU [...] here suffering simply goes on and on.
I You have your dignity.
TURIDRU Bah! Dignity without power or money is humiliation.
I Power without dignity is brutality [...] We are not happier for our growth, as you say. (129)

Their discourse moves on to the relationship between power and consumption; in particular, consumption of human beings, which Turidru prefers calling "to enjoy people," rather than to consume them. The I reminds Turidru that, once human beings have become an abstraction for the sake of consumption, like a TV set, or a new car, "then you can do anything you want to them. What do you think Hitler was all about?" Turidru refuses to accept that Sinatra may be part of a social system to which violence is intrinsic. The narrator is trying to alert Turidru to the consequences of abstracting a human being from his "humanity," of exerting power in the absence of dignity.[18] The I of "Ava Gardner's Brother-in-Law" is alerting Turidru to his responsibilities to the world around him. Gender roles, the consumption of women and of human beings in general, as well as the violence intrinsic to modern society are the pivots of the discussion between Turidru and the narrator. "Ava Gardner's Brother-in-Law" denounces unethical situations everywhere which are related to the place of women in patriarchal societies and in more modern ones, and denounces the impact of modernity on gender roles. These are problems for which, according to the narrator of Morreale's story, "[thinking] of an America that does not exist is no solution" (133).

What is relevant is not the peculiarity of the gender struggle itself, but the fact that, according to the narrator, the individual becomes and must feel responsible for an issue of global dimensions – the role of women in the history of the world – to which America, as a myth, will provide no solution. In "Ava Gardner's Brother-in-Law" the global takes the form of philosophical abstractions from the peculiarities of Sicilian and American societies, abstractions that, in the dialogue between the protagonists, become applicable to humanity at large.

Turidru is convinced that the role of women in Sicily keeps men playing the role of "roosters," as he says, and imagining themselves as the world's best lovers, a much-needed fantasy since "here we men are forced to live too much in our heads, because reality is not livable" (127). Which, in turn, is the reason why Turidru looks to America as the space for salvation. As already quoted above, the narrator is irritated by his affirmation.

The catalogue of evils that the I lists receives from Turidru a simplistic comment: "These are the difficulties of a society in transition [...] the turmoil of the emerging new way of life" (128). But the narrator does not let Turidru get away with it and demands that his interlocutor take his individual responsibilities: "Turi, how can you see so clearly about Sicily and yet be so muddled about America? [...] To think of an America that does not exist is no solution. Why have you given up on your writing?" (133). In these words we find again Jennifer Beals calling Nanni Moretti, who dreamed of being a dancer after watching *Flashdance*, "scemo," "stupid." In these words we find again the stupefied characters of *City*, outcast shreds of the "America Dream" itself who find no place outside of their abnormal exceptionality, as here we find again the stupefied eyes of the Albanians going to Italy in the film *Lamerica*. In the narrative discourses explored so far, the American dream unfolds as the projection of an individual's imagination onto spaces that she or he alters by superimposing hopes, ideas, and prejudices. We see this in the final scene of *Lamerica*, for example, in which Spiro is convinced that he is travelling to New York; we see it in the final scenes of *Non ci resta che piangere*, in our photographer's Arcadia, as much as in the possibly of a new island as conceived by Stromboli's mayor in *Caro diario*. These spaces so dramatically altered by a vision end up pointing at historical memory as the way out of the unviable dream. Those who do the pointing are obviously the intellectuals behind the stories.

Both the narrators of *L'arcadia americana* and "Ava Gardner's Brother-in-Law" indicate history as the antidote that should prevent the myth from prevailing in anyone's personal life. "Ava Gardner's Brother-in-Law" ends with the narrator finding some pictures and documents that tell the often painful history of those who left for America. Memory comes in both Lagorio's and Morreale's works as the necessary path for the development of viable ethics, and it is a memory that resides in the individual who is, in turn, responsible for it. America holds a role in the formation of subjective ethics only if the subject looks away from the myth and into history.

5 Historicizing the Dream: A Documented Eye on America

A New Perspective

The history of the Italian migration to the United States has received renewed and particular attention in some Italian artistic productions of the past ten years. The novel and the two films that I take under consideration in this chapter stage that history as the main character, which produces the elements of the fiction, not just the backdrop of the story. I focus on Melania Mazzucco's novel *Vita* (2003), on Nanni Moretti's documentary *The Last Customer* (2002), and on Emanuele Crialese's film *Nuovomondo* (2006). These three artistic productions are rooted in a narrative space where the stories of the individuals and history are inseparable, where the Italian tradition of narratives of the self recounts history with a clear intent, and in so doing reappropriates the phenomenon of migration to the United States.

"Migration represents a topic that Italian writers at large have considered marginal [...]" writes Stefania Lucamante (294). For paradoxical as it may seem, the Italian writers' lack of attention to the phenomenon of the great migration (ca. 1870–1921) is directly proportional to the large space that the American myth occupies in Italian literature, in its positive and negative representations, as well as in its problematization. These seemingly irreconcilable aspects are the two sides of the same coin – the Italian intellectual's modus operandi. Martino Marazzi, in commenting about the failure of Italian intellectuals to pay attention to the migration experience, which he calls "the long standing unease of the Italian intellectual toward another Italy" (*Voices* 292), explains that this other Italy, so far from home, is not "easily defined using the tools of abstract ideology, an Italy, therefore, that is not easily compatible with the ritual apologias and curses uttered in relation to the New World" (292). Echoing Marazzi, Lucamante writes, "Italian writers and their literary products are firmly tied to their social and political context, often driven by an ethical and ideological pursuit in their endeavors [...]" (295). It helps to quote again Giaime Pintor's essay on Vittorini's *Americana* as an example of what Marazzi and Lucamante state:

> In our words dedicated to America much may be ingenuous and inexact, much may refer to arguments extraneous to the historical phenomenon of the United States as it stands today. But this does not matter because if the continent did not exist our words would not lose their significance. This America has no need of Columbus, it is discovered within ourselves; it is the land to which we turn with the same hope and faith of the first immigrants, of whoever has decided to defend at the price of pains and error the dignity of the human condition. (244–5)

Pintor's America is an ideological mirror. As he admits that "the historical phenomenon of the United States" may be extraneaous to his discourse, he reclaims America as an object of desire charged with political significance, for he was writing in 1943, at the end of Fascism. The "hope and faith of the first immigrants" are thus removed from the historical, geopolitical context of the United States to become an analogy that illustrates and better explains the hope and faith of the Italians moving towards freedom. The historical habit of Italian intellectuals to rely on abstract ideology, together with the conspicuous role that such abstract ideology played in the building of the nation soon after the *Risorgimento*, have made it difficult for those intellectuals to take into consideration that distant, *"other"* Italy" (Lucamante 295),[1] until recent times.

In terms of narrative modes, the shift has happened at the level of the perspective, leaving untouched that solid Italian tradition of narratives of the self in search of identity, which means that there has been no abrupt movement from using images of America in order to talk about oneself to looking at history *tout court*. The American dream remains central to all these narratives that involve matters of identity and America. What shifts is the attention to *who* is dreaming the dream – and in these latest literary and filmic productions, the dreamers are the Italian emigrants. I will analyse the narrative shift by comparing *Vita* to *Sogni mancini*, *The Last Customer* to *Caro diario*, and *Nuovomondo* to *City*.

Vita

The epigraph to *Vita* is taken from Alain Resnais's film *Mon Oncle d'Amérique* (1980) and it reads, "L'America non esiste. Io lo so perché ci sono stato" (*Vita*; "America does not exist. I know it because I have been there"). The quotation is key to reading *Vita* on more than one level. The America to which the author points is the utopian dream that pushed many to cross the Atlantic at the beginning of last century, but it also represents the result of the experience of those who came back from America, after a few years of migration, some defeated economically and some deafeated, above all, in spirit. Such is the case for one of the two protagonists of the novel, Diamante, who arrived in the United States at age twelve and, not having found America, made it back to Italy about ten years later.

Diamante was looking for an America made of prosperity and well-being, and of companionship with his beloved Vita, the little girl who travelled to the United States with him when she was nine and whose name gives the novel its title. He, however, finds pain from the beginning: the poverty of an overcrowded boardinghouse in New York, in the Italian slums of Prince Street; a brief collaboration with the mobster organization Mano Nera; and exploitation, violence, and vexation on the railroad constructions of Ohio. Diamante gets entangled in some of the most terrible lines of American history. When, at eighteen, he is fetched almost dead from a street in Denver, Colorado, taken to the hospital, and diagnosed with nephritis, he understands that his American dream is over:

Il dottore gli incise la schiena per lasciar defluire il sangue e disse: Tu forse sai meglio di me come si chiama la tua malattia. Diamante rispose che lo sapeva.

La sua malattia è aver sognato un'altra vita, e da questa vita essere stato tradito. Averla persa, e aver perso persino il suo sogno. Non riuscire a ricordare. Credre che i suoi anni americani non siano mai esistiti. (362)

[The doctor lanced his back to bleed him and said, "You probably know better than I do what your illness is called." "Yes," Diamante said. He knew.

His illness was to have dreamed a different life, and to have to have had that life betray him. To have lost that life, and even the dream of it. To be unable to remember. To believe that his years in America never existed. (388–9)].

This passage plays on the double meaning of "vita," which refers both to life and to the name of the girl with whom Diamante is in love but who, in Diamante's absence, will end up choosing a different man.

Vita, based on the life of Melania Mazzucco's family, covers a span of time that runs through three generations. Its main focus is the American life of Diamante and Vita from 1903 to 1912, when Diamante returns to Italy. Melania Mazzucco, a grandchild of Diamante, is trying to understand the roots of her identity, roots that once attempted to find fertile ground in the United States:

> Un giorno di primavera del 1903 il quarto figlio dell'uomo delle pietre, un ragazzino di dodici anni, piccolo, furbo e curioso, arrivò al porto di Napoli e salì su una nave che apparteneva alla flotta della White Star Line [...]. Suo padre gli aveva affidato il compito di realizzare la vita che lui non aveva potuto vivere. Era un fardello pesante, ma il ragazzino non lo sapeva [...]. (11)

> [One day in the Spring of 1903, the fourth son of the man of stones, a twelve-year-old boy, small, clever, and curious, arrived at the port of Naples and boarded a ship of the White Star Line [...] His father had set him the task to live the life he'd been unable to live. It was a heavy burden, but the boy didn't know it [...]. (8)]

Vita is not only the story of Diamante and Vita, but also the account of Mazzucco's archival research on the footsteps of the two protagonists. The fictional part of the book was born in the cracks left open by the silence of what registers and archives could not account for. "La storia di una famiglia senza storia è la sua leggenda" (383; "The story of a family without history is its legend" 413), explains Mazzucco, whose family legend begins with the descent to the South of Italy of Diamante's grandfather, Federico, an official in Piedmont's army who fought for the unification of Italy in 1860. He was a dowser. Mazzucco finds out that Federico probably never existed, except in Diamante's imagination (*Vita* 384–5). Her aim is to reconstruct history, and to forego legend:

> Voglio sapere se è vero che Antonio ha ricomprato con i soldi americani di Diamante il pezzo di terra che la devastante crisi agraria degli anni Ottanta gli aveva tolto [...]. Se è vero che Vita voleva ricomprarlo a Diamante trentotto anni dopo [...]. Soprattutto cosa ne è stato di Vita – dove, quando è sparita. Perché, dopo la sua visita in Italia, ho perso le sue tracce. Al rabdomante, mitologico capostipite della famiglia, non penso mai. (384)

[I want to know if it is true that Antonio used Diamante's American money to buy back a piece of land that the devastating agriculture crisis of the 1880s had taken from him [...]. If it is true that Vita wanted to buy it again for Diamante thirty-eight years later [...]. Above all, what happened to Vita – where and when did she disappear? After her visit to Italy, I had lost all trace of her. As for the dowser, the mythological founder of the family, I never think of him. (414)]

However, Vita's birth or death records are not to be found in the archives of Tufo's old church (the existence of Vita is proven by several other documents and facts, and Roberto, Melania's father, met her):

La sua esitenza [Vita's] non è rimasta intrappolata in quei registri spietati. È sfuggita [...] agli ordinati archivi del tempo e della memoria. In un giorno di primavera, terso e azzurro come questo, ha affidato la mano a quella di Diamante, lo ha seguito su quell mare vicino e imprendibile che ogni giorno dalla finestra di casa sua deve aver guardato come una promessa, si sono infilati a capofitto nell'unica smagliatura della rete e insieme i due fuggiaschi hanno inventato un'altra storia. (389)

Her existence has not been trapped in those merciless registries. She has escaped [...] the ordered archives of time and memory. One spring day, with a clear blue sky just like today, she gave Diamante her hand and followed him out on to that far and elusive sea, which she must have seen every day from her window, and which she must have looked upon as a promise. They dove headfirst into the only gap in the net, and together these two fugitives invented another story. (420)]

The narrator of the text, whose voice overlaps with the authorial voice and with Mazzucco's voice itself, reports in her account the reasons why it became necessary for her to reconstruct the history of her ancestors: "Mi resi conto che non sapevo niente" (45; "I realized I didn't have any idea" 44). This occurs to her while she is in New York, for an academic commitment, and is reading ads for apartments located in the now fashionable Prince Street neighbourhood. Suddenly, the authorial gaze turns to the history of the Italian migration to the United States.

To understand the narrative shift that has happened in Italian literature and film with regard to the history of the migration, it is helpful to draw a parallel between the necessity of finding memory in *Vita* and in *Sogni mancini*. The need for this memory to be historical, and not simply individual, marks a crucial difference between the two novels; it marks the different positions of America, both as a myth and as a geopolitical space, in the two literary representations.

The Dream of the Fathers

Vita is dedicated to Roberto, Melania's father, whose tales about Diamante, will to write the family history, and papers related to it spurred Melania to write this novel. After Roberto's death, as it appears in the novel, it became relevant to Melania to re-establish the severed tie not only with her father but with his story and with history.

The death that initiates the story in *Sogni mancini* is maternal, and with her dead mother lies Martina's chance to recover the one lost memory that opens the gates to the tale: whether or not the protagonist had ever been left-handed. Yet, the dream that pushes the author to write a novel about the search for identity is paternal in origin, as is the ethical patrimony that pushes Martina to try and "undermine this damned identity" (*Left-Handed Dreams* 63):

> My protagonist is a woman like any other who travels through her memo-
> ries, cooks her food, strives hard for her career, takes care of her body, lives
> her romances, does her laundry, and faces her temptations. Meanwhile,
> she tries to open for all the doors to a specific region of the spirit that was
> her father's and mine [...].[2]

That region of the spirit, we know, is "then and *now* melancholically uninhabited [my emphasis]." There is a sense of the failure of that opening, which recalls its metaphorical counterpart in the novel: Martina's failed attempt at merging her dream and real lives, her failed attempt at understanding what her left-handed alter ego would have been like. We know Martina comes to terms with this failure and finds richness in her blurred identity, where her being Italian and her being American meet and combine in a very specific way.

Roberto, Melania's father, like all the Mazzucco men, is himself a melancholic figure: "I Mazzucco erano maschi – laconici, controllati, autoritari, tragicamente incapaci di comunicare. Gente di pietra" (45; "The Mazzuccos were males – laconic, controlled, authoritarian, tragically unable to communicate. People of stone" 44). Melania, who knows that her father had attempted to reconstruct, somehow, the family history, reads his personal notes in search of Diamante's story, but finds almost nothing. She will later discover that her father was on the wrong track: he thought he had found in Piedmont the small town where the Mazzuccos were probably from. He was wrong.

What had not been finished by the fathers would ideally be left to their daughters to be concluded. They both felt the responsibility to investigate matters of identity and to find memory, but Mazzucco and Duranti went in two different directions.

While in *Sogni mancini* history remains in the background of representation and the search for identity is conducted at the level of the narrator's inner life and of her immediate circumstances, in *Vita* the narrator's search for identity cannot be separated from the movements of history:

> Che c'entra allora il capitano, venuto a combattere in Italia con la 5ª armata, sul Fronte sud? Non l'ho mai incontrato, e non so se abbia pensato qualcosa di simile mentre, un giorno di maggio del 1944, prendeva possesso delle rovine di un villaggio chiamato, come la pietra di cui era fatto, Tufo. Fino a qualche anno fa non sapevo neanche chi fosse, e in verità non credo di saperlo neanche adesso. Eppure quest'uomo non mi è estraneo – e, anzi, la sua storia è così intrecciata alla mia che avrebbe potuto addirittura essere la stessa. Adesso so che quest'uomo avrebbe potuto essere mio padre, e che la scelta del ritorno a Tufo avrebbe potuto raccontarmela mille volte la domenica pomeriggio, mentre grigliavamo bistecche sul barbecue o tosavamo il prato nel giardino di una villetta del New Jersey. Ma non me l'ha raccontata. L'uomo che invece era mio padre mi ha raccontato un'altra storia. (10–11)

> So what about the captain who came to Italy to fight with the Fifth Army on the southern front? I never met him, and I don't know what thoughts were running through his head on that day in May 1944 when he took possession of a village called Tufo, like the stone from which it had been built. Until a few years ago, I didn't even know who he was, and it truth I don't think I know now. Yet this man is not irrelevant to me – in fact, his story and mine are so interwoven they could be one and the same. Now I know he could have been my father, and could have recounted his return to Tufo a thousand times as we barbecued steaks on a Sunday afternoon or did yard work at our house in New Jersey. But he never told me the story. Instead, the man who was my father told me another story. (7)]

This introductory chapter of the novel is entitled "I miei luoghi deserti" (7; "My Desert Places" 1). The story opens in the village of Tufo razed to the ground by the bombs of the Second World War. To have the story begin with an empty scene is not a random choice; it is also a metaphor for the lack of memory of her family history. The same title, "My Desert Places," is in fact assigned to the penultimate section of the book, where the legend and the history of the Mazzuccos are finally disentangled (the last two short sections are meant to be the closure to the three longer parts into which the story is divided). The way in which Melania comes to replenish her desolate, empty places is by filling them with the presence of history. These places, which are spaces of memory, are very different from the abstract desert island that Martina Satriano inhabits in *Sogni mancini* and that Francesca Duranti, the author, describes for us in her preface to the novel when she remembers her father's equanimity.

For the author of *Sogni mancini*, the island of which she dreams remains a utopian space that is neither American nor Italian but that translates, in the novel, into Martina's acceptance of her transcultural identity. For Melania Mazzucco, who enters her story as herself, her desert place needs history to come to life. Unlike Martina, she is not searching for a space where her ethicality and agency can assert themselves, assembling there what is the best of two worlds. On the ruins of what is lost, and following the story of what she herself calls the "losers" – those who have lost no matter what, both in Italy and in the United States – Mazzucco is in search of the history that has made her who she is.

In both novels personal identity remains the crux of the stories and their reason to be written; however, once the necessity for historical evidence overrides the need to find an ideal space (*Vita*), America stops being the utopian place to long for, or to blame for its non-existence. It stops being something far and foreign to be criticized, or praised (Baudrillard) for its absence of culture and history. It simply becomes part of Italy's history, as much as Italy is part of the United States' history. In *Vita*, the history of Italy and that of the United States become inextricable in the representation of the protagonists' lives.

Though the ways in which Mazzucco recounts history are varied, they always lead with individual stories. In the novel we find authentic documents and pictures related to the great migration to the United States, records of the trials that followed the accidental and man-provoked deaths of many Italians who worked on America's railroads and in its mines, with the names and stories of the victims, and the harsh lives of the immigrants in New York. Together with the history of Italian migration to the United States and its implications, we find Italian history; the detailed account of the Southern Front's conquest, in 1944, for example, as captain Dy (Diamante II, son of Vita) fights there; the history of Minturno, Tufo, and the Terra di Lavoro of which they were part; the history of Italy during Roberto's youth, and of its anti-American movement:

> Roberto si infiamma di politica, come è tradizione della famiglia di sua madre, scende in piazza a manifetsare contro Eisenhower, contro l'imperialismo degli Stati Uniti, prende manganellate in testa e viene portato in questura come molti suoi coetanei: scopre di non amare ciò che l'America rappresenta proprio negli stessi giorni in cui l'America bussa alle sue porte – proponendogli il sogno intramontabile di una felicità terrena, materiale, possibile. (218)

> [Roberto becomes inflamed with politics, as is the tradition in his mother's family; he demonstrates against Eisenhower and the imperialism of the United States, takes some blows on the head and is carted off to police headquarters along with many others his age. He discovers he does not love what America represents in precisely the same moment America comes knocking at his door, offering him the eternal dream of an earthly, material, possible happiness. (234)]

This Roberto could very well be the real flesh-and-bone counterpart of the imaginary Roberto whom Umberto Eco depicts for us in *La riscoperta dell'America*:

> Roberto abitava piuttosto il territorio extrapartitico delle attività culturali, delle case editrici, delle cineteche, dei giornali, dei concerti, è proprio in questo senso è stato culturalmente molto influente [...]. Roberto potrebbe essere nato tra il 1926 e il 1931. (Eco, Ceserani, and Placido 14)

> [Roberto inhabited a territory outside of any political party, made of cultural activities, publishing houses, film libraries, newspapers, and concerts, and in this sense he has been culturally very influential [...]. Roberto could have been born between 1926 and 1931.][3]

The real Roberto, Melania's father, was following the American dream while protesting against its implications, by trying to set up some lucrative business between the two countries together with Dy, who was an engineer. The author reports some of the letters that the two men were exchanging across the ocean, and in one of them, the American dream surfaces in its historicity:

> Delle sue lettere, appasionatamente burocratiche, pragmaticamente vincenti, ingenuamente ottimiste, m'è rimasta in mente la frase con cui coinvolge mio padre nel sogno Americano. Era questa, immagino, la lezione che mi avrebbe trasmesso. *"Io credo"* afferma Dy *"che noi due imbarcamo su una impresa che ne profitterà molto, sempre con l'aiuto di Dio e con LE FORZE E ENERGIE PROPRIE. Perché chi vuole cerca."* (221)

> [Of all his passionately bureaucratic, pragmatically winning, and naively optimistic letters the sentence that most sticks in my head is the one he wrote to involve my father in his American dream. This, I imagine, is the lesson he would have communicated to me. "I believe" Dy affirms, "that we two are embarking on an enterprise that will bring us great profit. Always with the help of God and with OUR OWN ENERGY AND STRENGTH. Because he who seeks, finds. (237)]

In *Vita*, the American dream regains its position in history. It is no longer the empty template for individual success; America, here, is not an isolated Arcadia (*L'Arcadia americana*), nor is it a comfortable apartment in Manhattan with basil on the balcony (*Sogni mancini*) or a swimming pool in Beverly Hills (*Treno di panna*). The history of what America truly meant for the Italian immigrants (whether or not, like Vita, they ended up being rich and successful) comes to the forefront, in *Vita*, and responds, ideally, to the concluding scene of "Ava Gardner's Brother-in-Law," in which the protagonist finds some pictures and documents that tell the stories of the early emigrants.

Nuovomondo

Of the literary and cinematic works I analyse, *Nuovomondo* certainly stages the dreamiest of the dreams considered.[4] Dreams and visions have the same value as factual reality in this turn-of-the-century rural Sicilian village, where syncretic culture fuses faith and religion with magic, and with medicine. The film's Felliniesque quality seems to give a perfect dimension to the dreams and hopes of those who left Italy seeking relief from extreme poverty. Set against the background of a dry and stony landscape, those dreams tell the inner story of the emigrants with poetic efficacy. If there was ever a moment when keeping the Aristotelian division between the function of poetry and that of history might be difficult, it is when watching *Nuovomondo*. The dream, in the form of visions, within its historical circumstances, is the protagonist of *Nuovomondo*. When, during a live interview for the online video magazine *Italics*, Anthony Tamburri compliments Crialese for his use of the oneiric element in *Nuovomondo*, the director responds: "I have great masters: Fellini, Pasolini, Antonioni. They had the courage to portray the dreams of men without being ashamed of being naïf." In this regard, he continues:

> What we have in common, all of us human beings, Chinese, American, Italian, is dreaming. I recuperate the dream because it's the best part of us and it's the purest part of us. The dream that I play in my movie is the dream that I thought this kind of people [poor emigrants] had – very simple, tied to food as they needed to eat; so … giant carrots, giant chicken, river of milk … because the first motivation [to leave for America], for these people, was not consuming, but surviving. (Crialese and Amato)

The poetic accent of the film manifests itself in the naïf elements of scenes where money falls from the sky and people swim in a river of milk or carry giant carrots – the voice of desire conjures images of a world of plenty completely unknown to those who decided to leave everything behind for it. Crialese calls these people heroes, since "[they] came here [the United States] without absolutely knowing what they were about to find – they were heroes because they didn't have super powers" (Crialese and Amato). Crialese opposes these heroes to the American fictional heroes who, instead, usually carry super powers of some sort. *Nuovomondo*, he declares, is homage to this kind of people. Yet, these people, just like Superman, can fly, even if it is only through their dreams. In the last scene of *Nuovomondo*, Salvatore and his sons, together with Miss "Luce," swim in an ocean of milk, joined by many fellow travellers; as the camera pulls back, thanks to an optical illusion the swimmers' black bodies moving through the white milk seem like birds flying in an open sky.

Visions and visualizations, in a narrated form, together with heroes stripped of super powers, also constitute the bulk of Alessandro Baricco's novel *City*. The world of *City* is filled with lonely characters who, one way or another, love to tell stories. Gould, the young, mentally ill protagonist, spends hours in the bathroom inventing the story of a boxer and narrating it, as if he were listening to it on the radio. Gould's caretaker, Shatzy Shell, records Western stories, because she would love to write a Western. The novel is filled with icons of America, and the city itself, which has no specific location, resembles an American city. Professor Bandini's *porch* is such an icon.[5] In *City*, America is a patchwork of literary and cinematic icons, confined to the world of narration, and as much outcast as the characters who narrate it. Baricco inscribes America within a literary realm, a realm of narratives as he says, "absorbed into the larger West."[6]

There was a time when images of America, far from being absorbed into the larger West, for some people had not even a name yet; and, far from being outcasts, they were sought after until they manifested, or not, in reality. In *Nuovomondo*, when in Ellis Island's facilities, a few Italian immigrants decide to climb on each other's shoulders in order to look at what lies beyond. From there, they (but not the film spectators) see ... what? Towers? Very tall houses, one of the men explains, where self-operating wooden boxes carry you to the upper floors, and, of course, they can carry animals too. While someone in the group is convinced that his house must be firmly attached to the ground, Salvatore, the protagonist, would very much like to have a house in the clouds. Besides Ellis Island's facilities, not one image of U.S. soil or environment is shown in *Nuovomondo* – the dream remains the protagonist.

Those who left for the New World were imbued with narratives about America, read in the letters sent by relatives overseas, and often seen in the pictures of magical plenty that were sent to Italy to lure women into arranged marriages. *Nuovomondo* looks at those stories and visions through the eyes of the individuals who crossed the ocean; the film takes a step away from the representation of the American dream on an ideological level, and a step into the investigation of its historical reality. In his introduction to *Nuovomondo* on DVD, Martin Scorsese reminds us that, yes, "Golden Door has the feeling of an epic journey, but it is seen through the perspective of the people who are making that journey, it's seen through their eyes." In this way the dream acquires its historical dimension.

As in the case of Melania Mazzucco and her *Vita*, Crialese's reasons for making his film are grounded in his curiosity about history and its individual protagonists, as he himself has stated on many occasions:

[D.] Qual' è stato il principio ispiratore di *"Nuovomondo"*?

[R.] Direi che le scintille sono state parecchie. A cominciare dalla mia permanenza negli Stati Uniti, poi gli studi su un luogo così particolare come Ellis Island. Ma soprattutto gli uomini, le fotografie, le lettere e le piccole grandi storie degli emigranti siciliani d'inizio secolo. (Gaudenzi)

[[Q] What was the inspiration for *Nuovomondo*?

[A] I'd say that the sparks have been many, beginning with my permanence in the United States, then my studies on such a particular place as Ellis Island. Above all the men, the photographs, the letters and the little and great stories of the Sicilian emigrants of the beginning of the century.][7]

Crialese studied Italian immigration to the United States for four years before making his film. One of the things he took away from all "the photographs, the letters, and the little and great stories" was the following: "These first-generation immigrants want their people back home to dream, they want to make their people believe in the dream; and that's what the American people have, as a power" (Crialese and Amato). This adds more dimension to the historical value of the dream that becomes the two-way connection between the Old and the New Worlds.

The film shows Salvatore Mancuso's family as they decide to leave Italy for the United States, which they call "la terra nova," the new land. They leave a dry, bare land that has reduced them almost to famine. The opening scene focuses on the details of such poverty: Salvatore and his older son Angelo are climbing barefoot, on stony ground, up to an improvised shrine (a cross made of two wooden sticks) in order to ask God whether or not they should leave for the New World. They carry in their mouths two stones as a token of faith for the divinity. As the camera zooms out, the two men become little figures against an empty, stony landscape. The last zoom-out of the film, where people become a flock of birds from a river of milk, plays as the counterpart to this scene and, stylistically, brings the film full circle.

From the beginning, the film brings to life a syncretic cultural environment where the boundaries between reality and the magic world of the unseen are blurred. Salvatore's mother, Fortunata, is in fact the healer of the village, "medica" as she calls herself, who performs magic rites to cure people of their physical and psychological conditions. This time around, she will heal a young lady who has been promised in marriage to a rich Italian American, overseas, by the village's priest.

The girl has been restless and anxious, having seen a few photographs sent from the New World reproducing a giant onion, trees growing money, and a gigantic chicken. She feels as if a snake were coiling inside her belly. Sure enough, with a short ritual, the symbol of desire will be extracted from the girl's womb – we see the old lady handling a snake; however, the pictures that have aroused that desire, and which Fortunata said should be burnt, are taken to Salvatore and Angelo by Salvatore's youngest son, Pietro. Salvatore interprets those images as the sign from God he was waiting for. That is the answer: they will leave.

More signs will reveal themselves to Salvatore in the form of visions, such as people carrying a giant carrot in the middle of a field, and money raining on him from the sky, after he buries himself in the ground to protest against his mother, who does not want to leave for the New World. She maintains that their dead have all come to visit the house in order to prevent the departure for the United States, at which Salvatore, overcome by rage, gives himself completely to the land that is starving them.

In Crialese's film, icons of plenty are manifestations of desire and accomplishment, signs of an imaginary world, America, that has its counterpart in its geopolitical reality, the United States. In *City*, these icons representative of America pertain to the world of narration (Shatzy's Western, Balloon Mac, the boxer's story, Bandini's analogy of the porch) and hence still to that cultural construct that has shaped the ideological form of America in Italian culture. In *Nuovomondo* these images of America, far less real than a porch or a western cowboy, are instead part of Italian history and of the migration of its people to the United States. This history is narrated to us through the vicissitudes of individuals and the details of their personal stories.

Agnès Godard, director of photography of *Nuovomondo*, makes a crucial observation on the centrality of the individual in the telling of the history of Italian migration, when she is interviewed by Jean Oppenheimer:

When Italian director Emanuele Crialese approached Godard about shooting *The Golden Door* […] he brought along a collection of turn-of-the-century photographs. In nearly every picture, at least one person was staring directly into the camera. It was as though the camera – and, by extension the viewer – was meeting their gaze. These photos served as visual guide for the film, and the idea was reinforced when Godard saw the Sicilian actors and extras who would play the key roles. "There was so much intensity, so much expression in their faces," she marvels. "It spoke to the deepest, richest idea of the film: the immigrant's desire to retain his singularity while becoming part of a new whole." (Oppenheimer 24)

The gaze to which Godard refers has the same function of exalting individuality as in the last scene of Amelio's *Lamerica* and in the opening lines of Baricco's *Novecento*. History, again, comes to the forefront within the well-established Italian tradition of narratives of the self.

Commenting on why we had to wait for Crialese's generation of artists and intellectuals to witness an interest, in Italy, in the history of migration to the United States, the Italian director says: "If you want to have an identity and you want to find yourself, you have to look back. There is no way you can formulate an identity if you don't have the courage to look at your past" (Crialese and Amato).

It is striking to notice how, even if they share the same respect for historical memory, artists of different generations, such as Crialese and Lagorio, can reserve a completly different place for America, and thus for the dream, in their ideology. For Lagorio and many of her generation, the American dream stands in opposition to the demands of history. For Crialese and Mazzucco, the American dream, as lived by individuals, is part of our history and they are not afraid of treating it as such. It is, in fact, the dream that gives their works, *Vita* and *Nuovomondo*, a hybrid quality: history and the dream both reside with equal dignity in the internal movements and bodily transitions of the individual. It seems to be the importance assigned to the individual in the great movements of history that makes the difference between the artists of the older and newer generations.

Lagorio learned from the Second World War that history resides in collective efforts and collective disasters and that memory is, first and foremost, the repository of both. Mazzucco and Crialese recognize the value of individual stories, in the collective experience, as inseparable from the collective. Poignantly enough, Crialese describes part of his path as an artist and the success of *Nuovomondo* as a product of the American dream.

While discussing his career, and particularly his years in New York, he comments: "For me New York opened the door of my imagination. For me the Golden Door is the door of my imagination and it is in this country that the door opened wide" (Crialese and Amato). Besides that door, there is a window, in Crialese's discourse: "I discovered New York through Martin Scorsese's films. He opened a window in my imagination." Crialese arrived in New York to follow his dreams. He describes Scorsese's introduction to *Golden Door* at its opening at Tribeca Film Festival, in New York, as the coming full circle of a dream.[8]

Scorsese is, in turn, the "cinematic chronicler of the epic of Italian America [...]. The subject matter of his Italian American films extends from the earliest days of immigration [...] No other artist has equalled Scorsese in giving a voice to the common experience of this group" (Casillo i). Crialese's *Nuovomondo* ends on Ellis Island; it is the link in the chain that connects the Old World to Scorsese's Italian American world.

Thanks to his personal path, Crialese understands the importance of an individual's dream in that moment of Italian history which brought so many to cross the ocean. Mazzucco, through a different experience, arrives at the same conclusion: there is no identity without looking at the past, and if this past includes America and the dream that brought many there, then we have to give the dream its place in our national and intra-national history.

In her short web-video lecture on "Immigrazione e letteratura" (immigration and literature) for the Treccani encyclopedia, Mazzucco explains:

Negli ultimi decenni c'è stato un rinnovato interesse verso il tema dell'emigrazione. E` come se l'Italia, [...] paese di grandissima emigrazione, [...] avesse però un po' rimosso la sua stessa storia [...]. C'e' stato una sorta di vuoto, di silenzio che ha fatto un po' dimenticare questa storia. E poi è come se improvvisamente avessimo sentito tutti insieme il bisogno di ritrovare le ragioni di quella storia passata quasi per spiegare ciò che stava succedendo nel nostro paese.[9]

[In the past decades there has been a renewed interest in the theme of emigration. It was as if Italy, [...] a country of great emigration, [...] had somehow forgotten its own history [...]. There has been sort of a void, silence that has made everyone forget this history. Then, all of a sudden, it seemed as if we all felt the need to find again the reasons for that past history in order to explain what was happening in our country.]

What happened in Italy in the 1990s were the two massive waves of immigration from Albania and the steady flows from North Africa and Eastern Europe, to which now we need to add the migration from Asia and South America. In Mazzucco's analysis, Italian historiography and literature begin to revisit the history of Italian immigration as necessary for understanding the present:

> Anche la letteratura italiana ha avuto un grande interesse per l'emigrazione nel momento in cui questa era in atto. Penso a De Amicis che scrive sull'oceano. Penso anche allo stesso Pirandello che scrive un racconto sull'emigrazione, a Pascoli che scrive il famoso poemetto "Little Italy." Poi, anche lì, è come se ci fosse una specie di silenzio e di rimozione. Siamo tutti tornati ad interessarci a questo tema, io stessa quando ho scritto *Vita* ... io, almeno personalmente, per una motivazione civile abbastanza forte. Vedevo che il mio paese era diventato un'America, una terra di approdo, un luogo nel quale centinaia di migliaglia di persone venivano a cercare un'altra vita, o il diritto a una vita. Pero` come italiani sembravamo aver dimenticato di essere partiti nelle stesse condizioni in cui erano partite le persone che ora stanno arrivando. Un po' per creare una sorta di specchio [...] anche per comprendere quello che ci stava sucedendo, io ho deciso di tornare indietro raccontando la storia dell'emigrazione di mio nonno che era andato all'inizio del Novecento negli Stati Uniti. (Mazzucco, "Immigrazione e Letteratura")

> [Also Italian literature has demonstrated a great interest in emigration while it was happening. I am thinking of De Amicis, who wrote about the ocean. I am thinking of Pirandello himself, who wrote a story on emigration. I am thinking of Pascoli, who wrote the famous poem "Little Italy." After this, in literature too, we have silence and distance. We have all taken a new interest in this theme, now; I myself, when I wrote *Vita* ... at least personally I did it because of a quite strong civil motivation. I noticed that my country had become an America, a landing place, a place where hundreds of thousands of people were coming in search of a new life, or in search for the right to a life. However, as Italians, we seemed to have forgotten that we had left in the same conditions in which the people who are coming now have left their countries. I decided to write *Vita* in order to create somehow a mirror [...] also to understand what was happening to us; that is why I decided to look back and tell the story of my grandfather's emigration, who had gone to the United States at the beginning of the nineteenth century.]

Mazzucco's words echo Crialese's on the importance of looking back in order to explore one's cultural identity. Her discourse is a clear example of how the commitment of an intellectual to a social cause, in her case the new immigration to Italy, expresseses itself through the re-enactment of history seen through the eyes of the individual and the involvement of what is personal (the story of her grandfather).

Those intellectuals who were founding a republican nation, Italy, on the ashes of Fascism and who continued to help the growth of the country through the collective struggles of the 1960s and the 1970s could not look at the American dream with a positive eye: the escape of the individual to a new land, where historical memory could be abandoned in the name of a new life, was not an acceptable solution and highlighted the political and economic weakness of the nation. Modern migrations due to the processes of globalization make it both easier and necessary to bring to the forefront of history what it meant for Italians to leave home. This allows us to understand and accommodate diversity. Italian intellectuals could not pay attention to the masses that had left Italy, until Italy became America and we all needed to remember who and what we had been.

Narratively, the American dream of *City*, powerless and shattered, regains its original strength when observed in its historical context. Even the end of a fully realized dream becomes powerful when addressed as a document. Compared to the work of Mazzucco and Crialese, Moretti's *The Last Customer*, although produced earlier, has taken the documentation of the dream a step further as the director witnessed the material destruction, piece by piece, of an American dream.

The American Dream and Globalization

In the passage from myth to history, things do not get any better for the American myth, as explored by Nanni Moretti; although, this time, Moretti is vouching for it. If, in *City*, Baricco confines the American dream to the realm of literature, the consequences of globalization seem to strip it of any right to a home at all; such is the message that Moretti's *The Last Customer* conveys, and it does so with a bittersweet taste.

The Gardinis, protagonists of the documentary *The Last Customer*, have indeed fulfilled their American dream, but they now must literally dismantle it, since the economic consequences of globalization have superseded the dream itself. A new building must replace their pharmacy in Manhattan Plaza, New York, which will be destroyed together with their home, and with the entire block. This is not simply a matter of replacing elements in a given space, for the Alps Drugtsore had gathered around itself a community of loyal patrons. As Laura

Rascaroli explains, "The transnational character of the new capital is, hence, ultimately responsible for the reduction and shedding of public spaces, places in which in the past it was possible to develop conversations and ultimately take part in a system of egalitarian justice" ("Home and Away" 191).

The Last Customer documents the days preceding and following the closure of the Alps Drugstore in 2002, the clearing of the shop, and the destruction of the building. Rascaroli explains that although this is a traditional documentary, "Moretti's presence is felt, particularly in the editing of the material" ("Home and Away" 189). At the beginning of the documentary we see a panning shot of old pharmacy bottles. The store is very elegant, and recalls an old Italian "drogheria" in its decor and in the display of the merchandise. We then see the demolition of the building and on this we hear Mrs Gardini tell the story of the pharmacy.

The Gardinis have owned the pharmacy and the building in which the shop is for a hundred years. They have remodelled the house with the birth of each child, making sure always to preserve the original look, just as they did with the pharmacy itself. "It really was our home," says Mrs Gardini, "and not only a place for business [...] It's very hard to let go." In the meantime, the spectators watch what the Gardinis said they would not – the demolition of the building. The music playing in the background is a version of Leonard Cohen's "Hallellujah," but the noises of the destruction are audible.

From the very beginning, the documentary intends to convey strongly the emotional drama of the Gardinis. Moretti relies on the details of the scenes and their sound to emphasize the discomfort of the moment. We see up close and hear plastic bottles being emptied and wooden vertical drawers being opened and closed in quick succession, while the man performing these acts comments, "This is a beautiful store." The visual and auditory magnification recalls the scene of Moretti's *The Son's Room* in which we watch and hear the boy's casket being sealed nail by nail. The drama of the end of an era, for the Gardinis and their customers, exudes from every detail of the documentary. Pathos figures as a founding element of the documentary's montage for a reason. The Gardinis' ability to be empathic with their customers and open to their problems magnetized a community around the pharmacy. The loss of the store is a loss of community that was built on a specific quality of communication.

Laura Rascaroli identifies three main characteristics of the documentary; one is the the Gardinis' Italianness, recognizable in their family values, in the style of the shop that calls to mind an old Italian pharmacy, and in the close, affective and caring relationships that they build with their customers. In this regard, the camera lingers on physicality – long embraces, tears, affectionate kisses, hands that reach out to reassure and comfort one another. After Mr Gardini has closed the shop's doors for the last time (and, again, we follow him in every detail that he has repeated since 1949), the camera spies, from behind some shelves, an embrace between him and his wife – the two cry in each other's arms, while Mrs Gardini thanks her husband repeatedly.

The second feature is the diversity of the community that the Gardinis have gathered around their shop, a diversity that, as Rascaroli puts it, is the expression of another fading "American myth – that of the inclusiveness of the melting pot, which is threatened by the increasing homogenization of urban areas and the displacement and ghettoization of different identities" ("Home and Away" 197). In *Nuovomondo*, on Ellis Island, we observe one of the beginnings of diversity as an enriching asset in the United States. We see women from all over Europe parading in their beautiful national costumes while walking together to meet their future husbands; and we see groups of men praying in different languages, within different religious traditions, one next to the other. In *The Last Customer*, we hear praises for the Gardinis from longtime customers of the most diverse ethnic and cultural backgrounds, who all refer to the Alps Drugstore as a community in spirit, a place where one can find understanding, help, support, and friendship. One of the customers comments that while the economic improvement of the neighbourhood is certainly a positive aspect, losing a familiar and welcoming space such as the Alps Drugstore is an irreparable loss.[10]

The customers are clearly preoccupied with the neighbourhood's loss of identity and history, which comes with economic growth. "What will go next?" asks one of the men in the store, "The Greek store, with its sacks of turmeric, and great, great sacks of spices? Do you know, there are still some glorious places around here; but, you wonder, are all their days numbered? They probably are, unless there is a great, great depression, which none of us yearns for." Paradoxically enough, now the American dream stands for the history that the globalized economy will sweep away, leaving room only for neighbourhoods that might have been built anywhere else in the world.

From the customers, we hear statements such as, "I think this has been a real piece of cement that's held these blocks together. And it's not that we're going to collapse, or anything like that; but it is going to make a difference"; and, "With them [the Gardinis] goes the real feeling of family and community we have in the neighbourhood." A man with a French accent recalls how Mrs Gardini helped "hundreds," he says, who were in fear and depressed when the AIDS crisis exploded. "This [the pharmacy] was a lighthouse," he adds, "in the tough, rough sea all around."

The third characteristic that Rascaroli individuates in *The Last Customer* is the in-betweenness, "in the sense that it is ideally and culturally positioned in between two places: Italy and America. The store is a 'home away from home,'" a piece of Italy as nostalgically remembered and idealized by the Italian immigrants. Rascaroli explains: "The pharmacy, in fact, was first home to diasporic Italians, and represented a cultural limen – being in-between a mythical Italy and a mythical America, consequently it also became home to other people living in a real or imaginary diaspora" ("Home and Away" 197).

In *Caro diario* the American dream is represented by pieces of what Italy has absorbed of the American culture. The mayor of Stromboli imagines an international, diverse community strolling along a Hollywoodian backdrop with palm trees from Los Angeles, lighting designed by Vittorio Storaro, and music by Ennio Morricone, à la Spaghetti Western. With a condescending smile, Moretti and his friend say goodbye to the mayor and his dream, while the poor man is contemplating his vision with eyes wide open. America here stands for that somewhere else where dreams come true and things are better. Moretti turns his back on this belief more than once in *Caro diario*. The episode in which he meets Jennifer Beals is another clear instance of his refusal.[11]

In *The Last Customer*, Moretti's attention turns to the "real" American dream, the one nurtured in the United States. History, then, comes to the forefront of Moretti's discourse – the director does not change the perspective of his *modus narrandi*: once again he chooses to look at an individual to tell a story – we can consider the Gardinis as a cohesive unit, in this documentary, all sharing the same feelings about the end of their business. What changes is the context of the discourse: from ideological to historical. This is, again, a major shift in the way Italian intellectuals and artists have looked at America so far. Yet, they do not abandon narratives of the self.

In the shift from ideology to historical documentation, images of America seem to lose the negative connotation that they bear in the previous works of art analysed here, where they are used to point at escapism and utopia as disputable values. Their utopian quality regains its more neutral place in history.

Conclusion

The final destination of the real and metaphorical voyages in the contemporary Italian literary and cinematic works that have taken America as their object and goal is not America, the land of unlimited possibilities for human accomplishment. The ultimate point of arrival is the person herself.

The protagonist of *Sogni mancini*, Martina Satriano, finds that the best solution for her is to live between two countries, Italy and America. She has lived in the United States for twenty years. Nonetheless, she calls herself Italian, but calls Manhattan home. The space that her oppositional halves inhabit – her left and right sides, her Lucanian and her Tuscan sides, her Italian and her American sides – cannot have rigid national boundaries. She makes moral choices relying on herself as individual, and on her own convictions, rather than on the group that surrounds her as society. She chooses an ethical displacement that will allow her to fulfil her human potential as she thinks best for herself and for the world around her. In order to do so, not only does she refuse to become fully American (which means, for her, to embrace an Anglo-Saxon ideal of America), but she also refuses the counter-dream that Professor Cerignola offers her: to go back to Italy as a successful and accomplished individual. She will keep on being a Leftist, and she will keep on living in between. The ethical self, in *Sogni mancini*, prevails.

So does the self protagonist of the film *Caro diario*, in which the idea of America is only tangential to Nanni Moretti's social and personal discourse about Italy, and about himself as an intellectual. Images of America are there to signify a utopian and somehow inauthentic world that does not represent a viable solution for the protagonist.

Several texts analysed in this book touch on the stereotypical European concept of American inauthenticity from different angles. In *Amérique*, Jean Baudrillard individuates the authenticity of American culture in its being inauthentic, where "inauthentic" ultimately means deprived of a European sense of history and culture. He sees the essence of America as a realized Utopia – de-linked from history, so without future, and hence without hope; a place where Europeans can finally experience a dizzy and liberating detachment from their sense of culture. Although he challenges Europeans to look at America without comparing it to Europe, Baudrillard's own discursive rhetoric about the United States is hopelessly built on a comparison with Europe. This same unavoidable comparison is pivotal in De Carlo's *Treno di panna* and Lagorio's *L'arcadia americana*. In the former, the narrating I, Giovanni, enters the Hollywoodian American dream and looks at it through all the baggage of European stereotypes about the emptiness of American culture. In the latter, the Italian photographer protagonist of the story visits the American sanctuaries of culture – its most prestigious universities – and describes them as utopian places far removed from the real world and from history. In different ways, and with different outcomes, the two photographers end up reinforcing their European / Italian identities because of a rhetorical strategy that builds the discourse on America as oppositional – America versus Europe, as it occurs in Baudrillard's *Amérique*.

In *Treno di panna*, Giovanni does not problematize the European component of his look upon America. It is there as a given, as a pretext underlying his narrative. On the contrary, the photographer of *L'arcadia americana* does question his prejudicial ideas about America, but his questioning shows itself to be only the rhetorical device that gives him more credibility and reliability as a commentator on the United States. One way or the other – in the light of history (*L'arcadia americana*), or apparently ignoring history (*Treno di panna*) – America can only be narrated as a construct heavily based on, and deeply rooted in, European culture. It is a construct that, in turn, defines European culture. In the end, as noted repeatedly, the "I" protagonists of these novels, and the authors behind them, take the opportunity to talk about themselves while they describe their America.

As far as this attitude of the Italian intellectuals goes, Ben Morreale's "Ava Gardner's Brother-in-Law" epitomizes the Pirandellian intellectual in conflict with society, who universalizes his ideas about humanity and the possibility of an ethical communication between subjects. In Morreale's short piece, this intellectual, the Sicilian Turidru, looks at America as the dream of salvation, but is obliged to confront it·in a conversation with an American subject, an accomplished American self, who asks him to abandon the dream and to remember history. The first-person narrator of "Ava Gardner's Brother-in-Law" points out to Turidru that the America the Sicilian is talking about is *his* idealized America, far removed from the social reality of the geopolitical one.

How much the New World can be an idea that does not necessarily entail the geopolitical space of the United States is the theme of Gianni Amelio's *Lamerica*. In the film, history repeats itself. The Albanians, who immigrate to Italy to flee the poverty of their country, are equated with the Italians who immigrated to the United States for the same reasons, at the turn of the twentieth century. Italy becomes *Lamerica* and, as "America," will not be able to save those who are searching for it.

In *City*, the cultural construct America becomes itself the protagonist of the novel, as such ironically denied by the author Alessandro Baricco. In a world – *City* – where the metaphorical voyage to America as accomplishment of the self is surpassed – where the subjects do not go anywhere but rather resemble sites on the World Wide Web – in this world, America as a narrative construct takes its definitive place as *narratum*. The American Dream represented in the characters Gould, Shatzy, and Professor Bandini becomes an outcast of Western civilization (partly absorbed into it, and partly rejected) to be confined to the realm of literature, and it shines in the beautiful narrative style of Shatzy's Western adventures, Gould's boxer's story, and Professor Bandini's individualist philosophy.

In the narratives I explored, those subjects who do not respond positively to Foucault's invitation to investigate what work one should do on oneself end up embracing a dream of only apparent fulfilment that will lead them to quixotic conclusions, as Roberto Benigni and Massimo Trosi show us in *Non ci resta che piangere*.

As far as the ethics of the subject go, and where images of America are concerned, the focus of my study has been the relation of the self to itself and to the space that surrounds the individual. This is a space constructed and defined by that same individual's gaze. We have seen how suitable the Italian tradition of narratives of the self is for such exploration of the subject. The historically weak Italian national identity allows the subject to focus on him / herself as a subject of the world, rather than a subject of only one nation, and a subject who, as an intellectual, feels the moral duty to be actively engaged in the improvement of civil society.

Although this weak national identity seems to strengthen when the individual deals with images of America as the elsewhere to run to for ethical accomplishment and salvation, the refractoriness of the Italian subject / intellectual to a rigid national identity, and the constant projection of her / his thought on a humanistic universal plane, allows him / her to discuss the significance of America far beyond its meaning in national culture. This peculiarity of the Italian intellectual makes him / her the privileged subject of *The Mirage of America* in the ways s / he is represented by the works here analysed, and in the ways these works are symptomatic of the intellectual standing behind them, and of her / his attitudes towards America. It is not by chance that the Italian intellectual talks about America to talk about her / himself. This inclination has deep historical roots in Italian culture, as Donald Heiney, Theodore Cachey, David Ward, and my own analyses of the narratives in this book point out.

As we take a perspective distance from the last chapter, from Gina Lagorio and Ben Morreale, who suggest that we should look into history and move away from the myth, we line up the two authors with all the fictional and real subjects of this book, who have for us that same suggestion. Hence we link them to Nanni Moretti's good-bye to the mayor of Stromboli and his artificial island; to Martina Satriano's refusal to forget her personal history; to the inconsistency of a dreamy cream train; to the Albanians who, going to Italy, are going to the wrong place, "Lamerica." To that same mistaken destination went Columbus, so Roberto Benigni and Massimo Troisi say, and having failed to stop him, all they can do is cry.

Alessandro Baricco finds a different solution to the inevitable: let's send America to that exceptional realm of literature and myth for good. That *City*, there. And let's forget about it, because *City* is not in America. America is in that larger, Western *City*. Or, we can choose to travel with Baudrillard, and then forget about history and culture if we really want to enjoy America.

In different ways and with different outcomes, in order to advance the ethical improvement of humanity, the works analysed in this study up to chapter 4 mark a divarication between America as a myth and the lessons of history. These works seem to point, directly or indirectly, at historical memory as the anchor that should save us all from the "American" myth: a salvation from the salvation ... Such a divergent look, because exclusive, risks endangering the necessary dialogue that Europe should have with its own mythic creation, America, in a globalized world that is still widely dominated by imperialisms and injustice. Hence, literary and filmic productions such as *The Last Customer*, *Vita*, and *Nuovomondo* are particularly welcome in how they relate the American dream to past and present history. That divarication between myth and history comes to an end when the myth is reinstated on its historical paths.

A development of this study, in fact, would further focus on the relationship between history and myth, as far as the cultural construct "America" is concerned in the European tradition. America is an integral part of Italian history and culture and, as such, belongs to the national collective imagery in the ways Italian artistic productions elaborate that history, in the ways they iconize that history. However, this national collective imagery also belongs to the international cultural scene in so far as Italian literature can go beyond national boundaries and can reflect upon humanity at large. As we have seen, Italian intellectuals have a tradition of perceiving and elaborating the concept of America as crucial to the understanding and improvement of human relationships, starting from the individual who sets out for America. This is particularly evident in the works by Moretti, Mazzucco, and Crialese treated here. Their elaborations spring from history and return to history – the historical aspect of America in European culture deserves further attention.

The authors and works I chose for this study are those that struck my imagination and with which I started a dialogue long ago. However, any further work that would look at images of America, as myth and dream, in Italian or any other culture, will have to consider how history has remodelled the myth from 9/11 on. In his "Le torri simboliche e il collasso della *fiction*: L'11 settembre 2001 e gli scrittori Italiani" (The Symbolic Towers and the Collapse of Fiction: 9/11 and Italian Writers), Francesco Longo writes:

Nella lettura di questi libri, si può dire, schematicamente, che la questione dell'11 settembre ruota intorno a tre temi fissi: l'intrecciarsi della Storia con le vicende private dei personaggi; la percezione dell'evento come di un fatto spettacolarizzato (il problema della realtà e della finzione); la differenza tra il mondo di prima e quello dopo l'evento. (246)

[Reading these books, one can tell, schematically, that the matter of September 11 revolves around three stable themes: the intertwining of

history with the personal vicissitudes of the characters; the perception of
the event as spectacularized (the issue of reality and fiction); the difference
between the world before and after the event.][1]

9/11 forced the flowing of collective history to the forefront of human
imagination and of international discourses again. Not surprisingly,
Italian literature has produced novels and short stories which weave
that history with individuals' accounts, in line with the Italian tradition
of narratives of the self. Andrej Longo's novel *Più o meno alle tre* (2002,
At around 3:00) tells the events of 9/11 from seventeen different points
of view. Considering the position of history in Mazzucco's, Crialese's,
and Moretti's (2002) works, the effects of 9/11 on Italian artistic productions, when concerned with America, seem to have reached beyond
those tragic events as Italian authors privilege a historical / documentary approach to tales of America. Through stories of individuals,
Italian literature and film have found a way to reposition America and
its dream in the telling of national history. Representation has thus been
critical to narratives of the past as much as the present. If migratory
fluxes to Italy have reminded the country of its own history of migration, and so have led Italians to feel closer to America, the tragedy of
9/11 has suddenly erased any distance between the Bel Paese and the
United States precisely because history was being told in the modes
of fiction, as Baricco pointed out ("Quando la storia si presenta come
un film").

The emotional element of the tragedy, amplified by the immediacy of
the television reports, has played a crucial role in how Italian people
perceived the United States and in the accounts of that perception:

> La distanza tra Europa e America era stata percepita come se fosse
> azzerata, come se lo spazio si fosse contratto a tal punto che gli Stati Uniti
> e l'Italia si avvertivano come sovrapposti. Un bersaglio solo, invece di
> due. [...] La tragedia, avvenuta in una zona geograficamente non italiana,
> si scopriva essere una zona così "emotivamente italiana," che, aiutata an-
> che dalla diretta televisiva, era capace di dissolvere i confini tra i territori
> e annullare la loro lontananza. Era *come se* l'11 settembre fosse una storia
> italiana. E il *molto lontano* per un po' ha coinciso col *qui* [emphases in the
> text]. (Longo 242)

> [The distance between Europe and America had been perceived as elimi-
> nated, as if space had shrunk to a point where the United States and Italy
> were perceived as overlapping. One only target, rather than two. [...] The

tragedy, which had happened in a zone geographically different from Italy, was now discovered to be such an "emotionally Italian" zone capable of dissolving the boundaries between the territories and of nullifying the distances, also with the help of live television. It was as if September 11 were an Italian story. And the *very far* has coincided with the *here*, for a while.]

That coincidence of near and far, although temporary, has changed forever the perceived distance between Italy and the United States, and between Italy and America. A further study on representations of America in contemporary Italian literature and film will have to scrutinize this dramatic change in perspective and its effects on when, how, and why images of America play a role in intellectual discourses in and on Italy.

Notes

Introduction

1 My translation. Unless otherwise indicated, all translations are mine.
2 The *New Oxford American Dictionary*.
3 The Quota Act limited the number of immigrants from Europe to about 350,000 per year, while the National Origins Act required potential immigrants to obtain visas from an American consulate abroad, which drastically reduced the number of people migrating to the United States. The number of immigrants remained relatively high, nonetheless. Mangione and Morreale explain, "By 1930, more than 4.5 million Italians had entered the United States" (33). Francesco Durante describes the phenomenon as follows: "È un progressivo svuotarsi di paesi e cittadine specialmente dei distretti rurali dell'Appennino, dell'Abruzzo, della Calabria, della Sicilia (9; "It is a progressive emptying of towns and villages, particularly of the rural disctricts in the Appennines, in Calabria, and in Sicily").
4 The narratological background of my textual analyses is to be found in, among other texts, Wayne C. Booth, *The Rhetoric of Fiction*; Roland Bouerneuf and Real Ouellet, *L'univers du roman*; Umberto Eco, *Trattato di semiotica generale*; Gerard Genette, *Figure III*; Philippe Lejeune, *Le pacte autobiographique*; Jurij M. Lotman, *Analysis of the Poetic Text*; Brian McHale, *Postmodernist Fiction*; James Phelan, *Reading Narrative: Form, Ethics, Ideology*; Gerald Prince, *Narratology: The Form and Function of Narrative*; and Seymour Chatman, *Story and Discourse: Narrative Structure in Fiction and Film*.
5 The lyrics of "Una Domenica italiana" were written by Gianni Boncompagni, creator and director of many successful television programs, and the music by Toto Cutugno, who also sang the song as the sound track of a Sunday television show. Cutugno is a very popular singer who,

for many years, has carried the flag of what popular culture calls "itali-anità," by singing lyrics that repeat stereotypes about Italy as icons of na-tional identity. One of his well-known songs is "L'italiano" (The Italian).

6 Let me repeat that by "America" I refer to a cultural construct that con-tains images of the United States as absorbed and re-proposed by the Italian cultural and historical context. The word is not used interchange-ably with "United States" or "USA."

7 The U.S. presidential election of 2008 certainly altered, if not reversed, the negative perception of the United States in Italian culture, which had worsened with the international political events that followed 9/11.

8 Botta's 1809 *Storia della guerra dell'indipendenza degli Stati Uniti d'America* was very successful in Italy, where it became a source of inspiration for the *Risorgimento*; in France; and in the United States, earning the praises of Thomas Jefferson and John Adams (see Teodori's "Storia della Guerra d'indipendenza USA").

9 On this topic see Zygmunt G. Baranski and Rebecca West, *The Cambridge Companion to Modern Italian Culture*; Stephen Gundle, *Between Hollywood and Moscow: The Italian Communists and the Challenge of Mass Culture, 1943–1991*; Vassilis Fouskas, *Italy, Europe, the Left: The Transformation of Italian Communism and the European Imperative*. These are just examples of a rather extensive bibliography in the field.

10 See Antonio Gramsci's *Prison Notebooks*.

11 I comment further on how Italian culture has looked, or not looked, at the great migration as part of its history in chapter 5.

12 Following the events of 9/11, the attitude towards American foreign pol-itics oscillated between a strongly accentuated anti-American feeling, dur-ing the Bush administration, and a sense of liberation and hope that came about with the election of Barack Obama to the presidency. That strong an-ti-American sentiment resurged in Italy among the Leftist intellectuals and the pacifist movements, including the Catholic ones, with the U.S. military intervention in Afghanistan. However, the Italian political establishment, meaning the centre-to-the right governing coalition and the centre-to-the-left opposition (with the only exceptions of "Verdi," "Comunisti Italiani," and "Rifondazione Comunista"), sided with the United States on the war on terror, and also with military action.

The perception of the United States in Italian culture, and throughout Europe, changed again with the election of Barack Obama, which was welcomed with hope as the sign of a possible real change in the political equilibrium of the world.

13 See Teodori, 100–20.

1. Wandering Subjects

1 See De Bernardinis 35.
2 Penta Film started as a joint venture in 1990 between what was then Silvio
   Berlusconi's Fininvest and Mario & Vittorio Cecchi Gori's Cecchi Gori
   Tiger Cinemat.
3 See Gian Piero Brunetta, Mario Sesti, and Manuela Gieri.
4 The song is on the album *Non tutti gli uomini* (Not Every Man), published
   by the CBS Dischi in 1988.
5 My translation. Unless otherwise indicated, all translations in the chapter
   are mine.
6 Entrepreneurs bribed political figures to obtain public contracts, some to
   evade taxes. This created a "Tangentopoli" – a polis (Milan at first, but
   then, indeed, the entire country) built through bribes. The legal operation
   that unveiled and investigated "Tangentopoli" was called "Mani Pulite"
   ("Clean Hands") and caused the fall of many political leaders who had
   governed the country, and of entire political parties such as the Partito
   Socialista led by Bettino Craxi.
7 Berlusconi gave birth to his political party, Forza Italia, in 1993, soon after
   the country had been shaken by "Tangentopoli." Forza Italia has converged
   in a larger political organism, Il Popolo delle Libertà, through a transition
   that went from 2007 to the beginning of 2009.
8 Michele becomes the neurotic "screaming actor / author / character"
   ("Landscapes" 51) on which Moretti's cinema focuses for some years.
   Gieri reminds us that "[…] Michele has progressively assumed multiple
   roles and thus became a reflection of an entire generation […]" ("Landscapes" 51). In *Palombella rossa*, Michele is a Communist leader with an
   identity crisis, undergoing losses of memory; but, "alla sua definizione
   contribuiscono elementi autobiografici quail il fatto che gioca a pallanuoto
   come il regista e che manifesta le tipiche idiosincrasie dell'autore (moral-
   ismo, intolleranza, fastidio profondo nei confronti della superficialità e
   della banalità contemporanea: ne è dimostrazione lo schiaffo dato all gior-
   nalista che pronuncia l'abusta parola *trend*)" (Bragaglia 72; "autobiographical elements contribute to his [Michele's] identity such as the fact that he
   plays water polo, like the director, and that he displays the author's typical idiosyncrasies (moralism, intolerance, deep impatience towards superficiality and the contemporary banality, a demonstration of which is the
   slap he gives to a woman journalist who utters the abused word *trend*.")
9 For a discussion of *Caro Diario* as a form of autobiography, see Mazierska
   and Rascaroli 31–45.

10 "Moretti's body," Gieri explains, "previously expropriated by Michele in the neurotic search for a generational identity, is now reappropriated by the director. That body is no longer a war machine, but here it becomes the point of departure for a global redefinition of the world of experience" ("Landscapes" 52).

11 In 2002, Moretti became an active symbol of political dissent: dissent against the mistakes of the Left, against Italian domestic and foreign politics, and against Berlusconi. He was actively involved in the leftist movement *I girotondi* that saw the participation of artists and intellectuals together with common people against the government's politics on justice, and later on public TV and on the school system, throughout 2002. *I girotondi*, literally ring-around-the-rosie, organized by different associations of citizens united by a common intent, were protest rallies that took place in major Italian cities. The participants would gather in circles around the buildings of some democratic institutions to symbolize their commitment to protecting those same institutions, as was the case around the palaces of justice in Milan and Rome, in January and February 2002. During two speeches delivered at different rallies that year, Moretti expressed his lack of confidence in the political skills of the leaders of the institutional Left and Centre-to-Left, which is symptomatic of the gap between many Italian leftist intellectuals and the political parties that form the Left.

   As an artist and an intellectual, Moretti has been by no means an isolated case of political involvement in Italy. The Italian Nobel Laureate for Literature, Dario Fo, and his wife, writer and actress Franca Rame, are politically active – they write a daily newsletter on their website that is a serious instance of alternative press. Roberto Benigni makes no mystery of his political creed and is a strong political satirist. A few years ago, another political satirist, Beppe Grillo, took a turn towards political activism and has been able to polarize thousands of people around his ideas ever since, also creating a movement of citizens, "Movimento a cinque stelle" (five-star movement), nowadays operative at the administration level of several Italian cities.

12 About Moretti's cinematic moral gaze, see also Roberto Escobar on *Caro diario* in "Riflessi nel grande schermo: Caro diario, la vita non è che leggerezza."

13 *Caro diario* won the David di Donatello and the Golden Globe awards for Best Film in 1994, and earned Moretti the Palme d'Or for Best Director at Cannes in the same year.

14 "Stupor" and "stupidity" share some meanings on the continuum of signification. Stupor, which is "admiring wonder" (*Oxford English Dictionary*)

as I use it in this text, is also "Stupidity, dullness of comprehension" (*OED*), where stupidity is "The condition of being deprived of the use of the faculties; a state of stupor" (*OED*).

15 Concerning Moretti's homage to Italian cinema, Laura Rascaroli writes: "Even though *Dear Diary* is a highly original film, the lessons of other filmmakers can be easily traced. In addition to the direct homage to Pasolini – who here represents a bygone era of Italian cinema which was not afraid to confront reality and to challenge mainstream beliefs and tendencies – the presence of two masters of Italian Neorealism, Roberto Rossellini and Cesare Zavattini, can be clearly felt. Rossellini is called to mind through the episode in Stromboli, the island that was the setting of Rossellini's eponymous 1950 film, although Moretti avoids direct quotations. It is interesting that the mayor, rather than turning to Rossellini for the 'beautification' of his island, thinks of the symbols of a much more commercial and popular (albeit refined) cinema, that of Morricone and Storaro. In general terms, Rossellini's attention to reality and to the contradictions of life is a lesson that Moretti uses wisely and widely in his film. More significantly, Zavattini's most radical neorealist and post-neorealist theories are evoked by *Dear Diary*. This occurs first through the idea of the shadowing (*pedinamento*) of a human being for a day filming all the things that happen to him or her. Moretti somehow repeats the same poetic practice, although he re-enacts the real events in his own life rather than shooting them as they happen (but the two practices co-existed in Zavattini's writings)" ("Caro Diario" 242).

16 Certainly so, but what comes to mind immediately, when watching that fake film, is Lawrence Kasdan's *The Big Chill* (1983) rather than any specific Italian movie. Like *The Big Chill*, Moretti's fake film portrays the moral decadence of a generation of unsatisfied ex-dissenters who have given up their ideals to embrace a middle-class lifestyle and values.

17 The English translation of *Sogni mancini*, published in the United States by Delphinium, is the work of the author herself, Francesca Duranti. In the United Kingdom, the English version has been published with an introduction by Nicoletta Di Ciolla McGowan, who also edited the translation. Neither English edition bears the preface to the Italian version which explains so much about the book and its author; although its content is deeply rooted in Italian history and culture, I do not believe that it is inaccessible to the American or British readers (a few explanatory notes would suffice). However, McGowan herself refers to this preface in her introduction (xvii). At various points Duranti's translation eliminates or changes some concepts on the basis of what seems a cultural prejudice

and not just a matter of translatability. Of Duranti's English version of *Sogni Mancini*, McGowan, who was in touch with the author, explains: "The English version […] has undergone a number of revisions for over four years after the Italian edition, Sogni Mancini, was published in 1996. The changes made on various occasions – for instance when the author was invited to read excerpts in universities in the US, and before she submitted the typescript to publishers – were intended to make *Left-Handed Dreams* read less as a translation and more as an autonomous text, a novel in its own right […]. By narrating such a story in English as well, the author – who herself lives in New York for most of the year – intended to give as authentic a voice as possible to the experiences of the protagonist, emphasizing the impact and effects of the North American society in which she has settled, and how they sedimented on, and reacted with, the substratum of values, memories and culture which are the patrimony carried forward from her native Italy. Therefore, although the author took great care to ensure the syntactic and lexical accuracy of the text – she in fact availed herself of the co-operation of an American friend whose task it was to 'de-italianize' her English – she insisted that certain linguistic quirks, neologisms, words that she (or rather her protagonist) created on the model of the Italian lexicon, be kept precisely to that effect" (McGowan 5–6).

18 The painful relationship with her mother is a substantial component of Duranti's work, even as a translator. Duranti's knowledge of German, English, and French, for which she has become an appreciated translator, is due to the several foreign governesses by whom she was raised in her Tuscan villa, while effectively removed from her mother, and to the fact that she wanted to please her parents by studying languages. Twice divorced, "Francesca Duranti has contributed to post–World War II Italian literature through her close examination of personal experiences, especially her relationships with her mother and husbands, and through her exploration of the dynamics of writing fiction. Duranti's novels show how life affords the material for art and how ones devotion to art can affect ones life" (Kozma).

19 For the importance and significance of food in this novel see Marina Spunta's essay "The Food of Tolerance in Francesca Duranti's *Left-Handed Dreams.*"

20 A note on why I do not make my discussion of *Sogni Mancini* gender-specific. In an interview released to Donatella De Ferra, a scholar in Women's Studies at the University of Hull, England, Duranti said: "Credo

che il femminismo sia una questione politica e come ogni fatto politico non è vero o falso. È opportuno o non è opportuno a seconda dei momenti. Allora ci sono certe cose che a mio parere oggi non sono più opportune: come per esempio questo insistere tanto sullo specifico della scrittura femminile. La scrittura femminile abbiamo dovuto affermare che esisteva e adesso lo sappiamo [...]. Esistono altri specifici: la scrittura giovanile contrapposta alla scrittura dei vecchi o degli adulti, esiste la scrittura di un credente rispetto alla scrittura di un ateo. Non si fanno queste altre divisioni, non esiste un corso universitario per scrittura anziana o per scrittura giovanile, allora l'insistere su questo specifico della scrittura femminile. ... C'è stato un momento in cui poteva essere utile proprio per la causa del femminismo [...], oggi forse non lo è più. Perché è come dare a noi stesse una specie di pista delle biciclette in cui corriamo tutte quante insieme, io preferisco correre con gli altri nella grande autostrada dove si cerca di andare più forte che si può, si cerca di battere gli uomini se possibile" (21; "I believe that feminism is a political matter and like every political matter is neither true nor false. It is either appropriate or inappropriate according to the moment. So, as far as I am concerned, there are certain things that are not appropriate any longer nowadays: as for instance, this great insistence on the specificity of feminine writing. We had to affirm that feminine writing existed, and now we know it [...]. There exist other specifics: juvenile writing as opposed to adult writing or old-age writing, there exists a believer's writing as opposed to a non-believer's writing. No one makes these distinctions, there is no university course about senile writing, or about juvenile writing, so to insist on this feminine writing. ... There was a moment when it could be useful for the cause of feminism [...], probably, today, it is not so any longer. It is like giving ourselves a cycling track where we run all together. I prefer running with the others on the large highway where everyone tries to run as fast as one can, where we try to beat men, if possible.")

I did not just limit myself to taking into consideration Duranti's idea on the specificity of women's writing. Her preface to *Sogni mancini* speaks of that "region of the spirit" that Martina explores in the novel as a space open to all. Abating rigid concepts of identity is the main goal of the protagonist's agenda. McGowan writes: "Martina Satriano is an exemplar of what Rosi Braidotti defines as the 'nomadic subject', a self which refuses to be drawn into the univocal configuration of an 'I', and is free to roam and to manifest itself in multiple and temporary configurations [...]. she discovers that to be able to be one and many grants her a flexibility that is the only way forward in a society which hopes to destroy all barriers and frontiers, and to become one big global environment, and where plurality and multiplicity demand openness and constant change" (xvii).

Besides the specific fluidity of matters of identity in *Sogni mancini*, more generally "[m]any Italian women writers claim a de-gendered literary status, clear of sexual polarisation, and demand recognition on exclusively artistic grounds. Nevertheless, whatever the ideological stance adopted, it would appear that the issue of personal identity, of the *making* of a self, still features very highly in the agenda of women writers" (McGowan xi). Analysing texts written by such women authors, and having to focus on their making of a self, means taking into consideration their wish for de-gendered discourses. This desire is one of the reasons why *The Mirage of America* presents contemporary Italian literature and film as the arena where reflections on ethics of the subject aim at negotiating and transcending differences for the good of global environments.

21 I think of singularity as that which Giorgio Agamben calls an individual's *ecceità* (*La comunità che viene*).

22 In her framing of her identity as a work in progress, Martina can be seen as the representation of what Foucault calls the work of the self on itself.

23 As said above, the author does not preface the English text, so I translate the Italian "Prefazione."

24 With regard to identity and identification, Emmanuel Levinas writes in *Entre Nous*, "No concept corresponds to the *I* as being. [...] The *I* does know itself as reflected in all the objective reality that has constituted it or with which it has collaborated; hence, it knows itself in terms of a conceptual reality. But if this conceptual reality exhausted his being, a living man would not differ from a dead one. Generalization is death; it inserts the *I* into, and dissolves it in, the generality of its work. The irreplaceable singularity of the *I* comes from its life" (*Entre nous* 26–7). See also Levinas's seminal work on the I, the Self, and the Other, *Autrement qu'être; ou, au-delà de l'essence*.

25 The line in the English edition "I didn't belong to any of the powerful ideological families" is absent from the original Italian text. For an explanation of the incongruencies of the translation see note 17 above.

26 Although the beginning of the first chapter of *Moby-Dick* should resonate in the minds of those who love books (like the first *terzina* of the *Commedia*), let me recall it here: "Call me Ishmael. Some years ago – never mind how long precisely – [...]."

With regard to Ishmael and Crusoe, and to Martina's shifting identity, Marina Spunta writes, "A further self-definition links Martina's identity with both American and British literary traditions, mixing *Moby-Dick*'s opening line with Defoe's shipwrecked character, Robinson Crusoe, thus merging the nineteenth-century English-language tradition of quests and travel writing with the postmodern notion of shifting identity" ("The Food" 236). This merging, oddly enough, actually replaces Ishmael, embodiment of a shifting identity (as a character and as a narrator), of tolerance, and of cohabitation of differences, with Crusoe, who is, instead, representative of all other conquering and mastering attitudes belonging to an entire social class very different from the *Pequod*'s crew. There can be no simple postmodern pastiche in "Call me Robinson," as I discuss in the text.

27 In his narrative, it is Ishmael who makes the reference to the "Bowditch's Navigator," the *American Practical Navigator* first issued by the mathematician and navigator Nathaniel Bowditch (1773–1838) in 1802.

28 "How it is, there is no telling, but Islanders seem to make the best whalemen. They were nearly all Islanders in the Pequod, *Isolatoes* too, I call such not acknowledging the common continent of men, but each *Isolato* living on a separate continent of his own. Yet, now, federated along one keel, what a set these Isolatoes were! An Anacharsis Clootz deputation from all the isles of the sea, and all the ends of the earth, accompanying Old Ahab in the Pequod to lay the world's grievances before that bar from which not very many of them ever come back" (*Moby-Dick* 216–17).

29 Agamben writes: "L'essere che viene è l'essere qualunque […] *quodlibet ens* non è 'l'essere non importa quale,' ma 'l'essere tale che comunque importa' […]. Il Qualunque che è qui in questione non prende, infatti, la singolarità nella sua indifferenza rispetto ad una proprietà comune (a un concetto, per esempio: l'essere rosso, francese, musulmano), ma solo nel suo essere *tale qual è*. […] l'esser-*quale* è ripreso dal suo avere questa o quella proprietà, che ne identifica l'appartenenza a questo o quell'insieme, a questa o quella classe (i rossi, i francesi, i musulmani) […] verso il suo esser-*tale*, verso l'appartenenza stessa" (*La comunità che viene* 9–10; "The coming being is whatever being [tale quale è] […] *quodlibet ens* is not 'being, it does not matter which,' but rather 'being such that it always matters.' […]. The Whatever in question here relates to singularity not in its difference with respect to a common property (to a concept, for example; being red, being French, being Muslim), but only in its being *such as it is*. […] such-and-such being is reclaimed from its having this or that property, which identifies it as belonging to this or that set, or this or that class (the reds, the French, the Muslims) – and it is reclaimed […] for its being-*such*, for belonging itself" *The Coming Community* 1–2).

30 I rely here on the concept of *quodlibet ens*, whatever being, as explained by
Agamben (see note 29).

A few pages further in his text, Agamben relates the "whatever in question" to singularity: "Qualunque è il matema della singolarità, senza il
quale non è possibile pensare né l'essere né l'individuazione [...] la singolarità non aggiunge nulla alla forma comune se non una *ecceità*" (*La comunità che viene* 19; "Whatever is the matheme of singularity, without which
it is impossible to conceive either being or the individuation of singularity
[...] Singularity adds nothing to the common form, if not an 'haecceity'"
The Coming Community 17). "Whatever," such as it always matters, is then
the basic concept (matheme) that allows the understanding and framing of
"singularity," because without the "whatever that always matters" singularity would be ethically meaningless, as it adds nothing to the common
form if not a formal characteristic that distinguishes, within a species,
one individual from another, which is what Duns Scotus called *haecceitas*,
heacceity. Martina is obsessed with the possible heacceities of her imagined selves while paradoxically trying to abate concepts of identity,
until she comes to the realization that only her being *tale qual è* matters.

31 Agamben writes, "Poiché l'amore non si dirige mai verso questa o quella
proprietà dell'amato (l'esser-biondo, piccolo, tenero, zoppo), ma nemmeno
ne prescinde in nome dell'insipida genericità (l'amore universale): esso
vuole la cosa con tutti i suoi predicati, il suo essere tale qual è. Esso desid-
era il *quale* solo in quanto è *tale*" (*La comunità che viene* 9–10; "Love is
never directed toward this or that property of the loved one (being blond,
being small, being tender, being lame), but neither does it neglect the
properties in favor of an insipid generality (universal love): The lover
wants the love *with all of its predicates*, its being such as it is" *The Coming
Community* 2).

32 Further in her essay Spunta writes, "Cooking and writing blend together
as essential ingredients of self-expression in her new life as an Italian-
American" (244).

33 Tamburri substitutes the usual hyphen with a slash when referring to the
several ethnicities who populate the United States. He wrote a booklet
about this choice in 1991, *To Hyphenate or Not to Hyphenate: The Italian/
American Writer: An Other American*, but I will quote from his preface to *A
Semiotic of Ethnicity: In (Re)cognition of the Italian/American Writer*: "A final
note: On the use of the slash (/) in place of the hyphen (-), I refer the reader to my *To Hyphenate or Not to Hyphenate*, where I considered, and still do,
the use of any diacritical mark in language steeped in ideology in the
broadest sense of the terms. It is basically an arbitrary decision that is

made according to a systematic set of ideas created by those who have the ability (read, also, power) to do so [...]. My reason in maintaining a diacritical mark – the slash – was to bring further light to the fact that a diacritical mark was, as a manner of speaking, *required*" (ix).

34 Another note on this at times puzzling translation. Talking about Proximum (for the use of unusual lexicon see above, note 17), Duranti introduces a concept that is absent from the original text. While the original says "The Proximum I was talking to you about in our last course," Duranti's translation changes that merely temporal reference into a judgment of quality, "one of our most boring class sessions," where "class session" is not even a course.

2. America Ubiqua

1 Alessandro Baricco is not only a novelist and a playwright but also a musicologist, an essayist, a columnist, and an expert on English and American literature. His novels *Ocean Sea*, *Silk*, and *City* are bestsellers, translated into many languages.

2 My translation. Unless otherwise indicated, all translations in this chapter are mine.

3 The contribution of Walt Disney to an idea of illusionary happiness was and is the main accusation formulated against him by his detractors in the United States. Remembering the criticism of Disney by American intellectuals, Neal Gabler writes: "The bill of indictment was, indeed, a long one. He had infantilized the culture and removed the danger from fairy tales in the process popularizing them for a mass market [...] He had promoted treacly values that seemed anachronistic and even idiotic in a complex, modern, often tragic world [...]. And at the same time he was commercializing his own country, he was regarded by his detractors as perhaps the primary example of America's cultural imperialism" (xviii).

4 Where not indicated otherwise, translations in this chapter are mine.

5 In 2003, Baricco recorded on CD a reading of *City*'s Western stories, with the music of the French group Air, released by the label Astralwerk.

6 The page number of the translation, 153, is the same as that of the original quote: it is not a mistake. The passages happen to be on the same page; and this occurs again for page 154, a few lines further down.

7 Baricco gives the Italian version of Bukowski's phrase, whose English original I borrowed from Sounes.

8 For a detailed version of the story see Matilde Hochkofler, *Comico per amore: la favola bella e crudele di Massimo Troisi*.

9 In his *A Philosophical and Political History of the Settlements and Trade of the Europeans in the East and West Indies*, Guillame Thomas Francois Raynal describes the peoples living in the Americas (natives and Europeans) as degenerate because of climate and geophysical conditions.

10 *Lamerica* won as best film at the European Film Awards, in 1994, and at the Goya Awards, in 1996.

11 In 2002, Italy was governed by a coalition of centre-right and right-wing parties.

3. On a Trip to America: The "I" Travels

1 Baudrillard's French version bears the same date: "chez les Pères Fonda-teurs du XVIIe siècle" (149). Given the context of his discourse, he seems to refer to the Pilgrim Fathers, rather than the eighteenth-century's Found-ing Fathers of the American nation.

2 For more extensive bio- and bibliographical notes on De Carlo, see Antonella Francini, "Andrea De Carlo."

3 Andrea De Carlo has been a very successful and prolific writer since the publication of his first novel. He was a photographer before entering the realm of literature, and he has always been a traveller. His fourth novel, *Yucatan* (1986), is based on his voyage with Federico Fellini in 1984 through Southern California and Mexico. The two met the anthropologist and cult figure Carlos Castañeda and travelled in Mexico to collect materi-als for a film based on Castañeda's books. Fellini did write a script that never became a film but was published in episodes in the daily *Corriere della sera*, with the title *Viaggio a Tulum* (Voyage to Tulum).

The friendship with Fellini began in 1982, when De Carlo collaborated with him as assistant director in *E la nave va* (*And the Ship Sails On*, 1983), and on that occasion also shot a documentary about Fellini's relationship with his actors, entitled *Le Facce di Fellini* (Fellini's Faces, 1983). De Carlo dedicated *Macno* (1984) to Fellini. This was his third novel, a political al-legory of present-day Italy focused on the corruption and hypocrisy of the political system and the power of well-constructed public images.

De Carlo's experience as director culminated in the making of the film *Treno di panna* (1988), based on his novel. The story, this time set in New York rather than in Los Angeles, radically changes the personality of the character. It is another story altogether, and very different on an artistic level.

De Carlo went back to drawing on his private life for material with *Due di Due*, 1989 (Two of Two); while in *Tecniche di seduzione*, 1991 (Techniques of Seduction), he explored again the Italian sociopolitical landscape of VIP environments and its corrupted paths to success. Since then, De Carlo has published *Arcodamore*, 1993 (Love Bow); *Uto*, 1995; *Di noi tre*, 1997 (About the Three of Us); *Nel momento*, 1999 (In the Moment); *Pura vita*, 2001 (Pure Life); and *I veri nomi*, 2002 (The Real Names). The United States appears again in *Uto* and *I veri nomi*.

4 To begin his account of the authors who changed the face of Italian fiction in the 1980s, Filippo La Porta writes: "E cominciamo proprio con lo scrittore che per primo ha fatto parlare di ripresa narrativa nel nostro paese: il milanese, allora neanche trentenne, Andrea De Carlo. Il suo romanzo d'esordio, *Treno di Panna* (Einuadi 1981), prendeva implicitamente le distanze sia dalla tradizione letteraria più vicina, sia da tutta la produzione narrativa e paranarrativa legata al 'movimento' (autobiografica e spesso lacrimosa)" (26) ("Let us begin exactly with the writer who first led to the recognition of a narrative revival in our country: the Milanese Andrea De Carlo, not even thirty then. His debut novel, *Treno di panna* (Einaudi 1981), implicitly took a distance from both the closest literary tradition, and the entire narrative and paranarrative production related to 'movement' (autobiographical and often pitiful).") (My translation. Unless indicated otherwise, all translations in this chapter are mine.)

5 The English title of the book is *The Cream Train*, but the image suggested by *Treno di panna* is that of whipped cream that can actually have a shape.

4. American Arcadia

1 A shorter version of this chapter appeared on *Forum Italicum*, with the title "Et in Arcadia Ego: Gina Lagorio's *L'arcadia americana* as the Reflection of a European Literary Self."

2 My translation. Where not indicated otherwise, all translations in the chapter are mine.

3 In 1987, Gina Lagorio was elected a deputy of the Independent Left in the Italian parliament, where she served for five years. In *Raccontiamoci com'è andata: memoria di Emilio Lagorio e della resistenza a Savona* (2003), she likes to remember that she entered the parliament with several other intellectuals (independent deputies) from different political backgrounds, among whom were the writer Natalia Ginzburg, Luigi Pintor, director of the Communist daily *Manifesto* until his death (2004), and two other prominent figures of the Italian literary and cultural landscape. On that same page (14), Lagorio reminds us that she has never possessed any party membership card but the Fascist one that she was obliged to take on

entering college. Although she has never officially belonged to any of the parties of the Italian Left, the Left is the ideological environment in which she carried out her political action, sometimes at odds with the leaders of the political parties. Lagorio discusses her experience in the Italian parliament and her refusal to belong officially to any party in Parazzoli, "Il coraggio di Gina," *Il gioco del mondo*. The book is a collection of interviews with famous Italian writers that Parazzoli made between November 1994 and February 1995. To him Lagorio confessed that she wanted the chronicles of her parliamentary life to be published only after her death.

4 Lagorio was questioned, in 2000, about the contribution of Italian intellectuals to the civil conscience of the country:

Q. Negli ultimi dieci anni si è notata l'assenza degli intellettuali nel ruolo di coscienza civile del Paese.

A. La politica è desolante e riflette una società civile altrettanto desolante [...]. Le grandi speranze sono naufragate e gli intellettuali hanno espresso questo vuoto, anche perché, diciamo la verità, non ci sono grandi figure di intellettuali; i giovani sono spesso nati dal nulla, come funghi a volte avvelenati. (Casagrande)

[For the past ten years the absence of intellectuals as interpreters of our country's civil conscience has been noticeable.

Politics is desolating and reflects a civil society as desolating [...]. Great expectations have vanished and intellectuals have expressed this void, also because, let's be honest, there are no great intellectuals; the young ones were often born out of nothing, like mushrooms that might be poisoned at times.]

This bitter realization of contemporary intellectuals' decadence is a preeminent feature of *L'arcadia americana*'s protagonist, who is as nostalgic for a more ethical intellectual past as his creator. Memory, in fact, plays a fundamental role for both.

5 One of Lagorio's last works, *Raccontiamoci com'è andata*, is a consecration of historical memory. The back cover of this small and captivating memoir reads, "Sono pagine di memoria tra pubblico e privato, forse il solo modo vincente di una narrativa etico-estetica che abbia un senso, ieri come oggi" ("These are pages of memories bridging the public and the private spheres, maybe the only winning way for an ethical/aesthetic narrative that is supposed to make sense, yesterday as today"). From these two sentences, the purpose of Gina Lagorio's entire narrative corpus emerges. In the preface to the same book, Furio Colombo counterpoints the title *Raccontiamoci com'è andata* with "È andata che adesso gli strumenti di lotta (non tanto più facili) sono scrivere, parlare, partecipare e non distrarsi mai" (12; "It

went so that now the tools for our struggle (not easy tools any longer) are writing, speaking, participating, and never getting distracted"). Gina Lagorio herself would have written so. Here is part of an interview that she gave to the literary magazine *Uomini e libri* back in 1977, and that frames her position as a writer in the civil society:

Q. Quale significato viene ad assumere per lei, nella situazione politico-sociale italiana, in un contesto letterario come quello italiano attuale, lo scrivere un romanzo?

A. Della crisi letteraria del nostro tempo le cronache sono, credo, la ri-prova piú evidente. Che senso abbia scrivere un romanzo in queste con-dizioni, me lo sono chiesto tante volte: con perplessità, con angoscia [...] Ma poiché tentare di fare meglio che si può quello che si sconosce, per cui si è nati, è già qualcosa, ho tentato, scrivendo un romanzo, di partecipare ai problemi del mio tempo [...] (36).

[What significance does writing a novel bear for you in the current Italian sociopolitical scenario, in a literary context such as the Italian one?

Chronicles are the best evidence of the literary crisis of our times, I think. I've often wondered, with perplexity and anguish, whether it makes sense to write a novel in such conditions [...] However, because trying and do-ing at our best what we can, what we were born for, is already something, and my job is to write, then I have tried to partake of the problems of my time by writing a novel [...] .]

6 The NATO forces intervened in the Balkans, in the tension between Serbia and Kosovo, on 24 March 1999.

7 I discuss Lagorio's definition of ethics in the Introduction.

8 To Anna M. Simm, who asks her, in January 2001, whether voting in polit-ical elections in Italy still makes sense, Gina Lagorio replies: "Sono scorata dalla mancanza di memoria e dalla corsa al potere spicciolo: destra e sinis-tra non sono uguali anche se stanno per diventarlo ma questo non è suffi-ciente per dimenticare [...] La viltà di certi rappresentanti della sinistra non mi fa però diventare di destra. Io sento rimorso per come sono qui ora, musica, torta, calda vestaglia ... Dunque vale la pena votare ancora, comunque" ("I am disheartened by the lack of memory and the race to power: right and left are not the same, although they are about to become so; however, this is not a good reason to forget [...] The cowardice of some representatives from the left does not push me to the right. I feel remorse for the way I am here and now – music, pie, warm bathrobe ... So, voting is still worthwhile, in whichever way").

Anna Simm is interviewing Gina Lagorio at the author's home, in an elegant apartment building in downtown Milan. Lagorio's remorse for her comfortable condition is the prick of conscience that prevents her from forgetting her history and Italy's history during Fascism, the war, and the Partisan Resistance. It is that same prick of conscience that makes hurtful the narrator's memory of the blissful hour spent in Barnes and Noble. The narrator and his author share a deep interest in jazz and in Hollywood cinema. Gina Lagorio came to love jazz through her husband, Emilio Lagorio, between the wars, and soon after the war, in July 1945, she published an article on Hollywood cinema in *Noi donne*, the magazine of the Unione delle Donne Italiane.

9   The essay was originally published as "Et in Arcadia Ego: On the Conception of Transience in Poussin and Watteau," *Philosophy and History, Essays Presented to Ernst Cassirer*, ed. R. Klibansky and H.J. Paton (Oxford: Clarendon Press, 1936) 223–54. It is now in Panofsky, *Meaning in the Visual Arts.*

10 Panofsky reaches this conclusion after having restored the correct meaning of "Et in Arcadia Ego," which in modern times, since the Renaissance, had been mistranslated as "I, too, lived in Arcadia." After going through a review of some Latin grammar, Panofsky explains, "The correct translation of the phrase in its orthodox form is, therefore, not 'I too was born, or lived, in Arcady,' but: 'Even in Arcady there I am,' from which we must conclude that the speaker is not a deceased Arcadian shepherd or shepherdess but Death in person" ("Et in Arcadia Ego" 307).

The aim of Panofsky's essay is to show how, though a mistranslation, the rendering of "Et in Arcadia Ego" as "I too, shepherds, lived in Arcady" came to embody the spirit with which literature and the visual arts represented the theme of Death in Arcadia in modernity.

11 Poussin painted the first version of his "Et in Arcadia Ego" presumably around 1630 (the painting is in the Devonshire Collection, England). The scene derives from Guercino's, although some elements were added, such as a shepherdess and the river god of Arcadia, Alpheus. The piece of masonry is now a tomb, and the skull is smaller than the one in Guercino's painting; "the picture still conveys, though far less obtrusively than Guercino's, a moral or admonitory message" ("Et in Arcadia Ego" 312).

Poussin produced the second version of his painting (now at the Louvre) five or six years later. About this version, Panofsky writes that it represents "a radical break with the Medieval moralizing tradition. The element of drama and surprise has disappeared [...] we have a basic change in interpretation. The Arcadians are not so much warned of an implacable future as they are immersed in mellow meditation on a beautiful past" (312–13).

12 For an analysis of women characters in Lagorio's novels see Blelloch and Vitti-Alexander.

13 See Biasin.

14 See Heiney's introduction to *America in Modern Italian Literature*.

15 Morreale is an Italian American short-fiction writer and essayist. Together with Jerre Mangione, he wrote *La Storia: Five Centuries of the Italian American Experience*, published by HarperCollins, New York, in 1992. "Ava Gardner's Brother-in-Law" was first published in 1991, in the anthology *From the Margin: Writings in Italian Americana*.

16 "Turidru" is an unusual spelling for what is probably "Turiddu," a nickname for Salvatore.

17 From now on, I will not use quotation marks to refer to the I – the character – of "Ava Gardner's Brother-in-Law," since I use quotations mark to refer to the "I" as a generic subject.

18 Giorgio Agamben widely discusses this concept in *Homo Sacer*. The idea is also central to Levinas's theory of the Self and the Other. Although in different ways, both Agamben and Levinas found their theories of the subject on the recognition of the Other as an essential part of the Self. If, for Agamben, the Other represents what an individual could *potentially* be (see in particular *The Coming Community*), for Levinas, the Other is the true foundation of the Self – the imperative responsibility towards the Other frames the individual.

5. Historicizing the Dream: A Documented Eye on America

1 Lucamante writes, "In an effort to build the young nation of Italy in the late nineteenth century and years thereafter, Italian intellectuals could not bring the displaced *other* Italy into their ideological paradigm – that Italy settling in the States and other foreign nations by the 1870s. For some, those Italians who migrated were not even conational. It appears that the mere discussion of migration during that time would have greatly damaged the ideology and construction of a unified nation [...]" (295).

2 Preface to *Sogni mancini*; see here, page 43.

3 This passage has already been discussed here, page 22.

4 *Nuovomondo* won several awards at the Venice Film Festival in 2006, including a Silver Lion for Crialese as a revelation, and at the David di Donatello Awards in 2007.

5 See here, page 69.

6 See here, page 65.

7 My translation. Where not indicated otherwise, the translations in this chapter are mine.

8 In this regard, during the interview with Tamburri, it is the actor and protagonist of *Nuovomondo*, Vincenzo Amato, who refers to the success of *Nuovomondo* in the United States as the realization of the American dream.

9 With regard to Italy's interest in the history of Italian immigration to the United States, Francesco Durante has written a monumental anthology in two volumes (to date) about the history and literature of the Italians in the United States, *Italoamericana*. In his introduction to the second volume, he explains, "L'indagine storica su questo fenomeno […] ha prodotto una ricchissima bibliografia […] che ha trovato nel volume di Emilio Franzina *Gli italiani al Nuovo Mondo* (1994) e nella grande Storia dell'emigrazione italiana (2004), curata dallo stesso Franzina con Piero Bevilacqua e Andreina De Clementi, la sua più aggiornata e completa esposizione (9; "The historical investigation of this phenomenon […] has produced a very rich bibliography […] that has found in Emilio Franzina's volume *Gli italiani al Nuovo Mondo* (1994) and in the great *Storia dell'emigrazione italiana* (2004), edited by Franzina himself together with Piero Bevilacqua and Andreina De Clementi, its most complete and up-to-date rendition").

10 "The creation of a transnational community is presented by Moretti's film as a coping strategy developed by individual in the face of global capital – a strategy which is nevertheless condemned to failure" (Rascaroli, "Home and Away" 197).

11 See here, page 39.

Conclusion

1 My translation.

Works Cited

Agamben, Giorgio, *The Coming Community* Trans. Michael Hardt. Minneapolis: U of Minnesota P, 1993. Trans. of *La comunità che viene*.

Agamben, Giorgio. *La comunità che viene*. 1990. Turin: Bollati Boringhieri, 2001.

Agamben, Giorgio. *Homo Sacer: Sovereign Power and Bare Life*. Trans. Daniel Heller-Roazen. Stanford: Stanford UP, 1998.

Alfano, Barbara. "Et in Arcadia Ego: Gina Lagorio's *L'arcadia americana* as the Reflection of a European Literary Self." *Forum Italicum* 40.2 (Fall 2006): 346–65.

Amelio, Gianni. *Lamerica: film e storia del film*. Ed. Piera Defassis. Turin: Einaudi, 1994.

Amelio, Gianni, and Goffredo Fofi. *Amelio secondo il cinema: conversazione con Goffredo Fofi*. Rome: Donzelli, 1994. 4–15.

Aprile. Dir. Nanni Moretti. Tandem, 1998.

Arciniegas, Gérman. *Amerigo y el Nuevo Mundo*. Madrid: Alianza Editorial, 1990.

Baranski, Zygmunt G., and Rebecca West, eds. *The Cambridge Companion to Modern Italian Culture*. Cambridge: Cambridge UP, 2001. http://dx.doi.org/10.1017/CCOL0521550343

Baricco, Alessandro. *City*. Milan: Rizzoli, 1999.

Baricco, Alessandro. *City*. Trans. Ann Goldstein. New York: Knopf, 2002. Trans. of *City*.

Baricco, Alessandro. "*City* e l'America." *Speaker's Corner: Alessandro Baricco – 28 agosto 2002. Senza Sangue*. 23 Sept. 2003. 17 Dec. 2012. http://www.labcity.it/Ipertesto/Echitrailettori/CitynellechatconBaricco/ChatSenzasangue2002/tabid/173/language/en-US/Default.aspx.

Baricco, Alessandro. *Next: Piccolo libro sulla globalizzazione e sul mondo che verrà*. Milan: Feltrinelli, 2002.

Baricco, Alessandro. *Novecento*. Milan: Feltrinelli, 1994.

Baricco, Alessandro. *Ocean Sea*. Trans. Alastair McEwan. New York: Random House, 1999. Trans. of *Oceano mare*.

Baricco, Alessandro. *Oceano mare*. Milan: Rizzoli, 1993.

Baricco, Alessandro. "Quando la storia si presenta come un film." *La Repubblica.it*. 12 Sept. 2001. 11 Oct. 2003. http://www.repubblica.it/online/speciale/dodicisettuno/dodicisettuno/dodicisettuno.html. N. pag.

Baricco, Alessandro. *Seta*. Milan: Rizzoli, 1996.

Baricco, Alessandro. *Silk*. Trans. Guido Waldman. New York: Harvill Press, 1997. Trans. of *Seta*.

Baudrillard, Jean. *America*. Trans. Chris Turner. London: Verso, 1988. Trans. of *Amérique*.

Baudrillard, Jean. *Amérique*. Paris: Bernard Grasset, 1986.

Biasin, Gian-Paolo. "Narratives of Self and Society." Baranski and West 151–71.

Blelloch, Paola. "Lagorio's Women Characters' Search for Self-Identity." *NEMLA Italian Studies* 17 (1993): 133–42.

Booth, Wayne C. *The Rhetoric of Fiction*. 2nd ed. Chicago: U of Chicago P, 1983.

Bouerneuf, Roland, and Real Ouellet. *L'univers du roman*. Paris: Presses Universitaires de France, 1972.

Bragaglia, Cristina. "Autobiografie e cari diari: Nanni Moretti e gli altri." *Annali d'Italianistica* 17 (1999): 69–76.

Brunetta, Gian Piero. *Cent'anni di cinema italiano: Dal 1945 ai giorni nostri*. Rome: Laterza, 1995.

Brunetta, Gian Piero. *Storia del cinema italiano: Dal miracolo economico agli anni novanta (1963–1993)*. Rome: Editori Riuniti, 1998.

Buccini, Stefania. *The Americas in Italian Literature and Culture: 1700–1825*. Trans. Rosanna Giammanco. University Park: Pennsylvania State UP, 1997. Trans. of *Il dilemma della Grande Atlantide*. 1990.

Cachey, J. Theodore, Jr. "Italy and the Invention of America." *CR (East Lansing, Mich.)* 2.1 (2002): 17–31.

Caro diario [*Dear Diary*]. Dir. Nanni Moretti. Sacher Film, 1994.

Casagrande, Grazia. "Intervista a Gina Lagorio. La memoria è un'arma per vivere il futuro." Downloaded document. *Cafè letterario di Alice.it*. 28 April 2000.

Casillo, Robert. *Gangster Priest: The Italian American Cinema of Martin Scorsese*. Toronto: U of Toronto P, 2007.

Chatman, Seymour. *Story and Discourse: Narrative Structure in Fiction and Film*. Ithaca: Cornell UP, 1978.

Crialese, Emanuele, and Vincenzo Amato. Interview with Anthony Tamburri. *Italics: Italian American Magazine* June 2007. 21 Jan. 2012. http://www.cuny .tv/show/italics/PR1008945.

Crowdus, Gary. "The Lack of Historical Memory: An Interview with Gianni Amelio." *Cineaste* 28.1 (2002): 14–18.

D'aquino, Antonella. "Caro Diario: A Modern Journey of Purification." *Rivista di Studi Italiani* 18.2 (Dec. 2000): 270–80.

De Bernardinis, Flavio. *Nanni Moretti*. Milan: Il castoro, 2001.

De Carlo, Andrea. *Arcodamore*. Milan: Bompiani, 1993.

De Carlo, Andrea. *The Cream Train*. Ed. John Gatt. London: Olive P, 1987. Trans. of *Treno di panna*.

De Carlo, Andrea. *Di noi tre*. Milan: Mondadori, 1997.

De Carlo, Andrea. *Due di Due*. Milan: Mondadori, 1989.

De Carlo, Andrea. *Macno*. Milan: Bompiani, 1984.

De Carlo, Andrea. *Nel momento*. Milan: Mondadori, 1999.

De Carlo, Andrea. *Pura vita*. Milan: Mondadori, 2001.

De Carlo, Andrea. *Tecniche di seduzione*. Milan: Bompiani, 1991.

De Carlo, Andrea. *Treno di panna*. 1981. Milan: Mondadori, 1997.

De Carlo, Andrea. *Uccelli da gabbia e da voleria*. Turin: Einaudi, 1982.

De Carlo, Andrea. *Uto*. Milan: Bompiani, 1995.

De Carlo, Andrea. *I veri nomi*. Milan: Mondadori, 2002.

De Carlo, Andrea. *Yucatan*. Milan: Bompiani, 1986.

De Ferra, Donatella. "Intervista con Francesca Duranti." *Bulletin of the Society for Italian Studies* 33 (2000): 14–22.

Defoe, Daniel. *The Life and Strange Surprizing Adventures of Robinson Crusoe*. London: W. Taylor, 1719.

Di Ciolla McGowan, Nicoletta. Introduction. Francesca Duranti. *Left-Handed Dreams*. Trans. of *Sogni Mancini*. 1996. Trans. Francesca Duranti. Ed. Nicoletta Di Ciolla McGowan. Leicester: Troubadour, 2000.

Down by Law. Dir. Jim Jarmusch. Key Video, 1986.

Durante, Francesco. *Italoamericana: Storia e letteratura degli italiani negli Stati Uniti. 1880–1943*. Vol. 2. Milan: Mondadori, 2005.

Duranti, Francesca. *La bambina*. Milan: La Tartaruga, 1976.

Duranti, Francesca. *Left-Handed Dreams*. Trans. Francesca Duranti. New York: Delphinium Books, 2000. Trans of. *Sogni mancini*.

Duranti, Francesca. *Sogni mancini*. Milan: Rizzoli, 1996.

E la nave va. Dir. Federico Fellini. Gaumont, 1983.

Eco, Umberto. Preface to the American Edition. *Travels in Hyperreality*. New York: Harcourt Brace, 1986.

Eco, Umberto. *Trattato di semiotica generale*. Milan: Bompiani, 1975.

Eco, Umberto, Gian Paolo Ceserani, and Beniamino Placido. *La Riscoperta dell'America*. Rome: Laterza, 1984.

Eder, Richard. "If They Give You Ruled Paper." *New York Times* 28 July 2002, late ed., sec. 7:6. *New York Times on the Web*. 21 Nov. 2003. http://www.nytimes.com/2002/07/28/books/if-they-give-you-ruled-paper.html. N. pag.

Escobar, Roberto. "Riflessi nel grande schermo: Caro diario, la vita non è che leggerezza." *Il Sole 24 Ore* 28 Nov. 1993.

Fante, John. *Chiedi alla polvere*. Trans. Maria Giulia Castagnone. Turin: Einaudi, 2004. Trans. of *Ask the Dust*. New York: Stackpole Sons, 1939.

Foucault, Michel. *Ethics, Subjectivity and Truth: The Essential Works of Michel Foucault 1954–1984*. Ed. Paul Rabinow. Trans. Robert Hurley et al. Vol. 1. New York: New Press, 1997. Trans. of *Dits et écrits*. Paris: Gallimard, 1994.

Fouskas, Vassilis. *Italy, Europe, the Left: The Transformation of Italian Communism and the European Imperative*. Brookfield: Ashgate, 1998.

Francini, Antonella. "Andrea De Carlo." *Dictionary of Literary Biography: Italian Novelists since World War II, 1965–1995*. Ed. Augustus Palotta. Vol. 196. Detroit: Gale Group, 1999. 101–8. *The Gale Literary Database*. 1 March 2003. http://galenet.galegroup.com/servlet/GLD/hits?r=d&origSearch=true&o=DataType&n=10&l=d&c=2&locID=psucic&secondary=false&u=CA&u=CLC&u=DLB&t=KW&s=1&NA=De+Carlo%2C+Andrea#MainEssaySection. N. pag.

Gabler, Neal. *Walt Disney: The Triumph of the American Imagination*. New York: Alfred A. Knopf, 2006.

Gaudenzi, Eva. "Orgoglio e dignità." *Filmit* 21 Sept. 2006. 3 Aug. 2011. http://www.film.it/articolo/emanuele-crialese-intervista. N. pag.

Genette, Gerard. *Figure III*. Paris: Editions du Seuil, 1972.

Gerbi, Antonello. *The Dispute of the New World: The History of a Polemic, 1750–1900*. Trans. Jeremy Moyle. Pittsburgh: U of Pittsburgh P, 1973. Trans. of *La disputa del Nuovo Mondo*. 1955.

Gieri, Manuela. *Contemporary Italian Filmmaking: Strategies of Subversion. Pirandello, Fellini, Scola, and the Directors of the New Generation*. Toronto: U of Toronto P, 1995.

Gieri, Manuela. "Landscapes of Oblivion and Historical Memory in the New Italian Cinema." *Annali d'Italianistica* 17 (1999): 33–54.

Gili, Jean A. *Nanni Moretti*. Rome: Gremese, 2001.

"Giova Fare a se stessi di tali incantesimi." Downloaded document *La Libreria di Dora*. 5 April 2000. 18 May 2004. http://www.italialibri.net/arretratis/intrw_0400.html. N. pag.

Giunta, Edvige. *Writing with an Accent: Contemporary Italian American Women Authors*. New York: Palgrave, 2002.

Gramsci, Antonio. *Prison Notebooks*. Trans. Joseph A. Buttigieg and Antonio
    Callari. New York: Columbia UP, 1992.
Guardì, Mario Bernanrdi. "Cardini fa l'eretico, ma è disposto a diventare 'or-
    ganico' di un partito no-global e anti-USA." Interview. Il Foglio 28 Feb.
    2002: 2.
Gundle, Stephen. *Between Hollywood and Moscow: The Italian Communists and
    the Challenge of Mass Culture, 1943–1991*. Durham, NC: Duke UP, 2000.
Hall, Stuart. "Who Needs Identity?" *Questions of Cultural Identity*. Ed. Stuart
    Hall and Paul Du Gay. London: Sage Publications, 1996. 1–17.
Hardt, Michael, and Antonio Negri. *Empire*. Cambridge, MA: Harvard UP, 2000.
Hardt, Michael, and Antonio Negri. *Labor of Dionysus: A Critique of the State-
    Form*. Minneapolis: U of Minnesota P, 1994.
Hardt, Michael, and Paolo Virno. *Radical Thought in Italy: A Potential Politics*.
    Minneapolis: U of Minnesota P, 1996.
Heiney, Donald W. *America in Modern Italian Literature*. New Brunswick, NJ:
    Rutgers UP, 1964.
"Ho tentato, scrivendo un romanzo, di partecipare ai problemi del mio tem-
    po." Interview. *Uomini e Libri* 64 (1977): 36.
Hochkofler, Matilde. *Comico per amore: la favola bella e crudele di Massimo Troisi*.
    Venice: Marsilio, 1996.
"L'impronta di una città qualsiasi." *Un libro e i suoi dintorni*. City di Alessandro
    Baricco. http://www.labcity.it/Ipertesto/Spazio/tabid/140/language/
    en-US/Default.aspx
Io sono un autarchico [*I Am an Autarchic*]. Dir. Nanni Moretti, 1976.
Johnny Stecchino. Dir. Roberto Benigni. Filmauro, 1991.
Jousse, Theirry. "Moretti ou Berlusconi." *Cahiers du cinema* 479/80 (May 1994):
    62–4.
Kadir, Djelal. "Global Time, Warped Space." Typescript. Literature and the
    Poetics/Politics of Space. The Fourth English Literature Conference at
    Eastern Mediterranean University, Cyprus. 10–11 May 2001. Keynote
    address.
Klarel, Mario. "Jean Baudrillard's *America*: Deconstruction of America and
    America as Deconstruction." *Amerikanstudien* 36.2 (1991): 227–40.
Kozma, Jan. "Francesca Duranti." *Dictionary of Literary Biography: Italian
    Novelists since World War II, 1965–1995*. Ed. Augustus Pallotta. Vol. 196.
    Detroit: Gale Group, 1999. 160–6. *Gale Literary Database*. 18 May 2004.
    http://galenet.galegroup.com/servlet/GLD/hits?r=d&origSearch=true&o
    =DataType&n=10&l=d&c=2&locID=psucic&secondary=false&u=CA&u=
    CLC&u=DLB&t=KW&s=1&NA=duranti%2C+francesca . N. pag.
Kristeva, Julia. *Étrangers à nous-mêmes*. Paris: Fayard, 1988.

Kristeva, Julia. *Nations without Nationalism*. Trans. Leon S. Roudiez. New York: Columbia UP, 1993.

Lagorio, Gina. *Approssimato per difetto*. Bologna: Cappelli, 1971.

Lagorio, Gina. "Arcadia." *1989. Il Silenzio. Racconti di una vita*. Milan: Mondadori, 1993. 105–26.

Lagorio, Gina. "Arcadia." Trans. Brenda Webster. *13th Moon*. 1993: 177–90. Trans. of "Arcadia."

Lagorio, Gina. *L'arcadia americana*. Milan: Rizzoli, 1999.

Lagorio, Gina. *Un ciclone chiamato Titti*. Bologna: Cappelli, 1969.

Lagorio, Gina. *Il polline*. Milan: Mondadori, 1966.

Lagorio, Gina. *Raccontiamoci com'è andata: memoria di Emilio Lagorio e della Resistenza a Savona*. Milan: Viennepierre, 2003.

Lamerica. Dir. Gianni Amelio. Cecchi Gori Group, 1994.

La Porta, Filippo. "Il Calvino dimezzato." *La nuova narrativa italiana*. Turin: Bollati Boringhieri, 1995. 23–40.

The Last Customer [*L'ultimo cliente*]. Dir. Nanni Moretti. Sacher Film, 2002.

Lejeune, Philippe. *Le pacte autobiographique*. Paris: Seuil, 1975.

Levinas, Emmanuel. *Autrement qu'être; ou, au-delà de l'essence*. La Haye: M. Nijhoff, 1974.

Levinas, Emmanuel. *Entre nous: Thinking of the Other*. New York: Columbia UP, 1998.

Levinas, Emmanuel. *Humanism of the Other*. Trans. Nidra Poller. Chicago: U of Illinois P, 2003. Trans. of *Humanisme de l'autre home*. Montpellier: Fata Morgana, 1972.

Longo, Francesco. "Le torri simboliche e il collasso della *fiction*: L'11 settembre e gli scrittori italiani." *Semestrale di studi (e testi) italiani. Apocalissi e letteratura* 15 (2005): 241–55. Dipartimento di studi greco-latini, italiani, scenico-musicali. Facoltà di Lettere e Filosofia – Università degli studi di Roma "La Sapienza." 25 July 2012. http://www.disp.let.uniroma1.it/contents/?idPagina=101

Lotman, Jurij M. *Analysis of the Poetic Text*. Ed. and trans. D. Barton Johnson. Ann Arbor: Ardis, 1976.

Lucamante, Stefania. "The Privilege of Memory Goes to the Women: Melania Mazzucco and the Narrative of Italian Migration." *Modern Language Notes* 124.1 (2009): 293–315.

Manacorda, Giuliano. *Storia della letteratura italiana. 1940–1996*. Vol. 2. Rome: Editori Riuniti, 1996.

Mangione, Jerre, and Ben Morreale. *La Storia: Five Centuries of the Italian American Experience*. New York: HarperCollins, 1992.

Marazzi, Martino. *Little America: Gli Stati Uniti e gli scrittori italiani del novecento*. Milan: Marcos y Marcos, 1997.

Marazzi, Martino. *Voices of Italian America: A History of Early Italian American Literature, with a Critical Anthology*. Trans. Ann Goldstein. Madison: Fairleigh Dickinson UP, 2004.

Marchese, Angelo. *L'officina del racconto*. Milan: Mondadori, 1983.

Marchesi, Simone. "Accumulazione e Sviluppo: il movimento della narrazione in *Caro Diario*." *Annali d'Italianistica* 17 (1999): 77–93.

Martini, Emanuela, ed. *Gianni Amelio: le regole e il gioco*. Turin: Lindau, 1999.

Masi, Stefano. *Roberto Benigni*. Trans. Eiko Tokunaga. Rome: Gremese, 1999.

Mazierska, Ewa, and Laura Rascaroli. *The Cinema of Nanni Moretti: Dreams and Diaries*. London: Wallflower Press, 2004.

Mazzucco, Melania. "Emigrazione e letteratura." *Treccani.it: L'enciclopedia italiana*. Web tv – Gli esperti rispondono. 21 Jan. 2012. http://www.treccani.it/webtv/videos/Int_Melania_Mazzucco_emigrazione.html.

Mazzucco, Melania. *Vita*. Milan: Rizzoli, 2003.

Mazzucco, Melania. *Vita*. Trans. Virginia Jewiss. New York: Picador, 2005.

McHale, Brian. *Postmodernist Fiction*. New York: Methuen, 1987.

Melville, Herman. *Moby-Dick*. 1851. Ed. Harold Beaver. New York: Penguin, 1972.

Messori, Vittorio. "Non con Bin Laden ma neanche con Bush." Interview with Michele Brambilla. *Corriere della sera* 28 Sept. 2001. 24 Jan. 2012. http://www.vittoriomessori.it/. N. Pag.

Morreale, Ben. "Ava Gardner's Brother-in-Law: A Word Play in Sicily." *From the Margin: Writings in Italian Americana*. Ed. Anthony Tamburri, Paolo A. Giordano, and Fred L. Gardaphé. West Lafayette, IN: Purdue UP, 1991. 125–37.

Non ci resta che piangere [Nothing Left but to Cry]. Dir. Roberto Benigni and Massimo Troisi. Mario e Vittorio Cecchi Gori, 1984.

Nuovomondo [*Golden Door*]. Dir. Emanuele Crialese. Rai Cinema, 2006.

Oberti, Renzo. "Intervista a Gina Lagorio: Viaggio intimo nell'Arcadia americana." *Giornale di Brescia* 1 Feb. 2001: 5.

Oppenheimer, Jean. "Chasing the American Dream." *American Cinematographer* 88.6 (June 2007): 24–31.

Palombella rossa [*Red Lob*]. Dir. Nanni Moretti. Titanus, 1989.

Panofsky, Erwin. *Meaning in the Visual Arts: Papers in and on Art History*. New York: Doubleday Anchor Books, 1955. 295–320.

Parazzoli, Ferruccio. *Il gioco del mondo: dialoghi sulla vita, i sogni, le memorie con Lalla Romano, Vincenzo Consolo, Luciano De Crescenzo, Giuseppe Pontiggia, Susanna Tamaro, Antonio Tabucchi, Lara Cardella, Gina Lagorio, Alberto Bevilacqua, Luce D'Eramo*. Milan: San Paolo, 1998.

Pavese, Cesare. "Yesterday and Today." *L'Unità* 3 Aug. 1947. Appendix. Heiney, 245–8.

Phelan, James, ed. *Reading Narrative. Form, Ethics, Ideology*. Columbus: Ohio State UP, 1989.

Il piccolo diavolo [*The Little Devil*]. Dir. Roberto Benigni. Columbia TriStar Films Italia, 1988.

Pintor, Giaime. "*Americana.*" *Aretusa* 2 (March 1945): 5–14. Appendix. Heiney, 243–5.

Porton, Richard, and Gary Crowdus. "Beyond Neorealism: Preserving a Cinema of Social Conscience. An Interview with Gianni Amelio." *Cineaste* 21.4 (1995): 6–13.

Porton, Richard, and Lee Ellickson. "Comedy, Communism, and Pastry: An Interview with Nanni Moretti." *Cineaste* 21.1–2 (1995): 11–15.

Prince, Gerald. *Narratology: The Form and Function of Narrative.* Berlin: Mouton Press, 1982.

Rascaroli, Laura. "Caro Diario." *The Cinema of Italy.* Ed. Giorgio Bertellini. London: wallflower press, 2004.

Rascaroli, Laura. "Home and Away: Nanni Moretti's *The Last Customer* and the Ground Zero of Transnational Identity." *New Cinemas: Journal of Contemporary Film* 3.3 (2005): 187–200. http://dx.doi.org/10.1386/ncin .3.3.187/1.

Raynal, Guillaume Thomas Francois. *A Philosophical and Political History of the Settlements and Trade of the Europeans in the East and West Indies.* Trans. J. Justamond. London: T. Cadell, 1776.

Riotta, Gianni. "La strategia della distensione" ["The Strategy of Distension"]. Foreword. *Treno di panna.* By Andrea De Carlo. 1981. Special Edition. Milan: RCS, 2003. 7–10.

Saada, Nicolas. "Et la vie continue…." *Cahiers du cinéma* 479/80 (May 1994): 52–4.

Saada, Nicolas, and Thierry Jousse. "Entretien avec Nanni Moretti." *Cahiers du cinéma* 479/80 (May 1994): 55–61.

Samueli, Anna. "L'unique pays au monde." Trans. Annick Bouleau. *Cahiers du cinéma* 479/80 (May 1994): 66–7.

Scorsese, Martin. Introduction. *Golden Door.* Dir. Emanuele Crialese. 2006. Videodisc. Buena Vista Home Entertainment, 2008.

Sesti, Mario. *Nuovo cinema italiano: Gli autori i film le idee.* Rome: Theoria, 1994.

Siebers, Tobin. *Morals and Stories.* New York: Columbia UP, 1992.

Simms, Anna M. "Incontro con Gina Lagorio." *Dialogo Libri* 13 Jan. 2001. 23 July 2004. http://www.dialogolibri.it/cont/interviste/lagorio.html. N. pag.

Son of the Pink Panther. Dir. Blake Edwards. Movies Unlimited, 1993.

Sounes, Howard. *Charles Bukowski: Locked in the Arms of a Crazy Life. 1998.* New York: Grove Press, 1999.

Spunta, Marina. "The Food of Tolerance in Francesca Duranti's *Sogni mancini.*" *Italianist: Journal of the Department of Italian Studies* 19 (1999): 228–50.

La stanza del figlio [*The Son's Room*]. Dir. Nanni Moretti. Sacher, 2000.

Stevens, Wallace. "An Ordinary Evening in New Haven." "The Auroras of Autumn." *The Collected Poems of Wallace Stevens*. New York: Vintage Books , 1990. 477–501.

Tamburri, Anthony J. *To Hyphenate or Not to Hyphenate. The Italian/American Writer: An* Other *American*. Montreal: Guernica, 1991.

Tamburri, Anthony J. *A Semiotic of Ethnicity: (Re)cognition of the Italian/American Writer*. Albany: State U of New York P, 1998.

Teodori, Massimo. *Maledetti americani: Destra, sinistra e cattolici: storia del pregiudizio antiamericano*. Milan: Mondadori, 2002.

Teodori, Massimo. "Storia della guerra di indipendenza U.S.A." *Il Sole 24 Ore* 3 Oct. 2010. 27 July 2012. http://www.massimoteodori.it/articoli/25-BOTTAguerraindipendenzaUSA.pdf. N. pag.

Toubiana, Serge. "Le regard moral. *Palombella rossa*." *Cahiers du cinéma* 425: 20–1.

Veneziani, Marcello. "Non voglio fare l'americano." *Il Giornale* 3 Oct. 2001: 1

La vita è bella [*Life Is Beautiful*]. Dir. Roberto Benigni. Cidif Cad, 1997.

Vitti, Antonio. "Albanitaliamerica: Viaggio come sordo sogno in *Lamerica* di Gianni Amelio." *Italica* 73.2 (1996): 248–61. http://dx.doi.org/10.2307/479366.

Vitti-Alexander, Maria Rosaria. "Gina Lagorio." *Dictionary of Literary Biography: Italian Novelists Since World War II, 1965–1995*. Ed. Augustus Pallotta. Vol. 196. Detroit: Gale Group, 1999. 160–6. *Gale Literary Database*. 18 May 2004. http://www.galenet.com/servlet/GLD/hits?r=d&origSearch=true&o=DataType&n=10&l=d&c=1&locID=psucic&secondary=false&u=DLB&t=KW&s=4&NA=gina+lagorio. N. pag.

Voltaire, François Marie Arouet de. *Candide*. Trans. and ed. Robert M. Adams. New York: Norton, 1991.

Ward, David. "Intellectuals, Culture, and Power in Modern Italy." Baranski and West 81–96.

Index of Names and Titles